The End of an Illusion

Comparative Studies of Health Systems and Medical Care

The End of an Illusion

The Future of Health Policy in

Western Industrialized Nations

**Edited by
Jean de Kervasdoué,
John R. Kimberly, and
Victor G. Rodwin**

UNIVERSITY OF CALIFORNIA PRESS
Berkeley • Los Angeles • London

University of California Press
Berkeley and Los Angeles, California

University of California Press, Ltd.
London, England

Copyright © 1984 by The Regents of the University of California

Library of Congress Cataloging in Publication Data

The End of an illusion.

(Comparative studies of health systems and medical care)
Contents: Health policy and the expanding role of the state, 1945–1980 /
Jean de Kervasdoué, Victor G. Rodwin -- Perspectives on the state /
Victor G. Rodwin -- Perspectives on prevention / John Ratcliffe . . . [et
al.] -- [etc.]
   1. Medical policy.   2. Health planning.
I. Kervasdoué, Jean de. II. Kimberly, John.
III. Rodwin, Victor G. IV. Series. [DNLM: 1. Health
policy. WA 540.1 E56]
RA393.S2813 1984   362.1   83-18030
ISBN 0-520-04726-5

Printed in the United States of America

1 2 3 4 5 6 7 8 9

Contents

Foreword

Publication of this book comes at an opportune time. We are in a period of rapid transformation in the organization and financing of health care in Western industrialized nations. Policymakers are challenging traditional assumptions, criticizing existing structures, and initiating significant reforms in the health sector. The health sector can no longer continue to grow in the future as it has over the past two decades. This "shock of recognition" is why the editors have called this book *The End of an Illusion*. The future of health policy will be characterized by powerful constraints and difficult choices. That is the sober conclusion of John Kimberly and Victor Rodwin in their final chapter.

In the United States, in 1981, the Omnibus Budget Reconciliation Act introduced major changes in the Medicaid program. It provided states greater freedom to determine eligibility and benefits for the medically needy, to make hospital payments less dependent on hospital costs, and to negotiate competitive contracts for some services. In 1982, the Tax Equity and Fiscal Responsibility Act (TEFRA) instituted a new system of payment for hospitals under the Medicare program. In contrast to the retrospective reimbursement of hospitals on the basis of per diem costs incurred, the new legislation mandates prospective payment on the basis of cases treated—discharges classified into 467 diagnosis-related groups (DRGs). The effect of these recent policy initiatives will be to reduce drastically the level of federal support to the hospital industry, particularly academic medical centers. And yet these measures only portend the kinds of changes we are likely to witness in the years to come.

The health policy shifts now occurring in the United States are not simply the result of the Reagan administration's conservative policies; they reflect the broader forces now transforming the health sector, both at home and abroad. For better or worse, physicians are working in a new environment. While the supply of physicians has been increasing rapidly, there have been major changes in the fiscal conditions affecting medical care and the practice of medicine. This book explains why this is true in the United States and in other Western industrialized nations. Its unique contribution is to provide a comparative perspective on current policy issues and the choices that lie ahead.

The End of an Illusion is the second policy oriented book in this series on comparative studies of health systems and medical care. It is a most useful companion to the previous book in the series, Victor Rodwin's appraisal of *The Health Planning Predicament*. Both books provide case studies of France, Québec, Britain, and the United States. Both combine scholarship with synthesis for the general reader. This book, however, provides case studies by different authors, each with his own perspective on the recent past and on the likely future.

The editors have avoided the typical limitation of a book of this sort: it is not a potpourri of essays connected only by a cover. The editors have persuaded the authors of the case studies to stay on target and have introduced the case studies with carefully focused essays on the changing nature of health policy. There are four main themes: (1) the contrasting perspectives on the role of the state in society, and their implications for health policy; (2) the place of disease prevention and health promotion in health policy; (3) the development and consequences of new medical technology; and (4) the ethical challenge of health care rationing. Whether or not one agrees with the views expressed in this book, the ideas will surely challenge preconceptions and provoke debate.

The editors of *The End of an Illusion* combine a wide range of skills and backgrounds. Jean de Kervasdoué, formerly a research fellow at the Center for Research in Management, École Polytechnique, is currently deputy secretary of hospitals in the French Ministry of Social Affairs and National Solidarity. John Kimberly is a faculty member in the Departments of Management and Health Care Systems at the Wharton School, University of Pennsylvania and is a specialist on the problems of organizational change. Victor Rodwin is a faculty member in the Institute for Health Policy Studies at the University of California, San Francisco, and a specialist on comparative issues in health policy.

Professor of Social Medicine   Philip R. Lee, M.D.
Director, Institute for Health
    Policy Studies
University of California,
    San Francisco

Preface

Can the Western tradition of individualism be reconciled with the principle of equity in health policy? How do our present institutions reinforce particular conceptions of health and illness and how might these conceptions change or be changed? What are alternative roles for the state in coping with issues of health policy? How are contemporary health systems and issues of health policy likely to be perceived in the future?

This book has its origins in the work of a group of scholars who tackled these questions at a seminar in Megève, France, in the Winter of 1979. They came from different disciplinary backgrounds; they did not all share the same political persuasions; and the systems with which they were familiar were in some ways quite different. More important than these apparent differences, however, they all came from Western industrialized nations and wanted to learn from one another.

Although the chapters of this book reflect our discussions in Megève, each is an independent contribution. An earlier version of this book was published in French under the title *La santé rationnée? La fin d'un mirage* (Paris: Economica, 1981).

We are grateful to all those who joined us in this collaborative venture. The sponsor of the seminar in Megève, the *Association Economie et Santé*—and particularly the enthusiasm of Patrick Lefrançois and Jean Soucaret—created a splendid setting for the participants. Jean-Marc Simon, then director of planning for the public hospitals of Paris—*Assistance Publique*—initiated the project in an intellectual and in a practical sense. The participants contributed through many hours of formal and informal discussions at Megève. Those who attended the seminar, in addition to the editors, include Eugene Bardach, Celia Davies, Robert Fetter, Daniel Friedmann, William Glaser, A. S. Härö, Dominique Jolly, Rudolph Klein, Jean-François Lacronique, Theodore Marmor, Edward Morse, Jose Aristidemo Pinnotti, Marc Renaud, Jean-Marc Simon, Paul Starr, Sandra Stein, Jean-Claude Stephan, Gosta Tiblin, Noel Tichy, and Karl Yordy.

Various people assisted us in the course of this project. Dr. Michel Manciaux provided us with valuable suggestions for chapter 3. Dr. Philip R. Lee, in addition to providing encouragement throughout, made helpful comments on our final chapter. Marian Phillip and the marvelous efficiency of the word processing system facilitated the typing of numerous drafts while John Kimberly was in the Health Systems Management Group at the School of Organization and Management, Yale. Eunice Chee, Les Gates, and the secretarial staff of the Institute for Health Policy Studies at the University of California, San Francisco were most helpful during the final year of the project. And Cindi Buoni and the staff of the Management Department at the Wharton School, University of Pennsylvania helped tie up loose ends in the final months of the project.

John R. Kimberly
Victor G. Rodwin

Contributors

Celia Davies is Senior Research Fellow in sociology at the University of Warwick. She has worked extensively in the field of organizational analysis with special reference to hospitals. Currently her research interests are the history of occupations in child health and organizational structures and opportunities for women. She has published many articles on the organization of health care and is editor of *Rewriting Nursing History* (London: Croom Helm; Totowa, N.J.: Barnes and Noble, 1980).

Francis Fagnani is currently director of a research unit dealing with prevention programs, risk assessment, and environmental health at the National Institute of Health and Medical Research (INSERM), Paris. He has worked in the fields of public health, environmental health planning, and health economics since 1969.

Jean de Kervasdoué is presently deputy secretary of hospitals in the French Ministry of Social Affairs and National Solidarity. While teaching and doing research at the Ecole Polytechnique in Paris, he worked for public administrations in the health and agricultural fields. He was adviser to the prime minister in 1981. De Kervasdoué has written articles on the sociology of scientific and technical organizations, the sociology of science, and the political economy of medical care.

John Kimberly taught at the University of Illinois and at Yale prior to joining the faculty of the Wharton School at the University of Pennsylvania, where he teaches in the Departments of Management and Health Care Systems. A member of the editorial boards of the *Administrative Science*

Quarterly, the *Journal of Health Politics, Policy and Law*, and the *Academy of Management Journal*, Kimberly has written extensively on problems of organizational change, managerial innovation, and health policy. He recently served on the Advisory Board for the Office of Technology Assessment's study *Technology and Handicapped People* and as a consultant to OTA's study of medical technology.

Rudolf Klein spent twenty years as a journalist, first with the *Evening Standard* and then with the *Observer*. Subsequently he became Senior Fellow at the Centre for Studies in Social Policy and, in 1978, Professor of Social Policy at the University of Bath. His research interests include public expenditure, the impact of economic recession on the relationship between the public and the private sectors of welfare, and health care politics. His latest book is *The Politics of the NHS* (Oxford: Longman Medical, 1983). He is joint editor of *Political Quarterly*.

Jean-François Lacronique, M.D., is Professor of Public Health at the University of Paris. A radiologist by training, he worked as a consultant on the use of computers in the field of health for the Ministry of Health in France until 1973, when he was appointed science attaché at the French embassy in Washington, D.C. Following that, he went back to France to become medical editor of the newspaper *Le Monde*. He returned to academia in 1980 and was appointed Deputy Director for Health and Hospitals at the Ministry of Health. He is currently Medical Director at the *Institut Pasteur Production*, a leading French pharmaceutical company in sera and vaccines.

Theodore R. Marmor taught at the Universities of Minnesota, Wisconsin, Chicago, and Essex before joining Yale's faculty as Professor of Political Science and Public Health and Chairman of the Center for Health Studies. He is the author of *The Politics of Medicare* and numerous articles on the politics and policies of the welfare state; and he is editor of the *Journal of Health Politics, Policy and Law*. Marmor served as special assistant to HEW's undersecretary in 1966, was on the staff of the President's Commission on Income

Maintenance Programs (1968–70), and served on the recent Presidential Commission on a National Agenda for the 80's.

John Ratcliffe has taught since 1979 at the University of California, Berkeley, School of Public Health, where he currently heads the Program in Health Education. Formerly he was with the World Bank in India, where he was responsible for a $32 million health and population policy research project and three economic sectors (population, health, and nutrition). He was also with the Ford Foundation in East Pakistan (now Bangladesh) where he was Codirector of the East Pakistan Research and Evaluation Centre, a population and health policy research project. He is the author of numerous articles on research methodology, peace, and health, and of a forthcoming book, *Population Control or Social Justice? The Determinants of Population Growth and Decline.*

Marc Renaud is Associate Professor in the Department of Sociology at the University of Montréal. He has published several articles on the politics of health, power, and medicine and on the unique Québec experience in reforming the health field. At present he is studying the social dynamic created by the recent Québec legislation in occupational health and analyzing the impact of the changes introduced by the Mitterand administration in France.

Christopher Robbins is Administrative Officer at the Council of Europe in Strasbourg, France, where since 1977 he has worked primarily on aspects of medical care that lend themselves to international cooperation. Prior to that he lectured in philosophy at the University of York for six years and spent nearly two years in the British Civil Service.

Victor G. Rodwin is Adjunct Assistant Professor at the Institute for Health Policy Studies, University of California School of Medicine, San Francisco. Over the past several years he has served as advisor to the Director of the principal French National Health Insurance Fund (CNAMTS) and as a lecturer in the School of Public Health and in the Health Arts and Sciences Program, University of California, Berkeley and in the Department of Organization and Man-

agement Studies, University of Paris IX (Dauphine). Rod-
win is the author of *The Health Planning Predicament: France,
Québec, England and the United States*. Berkeley, University of
California Press, 1984.

Paul Starr is Associate Professor of Sociology at Harvard
University. He is the author of *The Discarded Army: Veterans
after Vietnam* (1974) and more recently of *The Social Transformation of American Medicine* (1982). He frequently writes
about politics and social policy for general publications.

Jean-Claude Stephan, M.D., became a health economist
after practicing surgery for fifteen years. He is the author of
Economie et Pouvoir Médical (Paris: Economica, 1978) and
coauthor of *Hippocrate et les Technocrates* (Paris: Calmann-
Lévy, 1983). Stephan is currently Director of the French
National Center for Hospital Equipment and Technology.

Lawrence Wallack is Assistant Professor in the School of
Public Health, University of California, Berkeley. He is also
Associate Director of the Prevention Research Group, Medical Research Institute of San Francisco. He has published
numerous articles in the areas of social policy, mass media,
and prevention as seen from the perspective of alcohol and
other health related issues. He serves as a consultant to a
wide range of federal, state, and local agencies concerned
with public health issues.

Introduction
The End of an Illusion

Jean de Kervasdoué, John R. Kimberly, and Victor G. Rodwin

In Western society, everyone wants to live "normally" as long as possible. We ask physicians to do whatever they can to prolong life, be it only for months, or days, in the case of terminal illness. The arsenal of medical technology deployed to keep aging political leaders alive is but one example of this tendency. Physicians merely perform their duties and respond to the demands of the majority of people. Though the belief is widely held that health is the most precious thing a person has, most of us are loathe to analyze the collective consequences of this belief.

The most costly diseases are those for which there are presently no cures and which therefore require multiple diagnostic procedures, symptomatic treatment, and long-term care. Though the biomedical industry naturally invents and markets new machines and new drugs to improve diagnosis and treatment of these diseases, diagnostic and therapeutic procedures have only marginal effects on mortality rates. Nevertheless, hospitals have been built, new machines are purchased, and personnel continue to be trained and hired. All of this accelerates the rate of health care expenditures.

Such growth was easily tolerated when total health expenditures were well under ten percent of gross national product and when national economic growth proceeded at a rate of roughly five percent. Today, however, health care costs in many countries are increasing more rapidly than GNP, thus claiming an increasing share of the national product. As a result, new questions are being raised. Will it be possible to continue to remunerate the growing number of physicians at the levels to which they have become accustomed over the past two decades? Can health policies continue to encourage diffusion of new medical technologies? Will it be possible to support the biomedical industry and at the same time contain the growth of health care costs and achieve more equitable access to medical care?

The answer, we think, is that what was once believed possible may no longer be. The notion that the welfare state can provide an abundance of health services for all of its citizens is an illusion. In the future, social policy is likely to veer from idealism to realism, from opportunity to constraint. Difficult choices must be made. Our objective in this book is to identify the issues and themes around which debates about health policy will focus in the 1980s and beyond.

One has only to open a newspaper day after day to see that health and health policy revolve around questions of life and death, problems of suffering, and the ways Western societies have responded to these issues: through science, technology, bureaucratic organizations, professionalization, social security, health insurance, biomedical industries, and management. Rarely do we discuss suffering except where these responses are inadequate, as with the elderly and the physically or mentally handicapped. More typically, discussions of health policy focus on economic issues. Representatives of industry or of a ministry of finance argue that health care is too expensive, while physicians argue that government regulation of costs jeopardizes quality of care. Sometimes the discussion is political: some claim that a free enterprise system is more efficacious and more equitable than a nationalized system, while others argue the reverse. Sometimes the debate is technological: some claim that esoteric new technologies drive up the costs of health care even before there is solid evidence of their effectiveness. Others argue that new technology is essential for the practice of effective medicine.

This book contains three parts. Part 1 examines the recent

past: the expanding role of the state in the health sector of Western industrialized nations. In health systems of the 1980s the state defines the rules of the game and is also the principal actor. The state finances—directly or indirectly—a large part of the cost of health care. It also shapes policy in several critical domains: medical manpower and biomedical research, the purchase of equipment, the development of innovations, and the construction and modernization of hospitals. Curiously, it plays this public role while preserving, by and large, the notion that the practice of medicine is a very private affair—that the only obligation of the physician is to his patient. The state supplies funds, the ill demand care, and physicians command resources.

This highly individualistic conception of medicine is unlikely to survive during the present period of economic retrenchment. Retrenchment will force alternative conceptions of medicine. It is likely that, at first, as cost savings are sought, they will be found in the slack that has accumulated during the period of growth. Cost savings of this sort are not unlimited, however. When the fat has been cut away, it will be clear that the best way to save is not to spend.

Not to spend may involve questions of life and death. For example, should a child with a rare blood disease who requires transfusions costing in the neighborhood of $2,200 weekly be kept alive? Should pacemakers be made widely available to the elderly? Should renal dialysis be available to everyone who needs it? To raise these questions in a time of abundant resources would be—and has been—considered sacrilegious. Until social values have caught up with economic realities, it is likely that the medical profession can use deeply held beliefs about the value of life to great advantage; and as long as public opinion reflects a belief in the possibility of unlimited economic growth and infinite progress, these questions will provoke resistance of the most intense sort.

As the illusion of abundance wanes, however, the functioning of health systems, as well as the role of technology and the power of the health professions, will come under increasing scrutiny. The state is likely to extend its power. It will no longer merely finance and regulate the provision of goods and services in the health system; rather, it will be an arbiter in a debate about what is good, equitable, and right in the business of life and death. This debate will go beyond the domain of medicine, for well-being is not simply a byproduct of our health systems. Moreover, the debate will produce different results in different countries, as a consequence of historical, cultural, and institutional differences.

Part 2 of this book (chapters 2–5) elaborates on a number of these themes. Chapter 2 considers contrasting perspectives—radical, conservative and liberal—on the proper role of the state in society and explores their implications for health policy. The liberal perspective has dominated health policy in the West since World War II, but the conservative perspective now appears to be gaining ground. History has taught us to be modest, however, where prediction is concerned. We are therefore more inclined to indicate probable tendencies than to make predictions.

Chapter 3 discusses the state in relation to prevention policies. It begins with a historical analysis of disease prevention programs and the rise of clinical medicine and raises some of the key issues that have fueled health policy debates for years: Should disease prevention programs intervene largely at the individual level, or is there a case for collective action? Must they compete with curative medicine or are there new areas for growth (for example, in health education)? And, how can renewed interest in disease prevention avoid encouraging either victim-blaming, directed at individuals who fail to take responsibility for their health, or authoritarian state intervention to avert all potential risk factors? In resolving these issues it is helpful to distinguish between risk-taking and risk-imposing behavior and between strategies of health promotion versus health protection.

Chapter 4 analyzes the evolution of medical technology and its social impact. The precise nature of the medications, drugs, and equipment that will exist in the future is impossible to predict. What seems probable, however, is that research and development will be worldwide, and no one country will be able to control the development of new technology. A moratorium on technological development is therefore unlikely. Instead, each country will have to control access, which will raise a host of very difficult ethical issues.

Chapter 5 raises the specter of health care rationing as a mechanism for controlling access to health care and examines the ethical implications. There are already changes in doctrines relating to professional ethics and "the right to health." The concept of clinical freedom is unlikely to survive in an age of medical austerity. Physicians are increasingly aware that they must work in teams, accountable not only to their professional values and to individual patients but to a new public morality and new social and economic constraints. One common response to pressures for health care rationing is to advocate medical decision making based on a comparison of outcomes. One example is a utilitarian calculus that two years of additional life for an elderly person is less valuable than a longer period for a younger person. But such criteria for allocation of scarce medical resources are seriously deficient. This chapter explains why and proposes alternatives.

How will Western industrialized nations devise health policies in the future? Part 3 examines the recent past and probable future in three nations—France, Britain, and the United States—and in the Canadian province of Québec. Although each case is different, together they provide some indications of how current problems in the health sector may eventually be resolved. In a sense, these case studies are the heart of the book, because they demonstrate, singly and collectively, the range of alternatives before us.

Part 4, like Part 1, consists of a single chapter. We identify the common themes and variations in the case studies and speculate about emerging trends and the future of health policy.

Western societies are seriously questioning current assumptions about health, medicine, and individual and collective well-being. Our hope is that this book may help to explore the pathways that lie ahead and to avoid the quixotic jousting that tends to permeate the field of health policy.

Part I
THE RECENT PAST AND THE PRESENT PREDICAMENT

1

Health Policy and the Expanding Role of the State: 1945—1980

Jean de Kervasdoué and Victor G. Rodwin

Since World War II, in Western industrialized nations, the state has gradually expanded its role in the health sector. What was once the responsibility of the medical profession, charitable institutions, and local government now falls within the province of the nation-state. The state's responsibility has grown from enforcing minimal sanitary conditions and running public health programs to financing the provision of medical care, regulating the growth of the health sector, and reorganizing health care institutions. In some cases (e.g., Great Britain and Sweden), it has assumed even more control over the health system through nationalization of hospitals.

Until the early seventies, health policy focused on the problems of improving access to medical care and upgrading quality by narrowing the gap between new biomedical knowledge and its practical applications and availability. The goals were clear—to eliminate financial barriers to medical care and to construct and modernize hospitals—and there was widespread agreement on them. Although there were difficulties of coordination and financing, these objectives were largely accomplished; and the key actors involved—physicians, hospital associations, insurance companies, and government administrators—all benefited from the growth of the health sector. Over the last decade, however, the character of the problems, the goals, and the context of health policy have changed.[1]

3

The new problems are, paradoxically, the result of previous successes, rising expectations, and above all, the changing configuration of the health sector, as well as the fiscal crisis of most Western capitalist states.[2] Following a period of health sector growth, the problems of inequitable access and uneven quality of medical care have been exacerbated, and health care costs have exploded. Having succeeded in expanding and modernizing hospital infrastructure, state policies now focus on efforts to contain rising health care costs. At the same time, the goals of health policy have broadened and now involve hazy concepts such as "health promotion," "institutional innovation," "health planning," and "rationalization." But no one quite knows what the future health sector should look like or how to achieve control over the health system.

In addition to new problems and broadening goals, the growth of health professions and broader participation by consumers and interest groups have turned the health sector into a political arena for the resolution of competing claims. The medical profession has expanded through increased specialization, thus fracturing unity and increasing differences of opinion within the profession. New actors—paraprofessionals, labor unions, and the biomedical research establishment, no longer agree about what goals to pursue. The welfare state is no longer the angel of left-leaning social democrats; instead, it has become the target of the New Right, for social expenditures are presumed not merely to limit industrial competitiveness but also to be a source of waste and to strip social groups of their sense of responsibility.

How did this political situation evolve? How has the growth of the state's responsibility for health affected its policies? What tools are available to policymakers to plan and manage the health system, and which ones are most likely to be applied? To answer these questions, we will analyze two phases in the recent history of state intervention in the health sector.

PHASE ONE (1945−1970): GROWTH AND CHANGE

We will characterize phase one by focusing first on the similarities among Western industrialized nations during this period of growth and change. Next, we will review some of the differences between health systems and highlight two paradoxes of health sector growth: the problem of disparities in the distribution of medical resources and the uncertain benefits of medical care.

Similarities among Nations

Following World War II, infectious diseases that had previously been fatal could be cured in a matter of days. Naturally, it was hard to see beyond such progress despite the presence of incurable disease and the fact that the applications of medical research were strictly limited. In most Western industrialized nations, health policymakers focused on constructing and modernizing hospitals, promoting biomedical research and expanding access to medical care. In the context of resurging industrial economies, these policies succeeded in producing the health system's most striking characteristic: explosive growth. There was an extraordinary burgeoning of health sector employment, health care utilization, and health care costs.[3] The health sector responded to powerful new forces: changes in the demand for health care and changes in the supply structure of health services.

On the demand side, a number of factors account for the increasing utilization of health services. First, rapid economic growth resulted in increased per capita real income. For example, in the United States between 1950 and 1973, per capita disposable income increased by seventy-six percent (in constant 1958 dollars).[4] More disposable income means more money to spend on health services; and more money was spent.

In addition to private affluence, the state became actively involved in increasing and financing health benefits. In

Great Britain, following the Beveridge report in 1942,[5] the entire population was covered by the creation of the National Health Service in 1948. In France, the Social Security Ordinance of 1945 was passed, and over a period of thirty years national health insurance was gradually extended to cover the entire population. In Canada, hospital insurance was passed in 1958 and then extended to include ambulatory care in 1968. And in the United States, although there is no compulsory national health insurance, Medicare and Medicaid were passed in 1965 to provide health insurance for the elderly and the very poor. As medical technology brought new diagnostic and therapeutic procedures, these were covered under health insurance programs and contributed to increasing utilization of medical services. Moreover, as social problems became increasingly medicalized (e.g., long-term care for the elderly and alcoholism services), they were covered under health insurance.

Another factor that accounts for the increasing utilization of health services is the demographic change in the population of industrially advanced nations. Increased life expectancy at birth and declining birth rates greatly increased the percentage of the population over sixty-five. Since the elderly suffer from higher rates of morbidity than younger people, they tend to visit physicians more frequently and to have higher hospital admission rates. Still other factors that account for the increasing utilization of health services are the changing pattern of disease and the growth of medical technology. The major health problems in industrially advanced nations are no longer infectious diseases but chronic degenerative conditions, such as cardiovascular disease and cancer. This is partly related to the changing age structure but also reflects the evolution of industrial society and the social costs of economic growth and technological progress. For example, automobile accidents have increased the number and severity of emergency room cases. Also, the availability of new diagnostic procedures and therapies have led physicians to increase the range and quantity of medical procedures prescribed.

Finally, the demand for health services increased because of changes in socioeconomic characteristics—for example, changes in status: more white-collar and professionally trained workers; changes in level of education: more public information on the potential benefits of health care; and changes in geographic location: more people living in cities. These factors are closely correlated among themselves and with a high utilization of health services. They are a reminder of how much the activities in the health sector depend upon the larger socioeconomic system of which it is a part. After all, the health sector is mostly financed out of collective funds; it relies on the educational system for producing increasing numbers of diversified and highly skilled professionals; and it receives its patients according to the social system's changing, broader definitions of health.

On the supply side, there are also a number of factors that account for health sector growth. New biomedical knowledge, innovations in medical technology, and increasing medical specialization transformed traditional medical practice. The health sector evolved from a sort of cottage industry, composed of independent physicians, volunteers, and charitable institutions, to a major industrial complex centered around modern hospitals and supporting specialized and unionized staff and significant affiliated activities, such as the pharmaceutical industry, biomedical testing laboratories, and firms producing and marketing medical technology. Whereas in the late forties the general practitioner was the pivotal center of the health system, thirty years later the hospital, within which the specialist reigns, dominates the health system.

The hospital was transformed from a largely philanthropic institution caring for the indigent sick to a center supplied with basic medical infrastructure performing the highest functions of the health system—teaching, basic research, and diagnosis and therapy for complex illnesses. As late as the 1950s—at least in European nations—working in hospitals was considered largely a philanthropic activity. Hospital personnel were poorly paid or, in the case of religious hospitals, hardly paid at all; there were long working hours and no vacations. But as the state expanded its role in the financing and regulation of hospital activities, the institution grew into a bureaucratic organization with specialized functions, routine jobs, proper standards of remuneration, holidays and paid vacations.

In addition to changes within the hospital, new biomedical knowledge and medical technology brought a new corps of medical specialists, technicians, and paraprofessionals into the health sector, thus increasing the division of labor and the degree of hierarchy. The traditional specialties had an epistemological origin that preceded the rapid postwar growth of the biological sciences. They were distinguished by specialization in a technique (medicine or surgery), in an organ, or in a functional system (such as cardiology or neurology). It was only in the course of the 1950s that new medical disciplines emerged out of scientific disciplines such as biochemistry, biophysics, and immunology. Then, in the course of the 1960s, the hospital grew so important that organizational factors became a source of new medical disciplines. For example, the specialty of intensive care was not based on particular disease entities but rather on the need to provide care for the most severely ill patients in hospital wards.[6]

The splintering of medicine into compartmentalized specialties is painfully felt by the patient, whose most frequent complaint, as expressed by consumer movements, is that doctors care rather for organs and diseases than for complete human beings. Although these trends in the evolution of medicine are, no doubt, necessary given the growth of biomedical knowledge, they raise at least two fundamental issues, neither of which has been resolved in Western industrialized nations. The first is whether all graduates of medical school should have the right to practice all major forms of medical care throughout their entire lives. Should the right to practice be limited in time and therefore renewable only under certain conditions, or should it be limited to specific areas of competency? The second issue is whether the trend toward specialization should be encouraged or resisted. Is there still a place for the general practitioner in tomorrow's health system?

It would seem that the necessary counterpart to specialization would be the encouragement of coordination among specialties; but casual observation as well as empirical studies suggest that such coordination is minimal. In the future, regional health systems with networks linking hospitals and specialists to general practitioners and support services are likely to predominate. As for the present, the trend toward greater specialization continues in certain countries, though it is limited in others. Moreover, the evolution of medical specialties is associated with the emergence of new medical techniques and consequently a strong medical equipment industry and pharmaceutical sector. This growth, undoubtedly justified by some extraordinary medical accomplishments, has also led to extraordinary abuse. All industrially advanced nations have found it necessary to increase controls over these affiliated industries both to protect the consumer and to limit public expenditures.

In addition to changes in the demand and supply of health services, health system goals have broadened. Indeed, there are no clear limits to what activities a health system may encompass—a situation that has also contributed to the growth of the health sector.

Initially, health systems largely cured and cared for that portion of the population which demanded health services—the exposed tip of the so-called iceberg of disease. More recently, responsibility appears to have grown to encompass curing and caring for the portion of the population which is ill but does not seek help—the submerged part of the iceberg of disease.[7] Epidemiologic studies carried out in diverse nations—Lévy et al., in France; Wolfe, in Canada; Last, in England; and Bogatyrev, in the Soviet Union—amply confirm that for most conditions the submerged part of the iceberg is much larger than the known one.[8] As health system goals continue to broaden, the utilization of health services is likely to increase further. For example, health services will be provided not only to patients with heart disease but also to that portion of the population displaying high risk factors such as smoking, hypertension, and high cholesterol.

At the present time, health system goals are growing to cover the social components of disease at individual and community levels: alcohol-related problems, drug addiction and juvenile delinquency. Among the new areas covered are vocational rehabilitation, marriage counseling, sex therapy, and mental or nervous disorders reflecting postindustrial stresses such as the accelerated rate of social and technical change, large displacements to and from work, and frequent migrations in the course of a lifetime. The emerging phase in which most industrially advanced nations now find themselves is the expansion of the traditional health system's responsibility beyond that of caring for the submerged part of the iceberg of disease, beyond treatment of social pathologies, to its potential of assuring what the World Health Organization calls a "state of well-being." In this sense, a contraceptive, a sedative, a hallucinogen, or an antihypertensive is a symbol of the search for more choice, more self-control, more inner coherence. These new health system goals are especially valued in a postindustrial society in which traditional social networks, such as the family and the church, are eroding.[9]

During phase one, in Western industrialized nations, the organization of medicine was characterized by similar trends: the increasing utilization of services and medical techniques, the growing dominance of the hospital within health systems, and the rise of medical specialization. Despite such similarities, however, one should not overlook the differences between nations. They are due, in large part, to the fact that health systems are not isolated entities but are intricately tied to the organization of the state, which can either encourage or constrain their development.

Differences among Nations

EXPENDITURES

Per Capita Expenditures. As can be seen from table 1 per capita health expenditures vary from 1 to 3.5. These estimates are given in absolute values. However, since these values reflect the relative wealth of nations as well as exchange rates between currencies, it is worthwhile comparing health expenditures between nations as a percent of gross domestic products (GDP).[10]

Health Expenditures as a Percent of GDP. However much criticized, the concept of GDP is the principal indicator by which economists measure the wealth of nations. The percentage of GDP devoted to health expenditures is a conventional indicator of the relative investment of nations in the health sector.

In table 2, the taxonomy of table 1 is slightly changed. The disparities between nations decrease but vary, nevertheless, from 5.5 to 9.4 percent. One can also see that the richer countries (Sweden, the United States and Germany) have the largest health expenditures.

Structure of Health Expenditures. We have noted the variation of health expenditures between nations as indi-

TABLE 1

PER CAPITA HEALTH EXPENDITURES IN 1975 FOR SELECTED NATIONS

Per capita expenditures: 1975	*Corresponding nations in order of increasing expenditures*
$224, $226	Italy, United Kingdom
$491	Netherlands
$508, $518	Canada, France
$607, $638, $717	United States, Germany, Sweden

Source: Adapted from R. Maxwell, *Health and Wealth* (Lexington, Mass.: D.C. Heath, 1981), p. 33.

TABLE 2

HEALTH EXPENDITURES AS A PERCENT OF GPD FOR SELECTED NATIONS

Health expenditures as a percent of GDP	*Corresponding nations in order of increasing expenditures*
5 to 6	United Kingdom, Italy
7 to 8	Canada, France
8 to 10	Netherlands, Sweden, United States, Germany

Source: Adapted from R. Maxwell, *Health and Wealth* (Lexington, Mass.: D. C. Heath, 1981), p. 37.

cated by measures of both absolute and relative value; but the variation is even more striking when one examines the structure of health expenditures.

National health accounts usually distinguish several broad categories of health expenditure: hospitalization; ambulatory and home care (largely honoraria as well as wages of medical and paramedical personnel); and medical related goods (drugs, optometry, prostheses). There is also sometimes a category known as "other" which includes expenditures for administration, research, and certain forms of preventive medicine.

Table 3 reveals the great variation among nations in the structure of health expenditures. One might easily suppose that the hospital plays more or less the same role in these countries and that consequently the share of health expenditures devoted to hospitalization would be roughly the same. This is not the case, however, and if one adopts a purely technical view, it is difficult to explain why expenditures on hospitalization represented less than thirty-five percent of health expenditures in 1974 in both Germany and Belgium and more than sixty-five percent in Sweden.

Physician Income.   Despite the growing importance of specialized medical equipment and technology in modern medicine, the health sector is, above all, a labor-intensive industry. In hospitals, seventy percent of the budget is

TABLE 3
STRUCTURE OF EXPENDITURES FOR MEDICAL
GOODS AND SERVICES IN 1974
(or closest year)

	Hospital care − %	Ambulatory and home care − %	Medical related goods − %	Other − %
Germany (F.R.G.)	28.7	25.0	22.8	23.5
Belgium	29.1	35.7	19.8	15.4
United States	53.8	24.2	2.1	19.9
France	45.8	22.8	16.9	14.5
Italy	50.8	21.1	18.1	10.0
Netherlands	54.9	20.5	9.8	14.8
United Kingdom (1975)	63.5	23.1	9.1	4.3
Sweden	65.5	25.9	6.2	2.4

Source: OECD, *Public Expenditure on Health* (Paris, 1977), p. 15.

devoted to personnel, and this figure excludes physicians working in private practice.

The income of physicians varies widely between nations. One is struck by the great disparity in relative income between, for example, the average British and French physician. The former earns 2.7 times as much as the average production worker, whereas the latter earns 7 times as much, thus holding what may be a world record (see table 4).

MEDICAL CARE ORGANIZATION

The organization of medical care ranges from strong centralized systems (Britain and France) to great decentralization (Sweden, Canada, and the United States). More specifically, there are different mechanisms of physician remuneration, different distributions of hospital beds between the public and private sector, and different criteria for the allocation of health resources.

TABLE 4
RELATIVE IMPORTANCE OF PHYSICIANS' INCOME AMONG NATIONS
(1974 or near date)

Country	Ratio of average income of physicians to average gross earnings of production workers
Germany (1973)	6.1
Belgium	5.2
United States	5.6
France	7.0
Italy (1973)	6.8
Netherlands	6.3
United Kingdom	2.7
Sweden	3.5

Source: OECD, *Public Expenditure on Health* (Paris, 1977), p. 24.

Systems of Physician Remuneration.   Four systems of physician remuneration can be distinguished, each allowing for several variations.

(a) Fee-for-Service Payment.   This is the system of payment for physicians in private practice in the United States; physicians who refuse to accept nationally negotiated fees in France and Belgium; physicians not licensed by the health insurance funds in Germany; and physicians working outside the National Health Service in England.

(b) Fee-for-Service Payment According to a Fee Schedule.   Examples are Medicare and certain state Medicaid programs in the United States, and payment of most physicians in France, Germany, and the Netherlands.

(c) Capitation Payment.   This system remunerates physicians on the basis of the number of patients for whom they assume responsibility. It is the prevailing mode of physician remuneration for general practitioners in Britain and it is also widely used in the Netherlands.

(d) Salary Payment.   This system is most frequently used by public hospitals in France, Germany, and Italy. It is also used by public hospitals as well as many health maintenance organizations (HMOs) in the United States.

Distribution of Hospital Beds between Public and Private Sectors. Depending on the country, hospital beds in the public sector represent between one-fifth and almost all hospital beds.

In Britain and Sweden, almost all hospital beds are in the public sector; and in Italy there is a strong public sector. As for France, two thirds of all hospital beds are in the public sector, and roughly one-half of the other third are in the private proprietary sector.

Germany, the United States, and Belgium have a much smaller public hospital sector, representing roughly one-half of the beds in Germany, one-third in the United States, and barely one-fifth in Belgium. In contrast to France, however, the private nonprofit sector is relatively large in these nations.

Criteria for the Allocation of Health Resources.   A look at the health planning literature suggests that neither planners nor physicians know how much medical care is "needed" for particular populations, how much is lacking, or what is the best way of providing medical services.[11] What we know, on the basis of cross-national comparisons, is that different nations have organized their health services according to divergent conceptions of what is right. The level of health resources, as well as standards of medical care, differ greatly around the world.[12] Whether one looks at the number of physicians, hospital beds, or nurses per capita, there is considerable variation among nations (see table 5). Among industrially advanced nations, the relationship between lengths of stay and admission rates in hospitals reveals that those in geographic proximity have similar patterns of hospital utilization (figure 1). Overall, however, the amount of variation is tremendous.

Paradoxes of Health Sector Growth

Having outlined the similarities as well as the differences that characterize the pattern of health sector growth and

TABLE 5
VARIATION IN ACTUAL HEALTH RESOURCES

	General hospital beds per 1000 population 1971	Physicians per 10,000 population 1971	Nurses per 10,000 population 1970	Health expenditures as percent of GDP 1970
North America				
Canada	5.5[a]	15.1	45.9	7.2
United States	4.7	15.4	35.3	7.6
Britain				
England and Wales	4.1	12.7	30.7	4.6[b]
Scotland	4.9	15.6	35.5	
Scandinavia				
Sweden	6.9	13.9	40.7	7.3
Western Group				
Netherlands	5.4	13.2	19.2	6.0
Belgium	4.7[a]	16.0[c]	– –	
Luxembourg	5.9	10.8	19.6	9.3[d]
France	6.1	13.9	26.6	6.1

Southern Group				
Italy	4.8	18.4[c]	6.9	4.5
Spain	3.1	13.9[e]	6.7	4.1
Portugal	3.8	9.7	4.5	—
Central Group				
West Germany	6.7	17.8	23.1	5.7
Austria	6.0[a]	18.7[c]	20.3	5.4
Switzerland	6.0	15.0	22.8	7.0[d]

Source: Data on health expenditures are from the OECD *National Accounts 1952–1981*. Data on hospital beds, physicians, and nurses are from R. Maxwell, *Health Care: The Growing Dilemma. Needs v. Resources in Western Europe, the U.S. and the U.S.S.R.*, second edition (New York: McKinsey, 1975).

Note: The Organization for Economic Cooperation and Development (OECD) has recent data on health resources, but since our discussion concerns the 1970s, we are relying on 1970–1971 data for purposes of comparison.

[a]For 1970. [b]This figure is for the United Kingdom. [c]Includes those practicing in dentistry. [d]For 1975. [e]Registered personnel only.

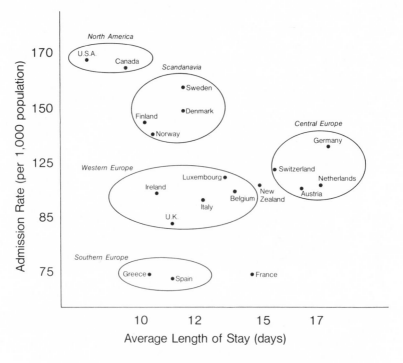

Fig. 1. Hospital lengths of stay and admission rates
in different nations.

*The data are from *World Statistics Annuals* (Geneva: WHO, 1973).

Source: J. F. Lacronique, "Cross-Sectional International Analysis of the Consumption of Short-Term Hospital Care," masters thesis (Sloan School of Management, Massachusetts Institute of Technology, June 1977), p. 34.

change, let us consider two questions: (1) Did the growth of medical resources improve access to health services? (2) Do the differences between health systems make for differences in health status?

ACCESS AND INEQUALITY

There is no agreed-upon indicator which can conclusively demonstrate the relative access to medical care that has been achieved by people at equal risk. As we have noted earlier, Western industrialized nations have succeeded in eliminating financial barriers to health services; however, there are still large disparities between regions in the distribution of health resources. Moreover, these disparities may well be exacerbated by progress in medical technology, for innovation is more readily adopted by the more urbanized areas and more privileged groups. Despite the growth of the health sector, the problem of inequitable distribution of medical resources is recognized in all Western industrialized nations.

Hospitals.   Inequalities in the per capita distribution of hospital beds are a good example. In Canada, the number of hospital beds per 1000 population varies from 5.4 to 10.9 among the twelve provinces.[13] In the United States the range among states is from 3.7 to 9.0, and in France, among administrative regions the range is from 11.0 to 17.0.[14]

Physicians.   Inequalities in the regional distribution of physicians are another illustration. In France, the number of physicians per 10,000 population varies from 9.4 to 21.8 among the twenty-two regions. In the United States the number varies among major regions from 13.1 to 17.9.[15]

In addition to such disparities in the distribution of health resources in all Western industrialized nations, there is clear evidence of inequalities in mortality rates by occupational groups. Moreover, in the United States there is evidence to suggest that the disparities in mortality between upper and lower classes have increased between 1965–1975, even in the face of higher levels of utilization by the poor.[16]

MEDICAL EFFICACY AND HEALTH STATUS

Can any differences in health status be attributed to the differences in expenditure levels and organizational characteristics of the various countries?

Life Expectancy.   We know that life expectancy at birth has increased dramatically in Western industrialized nations—from forty years in 1800 to seventy years today, for men, and seventy-eight years for women.[17] This upward trend began as a result of the public health movements that took place in the late nineteenth century throughout Europe; and during the twenty years following World War I life expectancy at birth increased at a rate of almost six months per year. Since World War II, this trend—which is attributable largely to the decrease in infant mortality—has practically stopped. People grow old, and although life expectancy at age forty-five has increased, we still have no cure for old age and the chronic and degenerative diseases that go along with it.

Among nations at similar levels of development there is little variation in life expectancy at birth: between 1968 and 1973 it varied from sixty-eight to seventy-two years for men and from seventy-four to seventy-seven years for women.[18] Of the nine countries of the Organization for Economic Cooperation and Development which we have been comparing, Sweden and the Netherlands have the highest life expectancy at birth and Germany and Belgium the lowest.[19]

Infant Mortality. Figure 2 shows the relationship between per capita health expenditures and infant mortality rates for nine OECD countries. The points are widely dispersed and there appears to be no correlation. Whereas Sweden has a low infant mortality rate and high per capita health expenditures, Italy has a high infant mortality rate and low per capita health expenditures. In contrast, Germany has both a high infant mortality rate as well as high per capita health expenditures; and Britain has relatively low indicators both for infant mortality and for expenditures.

There appears to be an absence of clear links between health care expenditures, medical care organization, and health status. In addition, we have seen that, with health sector growth, the problem of inequalities in the distribution of health resources has not disappeared. Nevertheless, neither of these factors is as critical in explaining the changing role of the state in the health sector as the problem of rising health care costs. The key theme during the 1970s

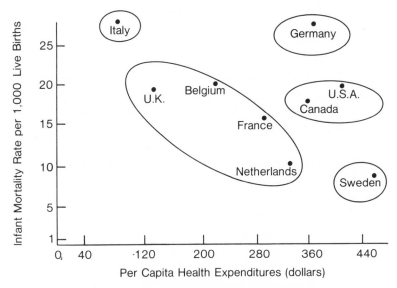

Fig. 2. The Relationship Between Infant Mortality and
Health Care Spending

Source: Institut National des Etudes Statistiques et Economiques (INSEE),
Annuaire Statistique de la France, 1976. The data on infant mortality rates are for
1973. The data on per capita health expenditures are for 1974.

became cost containment. The techniques used for achieving this goal can be summarized in two words: standards
and control.

PHASE TWO (1970–1980):
STANDARDS AND CONTROL

1970's

The second phase of state intervention in the health sector
coincides with a period of "tax-welfare backlash" in Western industrialized nations. During this period, governments have sought, sometimes successfully, to reduce
public expenditures for social programs, thus dismantling
key features of the welfare state. In Denmark in 1974, the
Progress Party of Mogens Glistrup led a strong movement
against taxes. In the United States, the antitax, antistate,
and antispending rhetoric of Ronald Reagan and George

welfare
backlash

Wallace dominated the 1976 presidential primaries and contributed to President Reagan's election in 1980. In 1978, the success of Proposition 13 in California provoked commentaries about an emerging American-style *Poujadisme*. In Canada, conservative Joe Clark rode a wave of fiscal conservatism in 1978, and in the province of Québec, Thomas Ryan has presented a serious threat to the Parti Québecois of Prime Minister René Lévesque. In France, the 1976 Plan of Prime Minister Raymond Barre well reflected the tax-welfare backlash, or what might be called the politics of retrenchment. And in Britain, Prime Minister Margaret Thatcher has led the way.

During phase two there has been a major shift in values with regard to medicine. Faith in technology and medical progress has begun to dwindle. The implicit search for extended life through modern medicines has gradually waned, for we are, after all, mortal in spite of machines, drugs, specialists, and health expenditures that have been growing at exponential rates for roughly twenty-five years. This recognition has promoted policymakers to emphasize, on the one hand, self-care and individual responsibility for personal health, and on the other hand, public health programs and population based planning.

The growth of medical specialization, which characterized the first phase of state intervention in the health sector, was largely a response to new technological possibilities and to patient demands. It is part of the individual tradition in medicine, in contrast to the social tradition, whose unit of analysis is not the patient but rather the population at risk.[20] The social tradition in medicine is exemplified by the early nineteenth-century reform movements: the sanitary movement in England, the medical police in Germany, and the public hygienists in France. These movements produced the first sociodemographic studies of mortality and morbidity. Their work was subsequently swamped by medical progress in the individual tradition, but during the second phase of state intervention there has been a renaissance of this social approach to medicine, for it provides a foundation for the design of health policy.

While promoting the ethic of individual responsibility, and reviving the social tradition in medicine as a long-run strategy for the containment of rising health care costs, policymakers have concentrated their efforts on short-term control mechanisms. Almost all nations have established formal administrative machinery to control costs. In nationalized systems such as the British National Health Service or the Swedish Health Service, classic budgetary tools have been deployed. In national health insurance systems such as those of France, Canada, and Germany, more complicated negotiating mechansims have evolved to establish reimbursement rates for physicians and hospitals.

In most European nations physicians' fees are generally negotiated between medical trade unions, the state, and health insurance funds. In the United States physicians are most often reimbursed on the basis of "usual, customary and prevailing charges" within a given geographic area. For hospitals the unit of reimbursement has generally been the patient day, whose value is usually calculated by dividing total operating expenses (either for an entire hospital or for separate departments)—including teaching, research, administrative costs, and a range of ancillary services—by the total number of patient days. In effect, this procedure is not so different from that of budgetary systems since the patient day is most often calculated on the basis of a projected budget and adjusted by the estimated number of patient days.

In addition to controlling provider fees, most nations have introduced some degree of cost sharing in the financing of health services. Private health insurance in the United States is known for its deductibles and copayments. National health insurance in France is known for its copayments. The effect of these mechanisms in controlling health care costs has been limited, however, for there have usually been exceptions in the case of catastrophic illness. In fact cost sharing is very unlikely to be effective for the majority of health service users, who are either very young, mentally ill, mentally handicapped, very old, seriously ill, or victims of an unexpected accident. It can only curb visits to doctors, it does not inhibit referrals. Moreover, in most European nations with national health insurance, the private sector responded by insuring the copayment through mutual aid societies and commercial insurance carriers.

As health costs have continued to rise, policymakers in most nations have come to realize that effective cost-control strategies must focus on the supply side. Consequently, they have resorted to defining standards of medical care and mechanisms for administrative control.

Standards of Provision

Standards of provision refer to ratios such as hospital beds per capita, medical equipment (e.g., computed axial tomography (CAT) scanners) per capita, or numbers of medical personnel per capita.[21] Aside from their role in limiting expenditures, such standards are most often justified on two grounds in the health planning literature: first, to assure equality of access to medical services; second, to assure quality of care. The relative importance of these justifications varies from one country to another.

In France, the Hospital Law of 1970 established institutional machinery for health planning and called for the creation of health regions (*secteurs sanitaires*), within which standards could be applied as criteria for the allocation of capital expenditures for medical care. In addition to its goal of containing health care costs, this law also sought legitimacy in its adherence to the principle of equality; however, as Aaron Wildavsky has observed, "Any effort to increase equality in one direction necessarily results in a decrease in another."[22] Thus, planning on the basis of hospital bed/population ratios penalizes regions with low population densities per square mile.

Upper limit standards justified on the principle of equality may also backfire with respect to cost-containment objectives. There are two reasons for this. The first has to do with the way standards are calculated; the second is related to the way they are enforced. The French experience illustrates this point.

Following the passage of the Hospital Law of 1970, standards for the proper number of hospital beds per capita were set in relation to existing patterns of hospital bed distribution. Based on analysis of average hospital occupancy rates in France and adjusted (slightly) for decreases in the average lengths of hospital stay per region, a rough standard was calculated which corresponded, in the final analysis, to the existing stock of hospital beds. Instead of leading to a more equitable distribution of hospital beds, this standard allowed regions whose hospital bed capacity was substandard to initiate hospital building programs (particularly in the private sector), without resulting in a corresponding decrease of hospital beds in regions that were above standard. It is not surprising that between 1968 and 1974 55,000 additional beds were added to the French hospital system.[23] One may wonder why no hospitals reduced their stock of beds; but a moment's reflection makes it difficult to imagine the government shutting down hospitals in order to conform to bureaucratic standards. Why shut down one hospital rather than another? And what about the resulting unemployment of hospital personnel?

In addition to standards that seek to promote equality of access, there are also standards that aim to assure quality of medical care. As an example, consider the professional standards review organizations (PSROs), which, ironically, were passed by the United States Congress as part of a strategy to contain rising health care costs.

A number of studies have indicated that a fee-for-service system of physician reimbursement runs the risk of tempting physicians to prescribe and perform medical procedures too generously. Bunker et al. have indicated that the number of appendectomies per capita is twice as high in the United States, as in England.[24] A number of studies provide strong evidence that reimbursement incentives affect physician behavior.[25] More specifically, in the United States studies have demonstrated that the existing reimbursement structure encourages costly institutional care, specialized services, and excessive use of technology.[26]

To prevent such potential abuse, the Social Security amendments of 1972 (Public Law 92–603) established 203 PSROs to encourage physicians to monitor medical practice. The legislation rests on two assumptions: (1) physicians are the most competent professionals to evaluate the quality of care; (2) administrative mechanisms and standards to conduct such evaluation must be devised at the local level.

Each PSRO has devised standards for various medical situations. For example, there are criteria by which to assess hospital admissions, lengths of stay, necessary medical procedures, and expected results. By comparing physician activities and patterns of patient utilization to the standards, a valuable system of monitoring and data collection has been established. The impact of PSROs is uncertain in the short run, however, and in the long run it is by no means certain that they would succeed in containing health care costs, even were they to survive politically.[27]

PSRO regulatory activities may eliminate some abuses— for example, unnecessary surgical and medical procedures; but it is exceedingly difficult to prevent physicians from pursuing modes of medical practice which fall outside the standard, for one would have to prove that their activities were useless. This is no easy task. Moreover, when there is doubt about the appropriateness of some medical procedures, there are always others that can be tried.

Suppose that PSROs could succeed in making existing patterns of medical practice correspond to quality standards. Even in this case, there is little reason to think that health care costs would be contained. In the name of equality, PSRO standards apply to all hospitals in a region—rural hospitals as well as regional teaching institutions. To the extent that standards result in upgrading quality in rural and community hospitals, they will increase costs further. Moreover, given the present state of the art, all medical practice cannot be rationalized into clear diagnostic categories with neat procedure standards. Despite great strides in medical science, there are still areas of medical practice in which knowledge is absent, demands are enormous, and there are virtually no established protocols for medical efficacy. In these areas, standards are likely to be arbitrary, partial, and difficult to enforce.

Mechanisms for Administrative Control

When standards are inadequate as tools to guide resource allocation in the health sector, what are the alternatives? All Western industrialized nations have made use of a rich variety of administrative control mechanisms in order to influence the behavior of consumers, providers, administrative institutions, or private firms—policy targets. These mechanisms may be summarized schematically in relation to three kinds of incentives: bureaucratic (which includes the elaboration of standards); market, and moral (see table 6).[28]

Each system of incentives reflects a set of social values as well as a theory of deliberate social change. For example, under a system of bureaucratic incentives individual free choice is allowed to operate within explicitly defined rules; in this context, there is a place for powerful state intervention in the health sector. Under a system of market incentives, individual free choice is thought to be maximized in a context of free markets, and the state's role is confined to promoting conditions in which markets are supposed to thrive. Under a system of moral incentives, the underlying assumption is that information is sufficient to influence human behavior. The state's role centers largely around educational campaigns.

Policymakers in all nations have had recourse to all of

TABLE 6

ADMINISTRATIVE CONTROL MECHANISMS IN THE HEALTH SECTOR

Targets	Instruments		
	Bureaucratic incentives	Market incentives	Moral incentives
Consumers: Subscribers Users	eligibility rules for health insurance	complementary insurance coverage cost-sharing (out-of-pocket payments)	health education programs health promotion campaigns
Providers: Hospitals Physicians	global budgeting limits of capital investment licensing standards utilization review peer review fees schedules	prospective reimbursement tax deductions subsidies advertising reduction in entry barriers	medical ethics
Administration: Ministries Subnational units	standards program planning evaluation	matching funds	demonstration projects social experiments
Firms	standards for health and safety standards for quality of drugs or food products	tax deductions (for health insurance premiums) merit rating in determination of health insurance premiums	prevention programs, e.g., screening

these incentive systems, but the relative importance of each varies from one country to another and has varied over time within specific nations. Great Britain has relied mostly on bureaucratic as opposed to market incentives, whereas in the United States it is the other way around. Margaret Thatcher has tended to be more keen on market incentives than her predecessors, however.

Health planning activities generally precede and follow the use of all the incentive systems noted in table 6. For example, health planners design and evaluate legislation and regulations, as well as market and moral incentives. As state intervention in the health sector has increased, the range and number of administrative control mechanisms and targets have increased as well. The optimal mix of such mechanisms is presumably one that would induce the critical actors in the health sector (targets) to behave in accordance with explicitly agreed-upon social goals. In practice, social goals are most often vague and conflicting, and there is no theory that relates administrative control mechanisms to social goals.

Just as there are debates in macroeconomics on the relative effectiveness of monetary versus fiscal policies, there are conflicting schools of thought in the health policy field with regard to the desirability of using regulatory mechanisms or market incentives. As the following chapter suggests, the modalities of state intervention—indeed, even the decision to intervene—are most often based on ideological predispositions.

CONCLUDING OBSERVATIONS

Since 1945, medical care organization in industrially advanced nations has been transformed. It is hard to imagine today, especially in Europe, the financial distress previously suffered by families without health insurance following prolonged illness. One can hardly remember the fears caused by bacterial infection before the advent of antibiotics. And yet these were the realities only yesterday.

The forces of transformation in all Western industrialized nations are the same, for they derive from scientific and technical progress and its consequences for Western values and societies. The organization of medical care, historically in the hands of religious orders and charitable institutions, was largely taken over by the mix of public and private sector arrangements described above. Though the state has been instrumental in generalizing access to health services during phase one, it appears that during phase two—despite its panoply of mechanisms for administrative control—the state has lost its grip on the transformation it helped to create. The continued explosion of health care costs preoccupies policymakers who know neither whether it will stop nor what the consequences will be.

What are the alternative roles for the state in the future health sector? Should disease prevention programs take the lead over curative medicine? Will the rapid rise of technological innovation in medicine force societies to make choices they have avoided because of the belief in perpetual progress? We now turn to a general consideration of these questions, before discussing more concretely how specific polities—France, Québec, Britain and the United States—are likely to resolve them.

NOTES

1. For further elaboration of this point, see V. Rodwin, *The Health Planning Predicament: France, Québec, England, and the United States* (Berkeley, Los Angeles, London: University of California Press, 1984), chap. 1.

2. J. O'Conner, *The Fiscal Crisis of the State* (New York: St. Martin's Press, 1973).

3. One of the central methodological problems in comparing health care costs involves identification of comparable data. For a recent discussion of these issues, see E. Lévy, ed., *Accounting for Health* (Paris: Economica, 1982). For an international perspective on the problem of rising health care costs, see J. P. Poulier, *Public Expenditure on Health* (Paris: Organization for Economic Cooperation and Development [OECD], 1974); T. Hu, ed., *International Health Costs and Expenditures* (Washington, D. C.: U.S. DHEW, Fogarty International Center, Pub. no. [NIH] 76–1067, 1976). For reviews of this problem in the United States and France,

see M. Zubkoff, *Health: A Victim or Cause of Inflation?* (New York: Prodist, 1976); E. Lévy, M. Bungener, G. Duménil, and F. Fagnani, *La croissance des dépenses de santé* (Paris: Economica, 1982).

4. Cambridge Research Institute, *Trends Affecting the U.S. Health Care System* (Washington, D.C.: Health Resources Administration, Pub. No. [HRA] 76-14503, 1975), p. 19.

5. W. Beveridge, *Report on Social Insurance and Allied Services* (London: HMSO, 1942).

6. J. de Kervasdoué and F. Billon, "Development of Research and External Influences: The Case of Cancer and Respiratory Diseases," *Social Science Information* 17, nos. 4 and 5 (1978).

7. V. Navarro, "Redefining the Health Problem and Implications for Planning Personal Health Services," *HSMHA Health Reports* 86, no. 8 (1971). Also, for a succinct statement on the broadening goals of health planning, see P. Lee, "The Frontiers of Health Planning," *American Journal of Health Planning*, 1, no. 2, (1976).

8. E. Lévy, M. Bungener, G. Duménil, and F. Fagnani, *Economie du Système de Santé* (Paris: Dunod, 1975); S. Wolfe et al., "The Work of a Group of Doctors in Saskatchewan," *Milbank Memorial Fund Quarterly* 46, no. 103 (1968); J. M. Last, "The Iceberg—Completing the Clinical Picture in General Practice," *The Lancet* 7279, no. 28 (1963); I. D. Bogatyrev, *Morbidity of Urban Populations and Standards of Therapeutic and Prophylactic Care* (New York: American Public Health Association, 1974).

9. L. Hirshhorn, "Toward a Political Economy of the Service Society"; and "The Social Crisis," Part II: *Social Services in the Transition to Post-Industrial Society*, Institute of Urban and Regional Development, University of California, Berkeley, Working Papers 229 and 252, See sections on health.

10. The data we have presented were chosen because they characterize the period 1970–1980. They are not the most recent comparative data available.

11. See, e.g., H. Blum, *Planning for Health*, 2d ed. (New York: Human Sciences Press, 1981); and A. Donabedian, *Aspects of Medical Care Administration: Specifying Requirements for Health Care* (Cambridge, Mass.: Harvard University Press, 1973).

12. R. Maxwell, *Health Care: The Growing Dilemma* (New York: McKinsey, 1975).

13. J. P. Poulier, *Public Expenditure on Health* (Paris: OECD, July 1977), pp. 44–48.

14. *Annuaire des statistiques sanitaires et sociales—1979* (Paris: Ministère de la Santé et de la Famille, 1979), pp. 75, 76. The data are for 1976.

15. *Health—United States—1980*, U.S. DHHS Publication no. (PHS)

81-1232 (Washington, D.C.: U.S. DHHS, 1980), p. 191. These data are for 1978.

16. M. Lerner and R. Stutz, "Have We Narrowed the Gap Between the Poor and the Non-Poor?" *Medical Care* 15, no. 8 (1977): 620–635.

17. *Public Expenditure on Health*, preliminary version (Paris: OECD, 1976).

18. Ibid.

19. Ibid.

20. Kervasdoué and Billon, "Development of Research and External Influences."

21. Relying heavily on the unpublished work of J. Dyckman, M. Myerson, H. Gans, and N. Glazer, Allan Blackman has written a useful summary of the advantages and disadvantages of standards in health planning. See "The Meaning and Use of Standards," in H. Blum et al., *Health Planning 1969* (San Francisco: APHA Western Regional Office, 1969), chap. 4.

22. Aaron Wildavsky, "Doing Better and Feeling Worse: The Political Pathology of Health Policy," *Daedalus*, Winter 1977.

23. J. de Kervasdoué, "La politique de l'Etat en matière d'hospitalisation privée, 1962–1978: Analyse des conséquences de mesures contradictoires," *Annales Economiques de Clermont-Ferrand* 16 (1979): 25–56.

24. J. Bunker, "A Comparison of Operations and Surgeons in the United States and in England and Wales," *New England Journal of Medicine* 282, no. 3 (1970): 135–144.

25. See, e.g., the classic paper by G. Monsma, "Marginal Revenue and the Demand for Physicians' Services," in H. Klarman, ed., *Empirical Studies in Health Economics* (Baltimore: John Hopkins Press, 1970). For a good review of the literature on this topic, see H. Luft, "Economic Incentives and Clinical Decision-Making" (Paper prepared for the Institute of Medicine, Washington, D.C., August 1982).

26. See, e.g., M. Blumberg, "Rational Provider Prices: An Incentive for Improved Health Delivery," in G. Chacko, ed., *Health Handbook* (Amsterdam: North Holland, 1979); and S. Schroeder and J. Showstack, "Financial Incentives to Perform Medical Procedures and Laboratory Tests: Illustrative Models of Office Practice," *Medical Care* 16 (1978): 289–298.

27. A. Dobsin, et al., "PSROs: Their Current Status and their Impact to Date," *Inquiry* 15, no. 2 (1978): 113–128.

28. This table was inspired by Eugene Bardach in the course of a discussion with C. Davies, R. Klein, T. Marmor and J. C. Stephan, on the occasion of our seminar at Megève.

Part II
THEMES FOR THE FUTURE

2

Perspectives on the State: Implications for Health Policy

Victor G. Rodwin

Over the next decade or two, the heated debates about appropriate levels of public financing for medical care as well as for health promotion and prevention programs are sure to continue. They will reflect conflicting schools of thought with regard to the choice of or the relative emphasis on regulatory mechanisms and market incentives. To understand such controversy it is helpful to review three orienting perspectives—conservative, radical, and liberal—with regard to the appropriate role of the state in society, and to explore their implications for health policy.[1]

CONTRASTING PERSPECTIVES ON THE STATE

The Conservative Perspective

In Western society, many of these beliefs may be traced to British social and political thought ranging from the traditionalist views of Edmund Burke to certain strands in the liberalism of Adam Smith and John Stuart Mill.[2] Conservatives value the importance of social order and authority. They respect the wisdom of the past as embodied in existing institutions and they want social change to proceed slowly, especially when little is known about the consequences. Conservatives categorically reject untested solutions to human problems.

A number of contemporary conservative beliefs are expressed today in the writings of Milton Friedman. His underlying values are libertarian and he emphasizes the social value of maximum individual freedom and of personal responsibility for achievement. Such values emerge clearly, for example, in Friedman's vision of the ideal society: "unanimity among responsible individuals achieved on the basis of free and full discussion. . . . The ultimate end is itself the use of the proper means."[3]

In practice, of course, unanimity among individuals is rare. Friedman's compromise is a political system based on majority rule. Most decisions, in his view, should be made by individuals through "voluntary exchange" in the context of a free market. Friedman claims that consumers should be sovereign because they know their own preferences better than anyone. He warns about the need to limit strictly the coercive power of the state, and he likens the ideal role of the state to that of an umpire and rule maker. To Friedman, the state is somehow above society—neutral—and charged with mediating the multiple demands of competing interest groups. In his essay "The Role of Government in a Free Society," Friedman emphasizes that

> the organization of economic activity through voluntary exchange presumes that we have provided, through government, for the maintenance of law and order to prevent coercion of one individual by another, the enforcement of contracts voluntarily entered into, the definition of the meaning of property rights, the interpretation and enforcement of such rights, and the provision of a monetary framework.[4]

Beyond these general functions of government, Friedman supports state intervention only in the presence of natural monopolies or externalities. In the case of natural monopolies, where it is technically efficient to have only one producer, he is prepared to choose between the evils of private monopoly, public monopoly, or public regulation. In the case of externalities, when the voluntary exchange of goods and services does not obey the "exclusion principle"—that is, when the actions of individuals have side effects on third parties for which it is impossible to compensate them (e.g., pollution)—Friedman is willing to consider the possibility of government intervention. He does this reluctantly, however, because in his view "every act of government intervention limits the area of individual freedom directly and threatens the preservation of freedom indirectly."[5]

Whereas liberals hold that equality promotes fraternal bonds and consequently assures greater social stability, conservatives hold that people are, by nature, unequal and that state intervention to achieve equality threatens personal freedom and weakens the economic incentives needed to promote economic growth: *in dubito, cum statu quo.*

The Radical Perspective

Radical beliefs are rooted in the nineteenth-century Hegelian—Marxist tradition. With respect to freedom and personal responsibility for achievement, radicals turn their attention away from the individual and emphasize the social. Whereas conservatives define freedom as the absence of restraint, radicals understand freedom as collective self-determination. Radicals argue that freedom and human development can be realized only if social inequalities are reduced. Analysts who hold conservative beliefs emphasize *equality under the law*; those who hold liberal beliefs advocate *equality of opportunity*; but those with radical beliefs tend to promote *equality of results*.

The radical perspective also has its ideal: a classless, stateless, cooperative society in which private property is abolished, exploitation is eliminated, and individual autonomy and potential are realized. This is communism. In practice, since the dream lies far in the future, contemporary radicals have concentrated on analyzing the problems of the modern capitalist state.[6] They reject what Paul Sweezy calls the "class-mediation" theory of the state,

> the tendency on the part of modern liberal theorists to interpret the state as an institution established in the inter-

ests of society as a whole for the purpose of mediating and reconciling the antagonisms to which social existence inevitably gives rise. . . . The class-mediation theory assumes, usually implicitly, that the underlying class structure, or what comes to the same thing, the system of property relations, is an immutable datum.[7]

Radicals view the system from a historical perspective. They see property relations as the outcome of class struggle. They are sympathetic to "class domination" theories. Instrumentalist theorists, such as Ralph Miliband, elaborate on the proposition by Marx and Engels that "the modern state is but a committee for managing the common affairs of the whole bourgeoisie."[8] Structuralist theorists, such as Nicos Poulantzas, reject the interpretation of the capitalist state as an instrument of the ruling class and emphasize the "objective" functions of state intervention within a capitalist economy.

More recent scholars sharing radical perspectives attempt to transcend these categories. Jurgen Habermas, for example, criticizes the modern capitalist state as heading toward a crisis of legitimacy.[9] In analyzing the need for the "accumulation-supporting state" to legitimate itself before the electorate, Habermas distinguishes several kinds of rationality. He explains how increasing societal demands on the state combined with limited intellectual, ideological, and organizational resources lead to "rationality deficits."

In contrast, James O'Connor proposes a three-sector model of the capitalist economy: the monopoly sector, the competitive sector, and the state sector. He explores the contradiction between the requirements of the state for expanded revenues and the maintenance of capital accumulation. In addition, he shows how accumulation and legitimation lead to demands for greater state expenditure; hence, the "fiscal crisis of the state."[10]

Probably the most innovative radical perspective on the theory of the state is Claus Offe's recent work on the "internal structure" of the state and its role in policy formation. He argues that the capitalist state has four principal attributes: (1) it is *excluded* from ordering and controlling production because enterprises are free; (2) it must deflect threats to accumulating units and *maintain* the conditions for capital accumulation; (3) in order to raise revenues and meet its obligations the state *depends* on the accumulating units for its own stability; (4) faced with the unstable functions of *exclusion, maintenance,* and *dependency,* it seeks to "convey the image of an organization of power that pursues common and general interests of society as a whole, allows equal access to power and is responsive to justified *demands*"—legitimation.[11]

Offe goes on to consider the character of state production. He distinguishes *allocative* from *productive* policies. After formulating "decision rules" for the process of policy formation, he indicates how the mechanisms necessary to maintain the structural attributes of the capitalist state change as capitalism evolves: as the capitalist state increasingly pursues "productive policies" (state production), it establishes planning and participatory machinery. Offe argues, however, that the capitalist state is incapable of planning.

> Planning. . . seems to be inherently impossible in the capitalist state as an internal mode of operation—impossible not in itself, but because of the acts of retaliation that planning provokes on the part of capital as a whole or individual accumulating units. Such acts of retaliation (the major forms of which are *absolute* disinvestment, or investment strikes, and *relative* disinvestment, or displacement of investment in time and space) tend to make the cure worse than the disease under capitalism, and are thus self-paralyzing in regard to state activity.[12]

The Liberal Perspective

Liberals, like conservatives, trace their beliefs to the British tradition of liberalism. Benjamin Ward summarizes the liberal theory of the nature of man in three concepts:

> hedonism, rationalism, and atomism. The first refers to the seeking of pleasure and the avoidance of pain, to human motivation as having a very strong materialistic, sensate

side. This side is sufficiently strong that it can be used as the basis for social analysis, though without losing sight of the nobler qualities that motivate humans from time to time.[13]

Although the underlying values of liberals resemble those of conservatives, there are some important differences. For example, personal responsibility for achievement is valued by liberals, but they do not insist that the link between effort and reward should be maintained for all goods and services. They consider some goods and services as a right rather than a reward; thus, the concept of merit goods in public economics.

Freedom, too, is valued, but there is also a broad role for state intervention. As Richard Tawney put it:

> There is no such thing as freedom in the abstract, divorced from the realities of a particular time and place. . . . It is still often assumed by privileged classes that, when the state refrains from intervening, the condition which remains, as a result of its inaction, is liberty. In reality, what not infrequently remains is not liberty, but tyranny. . . . The right to education is obviously impaired, if poverty arrests its use in mid-career; the right to the free choice of an occupation, if the expenses of entering a profession are prohibitive; the right to earn a living, if enforced unemployment is recurrent; the right to justice, if few men of small means can afford the cost of litigation.[14]

With regard to the theory of the modern state, post-World War II liberals depart significantly from conservatives, for they identify with social democratic ideals and with the principles of the welfare state. Representative writings in this tradition range from those of John Kenneth Galbraith, Gunnar Myrdal, and Richard Titmuss to those of Robert Dahl, Charles Lindblom, Richard Musgrave, and Andrew Shonfield.[15]

Liberals tend to view the state as a mediating force that somehow aggregates individual preferences and pursues the public interest. In so doing, the state is presumed responsible for providing services to the population. For example, in his analysis of the role of the state in the economy, Musgrave distinguishes three functions of government: allocation, distribution, and stabilization. Within this scheme, there are three justifications for state intervention in the economy: (1) to correct market failures; (2) to redistribute income; and (3) to manipulate fiscal and monetary policies in order to affect aggregate demand. Within the liberal system of beliefs, as Walter Heller claimed in the sixties, the government can achieve "any combination of government services, income redistribution, and economic redistribution and economic stability we set our sights on."[16]

Another vision of the state within the liberal belief system is the organic one. Such a view is grounded in Rousseau's concept of the "general will," which is not necessarily equivalent to the will of all. Like the French notion of solidarity, the organic vision of the state can serve to unify a nation around the idea of mutual aid, national cooperation, and planning. As noted by Robert Alford and exemplified in Galbraith's work, the ideal image of the liberal perspective is the planned society.[17]

IMPLICATIONS FOR HEALTH POLICY

Since the perspectives described above are broad orienting positions, the implications we will draw for health policy are not necessarily consistent with *all* the beliefs. Nevertheless, these perspectives are significant, for they command strong support and mirror deeply held world views.

The Conservative Perspective

Conservatives contend that state intervention in the organization of medical care should be strictly limited. They challenge health planning efforts insofar as they extend beyond such traditional issues of public health as immunization programs. The strength of the conservative critique lies partially in our ignorance. We do not know what constitutes a right distribution of health resources, and there may, in fact, be no such concept since, rather than being the solution of a technical problem, it would involve a decision about the kind of distribution we desire.

Planning requires some knowledge about what the future is likely to bring, some control over key actors in the health system, some agreed-upon criteria to evaluate the current delivery system for medical care, and some capacity to monitor the system being planned. Conservatives argue that these requirements are seriously deficient in the health sector. And, even if they were not, health planning would most likely reduce the role of free markets in resource allocation and increase state intervention and administrative control.[18] Moreover, health planning is likely to diminish both professional autonomy and consumer choice. It is not surprising, therefore, that conservative analysts are among the leading critics of planning: they believe it cannot work. Instead of a planning system, they prefer that health policy promote either of two models of medical care organization: the professional or the free enterprise model.

THE PROFESSIONAL MODEL

The professional model of medical care organization is advocated by associations of medical practitioners such as the American Medical Association (AMA) in the United States and the *Confédération des syndicats médicaux français* (CSMF) in France. It emphasizes the virtues of private medical practice on a fee-for-service basis—what the French call *la médecine libérale*. Professional medical associations have sedulously cultivated an image of private practice as a personal, symbiotic doctor-patient relationship. To defend their professionalism, they have appealed to the desirability of free market choice: selection of the physician by the patient, freedom of prescription by the doctor, professional confidentiality, and fee-for-service payment.

All aspects of the professional model have been systematically defended in a classic study by Mathew Lynch and Stanley Raphael. In answer to the question "Is there, then, any place for socialized medicine?" Lynch and Raphael conclude as follows:

> Since all experience shows and history attests to mankind's unquenchable thirst for freedom with justice, it follows that any system which limits freedom and justice, which imposes coercion and restricts voluntary effort toward self-betterment has no place in the advanced and just society. A system which commits its citizens to mental and fiscal imprisonment, which in its aim to abolish uncertainties unavoidably eliminates opportunity and challenge, and leaves only the boredom of a limited certainty—such a system can only be regarded as reactionary in the historic evolutionary process of man.[19]

The essence of the professional model comes forth in clarion tones when Lynch and Raphael assert that the "basic doctor-patient relationship, which is the *sine qua non* of good medical care, is destroyed by all schemes that remove responsibility from the patient"—and again when they find "attestation of the immutable nature of these truths" in the following citation from Plato:

> Athenian Stranger: And did you ever observe that there are two classes of patients in states, slaves and freemen: and the slave doctors run about and cure the slaves, or wait for them in the dispensaries—practitioners of this sort never talk to their patients individually, or let them talk about their own individual complaints? The slave doctor prescribes what mere experience suggests, as if he had exact knowledge; and when he has given his orders, like a tyrant, he rushes off with equal assurance to some other servant who is ill; and so he relieves the master of the house of the care of his invalid slaves. But the other doctor, who is a freeman, attends and practices upon freemen; and he carries his enquiries far back, and goes into the nature of the disorder; he enters into discourse with the patient and with his friends, and is at once getting information from the sick man, and also instructing him as far as he is able, and he will not prescribe for him until he has first convinced him; at last, when he has brought the patient more and more under

his persuasive influences and set him on the road to health, he attempts to effect a cure. Now which is the better way of proceeding in a physician?[20]

THE FREE ENTERPRISE MODEL

The free enterprise model of medical care organization is advocated by certain economists, principally D. S. Lees and Milton Friedman.[21] Like the proponents of the professional model, Lees and Friedman value free market choice and voluntary exchange. They differ from the former in that the traditional doctor-patient relationship is not important to them as long as new doctor-patient relationships allow market choice. Lees contends that medical care differs little in any of its characteristics from other goods and services and consequently defends the position that competitive markets in the health sector would produce an efficient allocation of medical resources. Friedman agrees. He also criticizes the monopoly of the medical profession over the delivery of health care and challenges the notion that, for reasons of technical efficiency in production (maintenance of standards), licensure is justified. Instead of licensure, Friedman advocates a system of voluntary certification in which anyone would be free to practice medicine "without restriction except for legal and financial responsibility for any harm done to others through fraud and negligence."[22]

Relying largely on the work of Reuben Kessel, Friedman criticizes the existence of price discrimination in medicine.[23] His argument is that the power of trade unions, including medical professional associations, restricts competition and results in artificially high medical fees. Friedman contends that the medical profession has preserved its monopoly position by severely limiting entry into medical schools and has retarded technological development both in medicine and in the organization of medical care. He interprets the growth of the professions of osteopathy and chiropractice as a reaction to medical monopoly power and argues that such alternatives might well be of lower quality than medical practice would have been without entry restrictions. He likens the high quality medical care required under current licensure standards to Cadillac standards in the automobile industry; and concludes that elimination of medical licensure would increase access and allocate medical resources more efficiently.

> Group practice in conjunction with hospitals would have grown enormously. Instead of individual practice plus large institutional hospitals conducted by governments or eleemosynary institutions, there might have developed medical partnerships or corporations—medical teams. . . . These medical teams—department stores of medicine, if you will—would be intermediaries between the patients and the physician. Being long-lived and immobile, they would have a great interest in establishing a reputation for reliability and quality. For the same reason, consumers would get to know their reputation. They would have the specialized skills to judge the quality of physicians; indeed, they would be the agent of the consumer in doing so, as the department store is now for many a product.[24]

The Radical Perspective

Like conservatives, radicals also oppose state intervention in the health sector; but they do so for different reasons. There are two main radical perspectives on health care: socialized medicine and deprofessionalized medicine. Proponents of socialized medicine criticize state intervention in general, and health planning in particular, within the context of capitalism. They contend that the role of the state is constrained by pressures of private capital accumulation and that planning serves as a tool of monopoly capital.[25] Consequently, to achieve significant change, those who favor socialized medicine argue that one must first begin by changing the capitalist system. Proponents of deprofessionalized medicine criticize state intervention and planning because it expands bureaucratic control over the health sector. Consequently, they attack not merely capitalism but socialism as well; and they advocate debureaucratization.

SOCIALIZED MEDICINE

The case for socialized medicine grows out of a critique of private medical practice and a commitment to equity in the provision of medical care. Proponents of socialized medicine criticize the presence of the profit motive in the capitalist health sector.[26] They claim that even if most goods and services are distributed on the basis of the consumer's willingness to pay, this should not be the way medical care is distributed. Medical care is different.[27] It should be distributed on the basis of some principle of fairness. After all, we are all part of the human family, and since a large part of illness falls on individuals due to fortuitous circumstances, they should not have to bear the costs alone. When health is threatened, since charity is insufficient to cope with our moral obligation to help those in need, the state must provide medical care to all. As Henry Sigerist put it many years ago:

> The goal of medicine is social. . . . Man has a right to health and is entitled to having this right secured. . . and everybody, rich and poor, should have all the medical care that science can give. There is only one way of achieving this: the physician must be removed from the sphere of competitive business.[28]

In contrast to proponents of the professional model who claim that the doctor will look after the interest of the patient where there is a fee for services rendered, advocates of socialized medicine argue that the professional fee distorts the doctor-patient relationship. They contend that fee-for-service medicine tempts the doctor to pursue his own interests before those of the patients. As George Bernard Shaw put it:

> That any nation, having observed that you could provide for the supply of bread by giving bakers a pecuniary interest in baking for you, should go on to give a surgeon a pecuniary interest in cutting off your leg, is enough to make one despair of political humanity.[29]

Those who favor socialized medicine scoff at the notion that medical care should be bought and sold like a commodity.

> It cannot be maintained that the public interest is adequately safeguarded when any doctor can set up wherever he likes, with whatever equipment he likes. In the absence of any overall organization, medical services lack cohesion and continuity; they remain incomplete; they are accompanied by considerable waste of time and high expenditure.[30]

A nationalized health service such as that in England (see chap. 8) involves public ownership of the hospital sector and allows a limited amount of private practice; but under socialized medicine such as in the Soviet model, private practice is prohibited by law, and all physicians work on a salaried basis for the state. In theory, such a model requires central planning and regionalization of health resources and is possible only in a socialist society.

DEPROFESSIONALIZED MEDICINE

The case for deprofessionalized medicine grows out of a critique of professionalism and bureaucracy in industrially advanced nations. Ivan Illich argues that damage done by medical providers—what he calls *iatrogenesis*—reflects the failure of our medical care system.[31] Illich advocates a total debureaucratization of industrial society.[32] He delivers unsparing criticism at industrialism and claims that our medical delivery system has reached a point where advances in medical technology result in an increasing incidence of iatrogenesis:

> Medicine began to approach the second watershed. Every year medical science reported a new breakthrough. Practitioners of new specialties rehabilitated some individuals suffering from rare diseases. The practice of medicine became centered on the performance of hospital-based staffs. Trust in miracle cures obliterated good sense and traditional wisdom on healing and health care. The irresponsible use of

drugs spread from doctors to the general public. The second watershed was approached when the marginal utility of further professionalization declined, at least insofar as it can be expressed in terms of the physical well-being of the largest numbers of people. The second watershed was superseded when the marginal *disutility* increased as further monopoly of the medical establishment became an indicator of more suffering for larger numbers of people.[33]

For Illich, there are three kinds of iatrogenesis: clinical, social, and structural. Clinical iatrogenesis results from pain, sickness, or death provoked by the provision of medical care. Social iatrogenesis results when health policies reinforce an industrial organization that generates dependency and ill health. Structural iatrogenesis results when "medically sponsored behavior and delusions restrict the vital autonomy of people by undermining their competence in growing up, caring for each other and aging."[34]

Illich proposes to limit the dependency that industrial society imposes by fostering self-reliance, self-care, and consumer control over the provision of health services. This is strangely reminiscent of Friedman's free enterprise model of medical care organization; but it differs in that Illich is not as concerned with free choice and pluralistic modes of health care delivery as much as he is concerned with reducing dependence on professional services and increasing individual autonomy and self-sufficiency.

The Liberal Perspective

In contrast to conservatives and radicals, liberals support both state intervention in the health sector, in general, and health planning, in particular. Liberals do not seek fundamental changes in the present role of the modern welfare state. They accept the present institutional arrangements for financing and organizing health care; consequently, they focus their attention on pragmatic state intervention to minimize current problems. In the United States, although there are no clearly articulated models of how a liberal health sector would look, liberals would most likely support a national health insurance program to improve access to health services and a range of administrative controls and financial incentives to contain rising health care costs.

In a sense, liberals occupy a position midway between conservatives and radicals. They support aspects of the conservative's professional and free enterprise models of medical care organization; at the same time, they are sympathetic to aspects of socialized and deprofessionalized medicine. For example, along with advocates of the professional model, liberals support the enforcement of minimal licensing standards for health professionals and hospitals. Along with advocates of the free enterprise model, they favor the use of market incentives to improve efficiency in the allocation of health resources. In addition, liberals share the equity concerns of advocates of socialized medicine and they support the concerns about self-reliance and consumer control expressed by advocates of deprofessionalization.

Debate among liberals and conservatives about the proper role of the state in the health sector usually centers around the following questions: How extensive is market failure in health care? And, how great is the inability of the market to satisfy the rights of individuals to medical care? At one extreme, left-leaning liberals advocate a state controlled national health service along the lines of the English model. At the other extreme, right-leaning conservatives advocate private health insurance allocated on the basis of ability to pay market premiums.

Economists have noted the special characteristics of medical care which make it an uncertain candidate for efficient allocation by the market mechanism.[35] To view the matter only from the economic perspective does not provide a satisfactory basis for evaluating the proper role of the market versus the state in the organization of medical care. Economist Anthony Culyer put it this way:

> Nothing scientific can (at the moment) be said about the relative desirability of the NHS (or any other system) and consequently. . . social scientists (or any other kind) who

believe that they have shown that general circumstances can determine the best form of organization of medical care, are in fact, wittingly or unwittingly, lending spurious support to what amounts to no more than an ideological assertion.[36]

Liberals and conservatives do not disagree about the extent of market failure in the health sector. Rather, they have different criteria for evaluating the appropriateness of state intervention and planning. The liberal perspective is characterized by three central criteria that they believe should guide state intervention in the health sector: rationality, equity, and accountability.

RATIONALITY

Max Weber distinguished between two kinds of rationality: substantive rationality, which refers to the value of desired goals; and formal rationality, which refers to the effectiveness of particular means used to advance any specified end.[37] Liberals concentrate on the latter category: the relation between means and ends. Conservatives argue that the formally rational behavior of individuals pursuing their own self-interest tends to promote a notion of public interest that is substantively rational. In contrast, liberals note that a society whose members act in a formally rational way, or even one whose members are individually substantively rational, is not necessarily a rational society in the sense of successfully achieving its shared values. Along with Weber, liberals would interpret state intervention and planning as attempts to harness the market for purposes of improving economic efficiency and achieving a "rational society."

Planners tend to adopt a cognitive style of defining goals, assessing alternative strategies to achieve them, and evaluating the impact of these strategies. For example, health planners have emphasized a broad definition of health, evaluated the effectiveness of medical care, and urged more comprehensive state efforts to shape forces outside the medical sector affecting health. To the extent that they have set priorities, analyzed perceived problems, and evaluated alternatives and results, they may be said to be acting rationally. With this justification, Liberals have sought comprehensive planning and state intervention to rational-ize the health sector.

EQUITY

In addition to their concern for formal rationality, liberals appeal to ideals about what a good health system should do. They tend to use the notion of equity to encompass a range of these ideals. Social, political, and moral theorists, for example, appeal to the notion of rights as well as to justice and fairness.[38] Often these criteria have been used to justify the redistribution of health resources from groups who have plenty to groups who are in need—for example, from relatively overserved to underserved regions of the country, or from the affluent to the poor. In this sense, it is important to distinguish equity from equality. Whereas equality of medical care implies an equal amount for all, equity implies a distribution based on such principles as, "To each his due"; or, "To him that hath, from him much shall be required"—that is to say, care in accordance with some criterion of need, not ability to purchase.[39]

The equity criterion can be used to justify state interven-tion even when the market results in an efficient allocation of resources, for such a result is not necessarily equitable. To the extent that liberal theorists rely on equity as a cri-terion for state intervention when the market would other-wise operate efficiently, they agree with radicals; but when there is evidence of market failure, the liberal's appeal to equity is strengthened. In the absence of the free market's obtaining an efficient allocation, an even stronger case can be made for the pursuit of justice.

ACCOUNTABILITY

Often the pursuit of equity has led liberals to advocate greater centralization of planning, such as the elaboration of national standards for the allocation of new medical technology. Centralization, however, conflicts with goals of local autonomy and raises the issue of accountability.

The market distributes resources in response to impersonal forces; and political decisions are responsive to interest groups, institutions, and corporations which have power. To offset these forces, liberals try to design institutional mechanisms to hold health care providers and planners accountable and responsive to key actors in the health sector. The challenge in making these mechanisms operational lies in defining the relevant groups—for example, residents of a region, subscribers to insurance, health care workers, consumers, or some combination of these.

CONCLUDING OBSERVATIONS

The basic differences in perspectives on the state can neither be resolved nor ignored. The liberal system of beliefs accepts the legitimacy of the state as problem solver, whatever the institutional context. It emphasizes the value of state intervention for making marginal improvements. Conservative and radical beliefs are useful for illuminating the inadequacies of existing health policies; neither system of beliefs, however, is helpful as a guide for investigating how to improve policy. And neither liberal beliefs nor conventional price theory provides an objective basis for evaluating the market versus the state in the organization of medical care.

Conservative, radical, and liberal perspectives on the state tell us nothing about the relative merits of alternative modes of state intervention or about the specific policies that ought to be promoted in the health sector. For policy prescriptions we will have to look elsewhere. To evaluate policy problems in the future, however, it is essential to have a clear understanding of these competing perspectives—if only to discern how the choice and formulation of health policies reflects political beliefs about the proper role of the state in society.

NOTES

1. This chapter is drawn almost entirely from my book *The Health Planning Predicament: France, Québec, England, and the United States* (Berkeley, Los Angeles, London: University of California Press, 1984), chap. 2. The terms *conservative, radical,* and *liberal* have been used differently by different authors. For more detail on the tradition of conservative, radical, and liberal world views, see B. Ward, *The Ideal Worlds of Economics* (New York: Basic Books, 1979). See also, R. Alford, "Paradigms of Relations Between State and Society," in L. Lindberg et al., eds., *Stress and Contradiction in Modern Capitalism* (Lexington, Mass.: D. C. Heath, 1975); and D. Gordon, ed., *Problems in Political Economy: An Urban Perspective* (Lexington Mass.: D. C. Heath, 1971), chaps. 1, 6.

2. E. Burke, *Reflections on the Revolution in France* (Garden City, N.Y.: Doubleday & Co., 1961); J. S. Mill, "On Liberty," in M. Lerner, ed., *Essential Works of J. S. Mill* (New York: Bantam, 1961); A. Smith, *An Inquiry into the Nature and Causes of the Wealth of Nations* (New York: Modern Library, 1937).

3. M. Friedman, "The Role of Government in a Free Society," in *Capitalism and Freedom* (Chicago: University of Chicago Press, 1962), p. 23.

4. Friedman, "The Role of Government," p. 27.

5. Ibid.

6. Today there is a flourishing literature in this tradition. See, e.g., J. Habermas, *Legitimation Crisis* (Boston: Beacon Press, 1973); R. Miliband, *The State in Capitalist Society* (London: Quartet Books, 1973); J. O'Connor, *The Fiscal Crisis of the State* (New York: St. Martin's Press, 1973); C. Offe, "Structural Problems of the Capitalist State," in K. von Beyme, ed., *German Political Studies* (London: Russel Sage, 1974); C. Offe, "The Theory of the Capitalist State and the Problem of Policy Formation," in Lindberg, *Stress and Contradiction*; and N. Poulantzas, *Political Power and Social Classes* (London: New Left Books, 1978).

7. P. Sweezy, "The Radical Theory of the State," in D. Gordon, ed., *Problems in Political Economy: An Urban Perspective* (Lexington: D. C. Heath, 1971), p. 25.

8. K. Marx and F. Engels, *The Communist Manifesto* in K. Marx and F. Engels, *Selected Works* (Moscow: Progress Publishers, 1977), pp. 110–111.

9. Habermas, *Legitimation Crisis*.

10. O'Connor, *Fiscal Crisis*.

11. Offe, "The Theory of the Capitalist State."

12. Ibid., p. 143.

13. B. Ward, *The Liberal Economic World View* (New York: Basic Books, 1979).

14. R. Tawney, *The Radical Tradition*, cited by A. Donabedian in *Aspects of Medical Care Administration: Specifying Requirements for Health Care* (Cambridge, Mass.: Harvard University Press, 1973) pp. 260, 261, 267.

15. R. Dahl and C. Lindblom, *Politics, Economics and Welfare* (New York: Harper and Brothers, 1953); J. Galbraith, *The New Industrial State* (New York: Houghton Mifflin, 1967); R. Musgrave, *The Theory of Public Finance* (New York: McGraw Hill, 1959).

16. W. Heller, "Reflections on Public Expenditure Theory," in Gordon, *Problems in Political Economy*, p. 39.

17. R. Alford, "Paradigms of Relations."

18. As noted in chapter 5, planning is often defined as an administrative mechanism for replacing the market. However, this is not its only function. In some cases, for example antitrust policy and certain government regulations, planning can serve to foster market competition. Even if planning reduces the role of economic markets, there might remain significant competition in the form of political markets—e.g., when organized interests put pressure on elected representatives or when logrolling occurs in regional health planning bodies.

19. M. Lynch and S. Raphael, *Medicine and the State* (Springfield, Ill.: Charles Thomas, 1963), p. 422.

20. Ibid., p. 414

21. D. Lees, "Health Through Choice," in R. Harris, ed., *Freedom or Free-for-all* (London: Institute of Economic Affairs, 1968); Friedman, *Capitalism and Freedom*, chap. 9.

22. Friedman, *Capitalism and Freedom*, p. 158. Physicians are, in fact, liable for any injury which is the proximate result of their negligence, where negligence is established based on what the ordinary physician would do under similar circumstances. In addition, physicians may be liable for subjecting patients to risk without informed consent. The widespread presence of insurance against malpractice, however, raises questions as to whether liability actually deters negligence when the physician does not bear the full financial consequences.

23. R. Kessel, "Price Discrimination in Medicine," *Journal of Law and Economics* 1 (October 1958).

24. Friedman, *Capitalism and Freedom*, pp. 158–159.

25. See, e.g., V. Navarro, "Political Power, the State, and Their Implications in Medicine," in J. Salmon, "Monopoly Capital and the Reorganization of the Health Sector," *The Review of Radical Political Economics* 9, no. 1 (1977).

26. See, e.g., B. Ehrenreich and J. Ehrenreich, *The American Health Empire: Power, Profits and Politics* (New York: Random House, 1970).

27. For an economic analysis of how medical care is different from other goods and services, see K. Arrow, "Uncertainty and the Welfare Economics of Medical Care," *American Economic Review* 53, no. 5 (December 1963). Also see A. Culyer, "Is Medical Care Different?" in M. Cooper and A. Culyer, eds., *Health Economics* (Middlesex, England: Penguin, 1973).

28. Cited by Lynch and Raphael, *Medicine and the State*, p. 8.

29. G. B. Shaw, *Doctor's Dilemma* (London: Constable, 1930), preface.

30. R. Sand, cited by Lynch and Raphael, *Medicine and the State*, p. 9.

31. I. Illich, *Medical Nemesis: The Expropriation of Health* (London: Calder and Boyars, 1975).

32. Illich's critique of industrialism has annoyed Marxist analysts in the health field and has led the French magazine *Le Nouvel Observateur* to call Illich a "petit réactionnaire." See, e.g., V. Navarro, "The Industrialization of Fetishism or the Fetishism of Industrialization: A Critique of Ivan Illich," in V. Navarro, *Health and Medical Care in the U.S.: A Critical Analysis* (Farmingdale, N.Y.: Baywood, 1977).

33. I. Illich, "Two Watersheds," in *Tools for Conviviality* (New York: Pantheon, 1973), p. 6.

34. Ibid, p. 165.

35. K. Arrow, "Uncertainty and the Welfare Economics of Medical Care," *American Economic Review* 53 (1963): 941–973; A. Culyer, "The Nature of the Commodity 'Health Care' and Its Efficient Allocation," *Oxford Economic Papers* 23 (1971): 189–211.

36. A. Culyer, "The 'Market' Versus the 'State' in Medical Care," in G. McLachlan, ed., *Problems and Progress in Medical Care* (London: Oxford University Press, 1972), p. 6. Also, see A. Culyer, "The NHS and the Market: Images and Realities," in G. M. McLachlan and A. Maynard, eds., *The Public/Private Mix for Health* (London: The Nuffield Provincial Hospitals Trust, 1982).

37. M. Weber. *The Theory of Social and Economic Organization*, trans. A. Henderson (New York: Free Press, 1968).

38. On the notion of rights, see R. Dworkin, *Taking Rights Seriously* (Cambridge: Harvard University Press, 1977). On the notion of justice, see J. Rawls, A Theory of Justice (Cambridge: Harvard University Press, 1971).

39. I am grateful to the Reverend Paul Lehmann for bringing this formulation to my attention.

3

Perspectives on Prevention: Health Promotion vs. Health Protection

John Ratcliffe, Lawrence Wallack, Francis Fagnani, and Victor G. Rodwin

Despite differences in the organization of health services in Western industrialized nations, efforts to prevent disease have evolved in similar ways. The impact of vastly improved medical technologies, prevailing disease patterns, and professional and social ideologies is sufficiently similar in industrialized nations to allow us to discern some common trends. This chapter begins with a historical perspective, after which we identify the institutional and ideological issues related to prevention strategies and distinguish two contending strategies: health promotion versus health protection. Since these two approaches have very different implications for public policy, we evaluate them first from the standpoint of evidence about the determinants of disease and mortality, and second, from the standpoint of the relationship between risk-taking and risk-imposing behavior. Finally, we attempt to reconceptualize the problem of disease prevention and provide guidelines for future action.

From the outset it is useful to distinguish among primary, secondary and tertiary prevention.[1] *Primary prevention* refers to all measures that prevent the outbreak of a disease. It is, of course, not limited to medical procedures. Primary prevention can be accomplished either by reducing exposure to the causal agent or by altering the susceptibility of the individual at risk. Examples range from the spraying of mosquitoes, to water purification, basic sanitation, and traditional public health education. *Secondary prevention* is the detection and diagnosis of disease at an early stage, usually through screening procedures. It focuses on individuals who are identified as being at risk for particular diseases, and it provides remedial action so that the problem will not worsen. *Tertiary prevention* is the amelioration, treatment, or cure of clinical disease. It aims to prevent impairments and handicaps and to readapt the patient as well as possible to his social context.

A BRIEF HISTORICAL PERSPECTIVE ON PREVENTION

In the past there were at least three kinds of disease prevention strategies, all of which are still promoted today. One was concerned with the quality of the physical environment and with sanitary measures to control communicable diseases. Another involved measures of a social nature, such as regulation of working conditions or protection of particular social groups—for example, women and children. These measures gradually resembled secondary prevention programs as knowledge and techniques improved. A third kind of prevention strategy concentrated on specific diseases whose importance was such that public pressure led to the creation of specific programs and even to the construction of special facilities. The best known European example is that of sanatoria for the treatment of tuberculosis.

Public health movements in Europe were well underway long before the technical efficacy of medicine was demonstrated. One of the basic principles of these movements was already apparent during the eighteenth century. Michel Foucault notes that "health and the general well-being of the population became one of the essential goals of the political authorities."[2] However—and this explains why the problem of medical efficacy was not evoked at the time—this goal was conceived less in terms of cure and recovery from disease than in terms of social and economic assistance.

Apart from strict regulations to control the spread of epidemics, "medical services were only one component of aid to the poor. . . . At that time, the therapeutic role of hospitals was limited, compared with their role in furnishing material aid and administrative control."[3] As the therapeutic potential of hospitals evolved during the eighteenth century, illness among the poor slowly became part of the more general problem of public health. According to Foucault, public health workers assumed an important role in policing the body politic as well as regulating the economy and maintaining order.

> The tremendous demographic surge in Western Europe during the eighteenth century, the necessity to coordinate and to integrate the growing population into the productive system, and the urgent need to better adapt and to tighten forms of social control, turned the notion of 'population' not only into a theoretical problem but also into an object of surveillance, analysis and programmed action.[4]

In this context, two areas became ideal targets for action: on the one hand, child rearing and health, both of which were linked to the organization and normalization of family life;[5] and on the other hand, public health programs, which both prompted and justified numerous government measures to improve hygienic conditions.[6] As Foucault notes, "It was the doctor's role as a hygienist more than his prestige as a healer that ensured his strong political position in the eighteenth century, which by the nineteenth century had become economic and social."[7]

Public authorities in the eighteenth century were concerned with such technical improvements as better sewerage and clean water, but they also had moral aims. Family policy, for example, tried to instill a new ethic in the lower classes, one that sought both to make the family serve the needs of economic development and to improve the social conditions of the growing number of men, women, and children obliged to work in industry. As far as public health was concerned, efforts centered on places that were particularly favorable breeding grounds for infections and diseases, such as prisons, ships, port installations, and hospitals. The city was seen as a priority area for disease prevention efforts, but subsequently the factory and the home were included as well. These various activities led naturally to the comingling of medical and political authorities. Medicine became as much a technique for social control as a service for the art of healing and took on greater and greater importance in administrative structures and in the machinery of power that, during the course of the eighteenth century, continued to expand and become entrenched.

In the latter part of the nineteenth century, the emergence of clinical medicine, narrowly focused on examination, diagnosis, and treatment, as well as the development of private, entrepreneurial fee-for-service practice, were a response to the growing demand for medical care on the part of individuals and families. Growing demand could not have come about if broader and broader segments of the population had not internalized the values on which clinical medicine rested. Foucault notes that, "In the space of a century, the medical profession succeeded in converting everyone to the idea that life was not possible without regular recourse to medicine, that even benign medical trouble needed attention, and that the notions of self, the body, health and sickness could not be distinct from the discourse of medical ideology."[8]

In the period following World War II, medicine gained ascendancy as previous forms of institutional control of the physical environment gradually disappeared in the wake of the eradication of the major diseases that had plagued former generations. The efficacy and prestige formerly attached to preventive forms of public health intervention became associated with the rise of modern medicine. Concurrently with the rise of medicine, the concept of disease prevention began to show signs of disintegration.

THE DISINTEGRATION OF DISEASE PREVENTION AND THE EMERGENCE OF NEW POLICY ISSUES

One of the first signs of disintegration was the emergence of professional and institutional boundaries between curative and preventive medicine. In principle, a medical procedure includes preventive as well as curative aspects. In the past, this integration of prevention and curative medicine was part of the family doctor's job. But, as the role of the general practitioner receded behind that of the growing number of specialists, children began to be examined by child health doctors, students by university doctors, draftees by army doctors, and workers by occupational doctors. Disease prevention programs no longer seem to be the monopoly of a well-defined professional group.

In addition, although the difference between curative medicine and disease prevention can sometimes be ambiguous, there tend to be institutional conflicts between these two approaches to health care. Curative medicine roughly corresponds to entrepreneurial fee-for-service medical practice and is based on the principle of the patient-consumer's sovereignty; disease prevention corresponds to a more socialized approach to health care and is based on the principle of the state's right to intervene for the collective good.[9] The organization of medical services reflects this dichotomy in a number of countries. In France, for example, curative medicine is institutionally separate from disease prevention—it is still the domain of private practice—whereas prevention programs are, by and large, organized by the state. (One notable exception is that costs of occupational medicine are covered by firms.)

A second sign of disintegration is the lack of a clear differentiation between the services rendered by traditional primary and secondary prevention programs and those of the numerous helping professions that claim to provide information, resolve personal problems, and promote well-being. Over and above a core of procedures reserved for the medical profession, a gamut of primary prevention services has developed in the huge arena of insurance, job training, physical therapy, counseling, and other personal, psychological, and pedagogical services.

A third sign of disintegration can be attributed to controversy about the proper role of the state in prevention programs (see chap. 2). Since the aim of secondary prevention is to detect diseases not as yet perceived by the patient, its practitioners have favored a system and a form of organization that—depending upon the relationship sought between individual freedom and the collective welfare—either encourages or requires frequent check-ups of the population. In Western industrialized nations this form of coordinated action has been resisted, largely because of the specter of a "big brother" state with a central health file on each citizen. This raises a major dilemma for the future of disease prevention: it either must develop into an authoritarian activity based on professional expertise and the tutellary action of state agencies, or into an active form of individual responsibility and education.[10]

Beyond the disintegration of disease prevention activities, the leading policy issues today concern the role of primary prevention efforts. There are two contending strategies by which primary prevention can be achieved: health promotion and health protection. Health promotion aims at altering individual behavior. Health protection aims at altering sociopolitical and economic structures. In the United States and Britain, health policymakers have released official documents that emphasize a strategy of health promotion.[11] In contrast, in France and Québec health policymakers have released documents that place greater emphasis on health protection.[12]

Advocates of health promotion argue that the major killers of today—heart disease, cancer, and stroke—are primarily a consequence of an unhealthy life-style. According to this view, such personal factors as stress, improper nutrition and excercise, and the abuse of alcohol and tobacco, are the primary causal agents in the etiology of disease. Although this approach recognizes the multifactorial nature of etiology, it still conceives of disease as a personal event that occurs inside—and is fundamentally under the control of—the individual person. As John Knowles, president of the Rockefeller Foundation, observed:

> Prevention of disease means forsaking the bad habits which many people enjoy—overeating, too much drinking, taking pills, staying up at night, engaging in promiscuous sex, driving too fast, and smoking cigarettes—or put another way, it means doing things that require special effort—exercising regularly, improving nutrition, going to the dentist, practicing contraception, ensuring harmonious family life, submitting to screening examinations.[13]

Advocates of health protection hold that our major chronic diseases are the consequence of social organization in general, and economic structure in particular. They tend to relate modern modes of industrial production to observed disease patterns through occupational stress and environmental pollution. A strategy of health protection would focus on occupational exposures to carcinogens and other toxins; the pollution of air, water, and soil by chemical, radioactive, and incinerated wastes; and exposure to inorganic fertilizers, pesticides, and food additives. It would also link public policies to patterns of disease by suggesting that the unequal distribution of social goods and resources among competing social groups is primarily responsible for the differential distribution of disease among different social classes. As Leon Eisenberg, of Harvard Medical School, argues:

> The new converts to prevention, having discovered that behavior affects health, focus on the responsibility of the individual for illness prevention by eating and drinking in moderation, exercising properly, not smoking and the like. Surely, in the final analysis, it is the individual who carries out these actions. But what does it mean to hold the individual responsible for smoking when the government subsidizes tobacco farming, permits tax deductions for cigarette advertising and fails to use its taxing power as a disincentive

to smoking? What does it mean to castigate the individual for poor eating habits when the public is inundated by advertisements for "empty-calorie" fast foods and is reinforced in present patterns of consumption by federal farm policy?[14]

Advocates of health protection tend to support far-reaching social reform. Since they believe that disease is socially caused, they argue that its prevention requires social change.[15] The social chain of disease causality is forged in three ways. First, advertising is concerned more with selling the product than with the health of the buyer, so potential adverse effects of the product advertised are systematically minimized. Second, firms tend to "externalize" their production costs as much as possible (i.e., they dump as large a portion of toxic by-products as possible into the environment so that the product can be sold for a lower price than if the cost of by-product containment and disposal had to be borne by the producer). Third, government policies—which allocate resources, risks, and benefits among social groups—are heavily influenced by powerful and wealthy groups.

In summary, advocates of health protection tend to place responsibility on the state and on industry.[16] Their unit of analysis is a population group (e.g., the nation as a whole, a particular group of workers, or a social class), not the individual. In their view, primary prevention entails changing sociopolitical and economic structures so that environmental hazards are reduced at their source and life-styles change in response to a reallocation of resources, risks, and benefits. Because it challenges the status quo, health protection is an explicitly political strategy. It therefore differs from health promotion, which gives the appearance of being politically neutral because it does not challenge existing arrangements.

The major reason for disagreement over what constitutes an appropriate disease prevention strategy is owing to personal and societal values—the implicit, taken-for-granted feelings and beliefs that reflect the basis of social organization. It is this network of values, combined with their underlying assumptions about human nature and disease causality, which guides our activities in the field of prevention. In addition, the judgment about the relative effectiveness and efficiency of health prevention programs is largely determined by one's institutional vantage point. For example, in the United States, the primary concern of management is to cut back on expensive health benefits and to urge individuals to take more responsibility for their health. In contrast, the primary concern of the health care industry is to promote high technology health promotion services.

In Western industrialized nations there is a growing public skepticism about the efficacy of medical treatment for dread diseases such as cancer, and a deepening fear that we are not in control of the forces that determine our health. Tempted to turn to primary prevention as the ultimate solution to health problems, the public is faced with the difficult task of choosing between contending prevention strategies about which the experts are seriously divided. This choice is made more difficult because the public—and many health professionals—are largely unfamiliar with the primary determinants of disease and mortality and therefore lack the knowledge on which to base the decision.

THE DETERMINANTS OF DISEASE
AND MORTALITY

The medical approach to health and disease assumes that mortality rates and health status are determined primarily by the interaction between the individual and disease agents in the environment. In addition, it assumes that modern medical technology and ancillary services are primarily responsible for observed declines in mortality and improvements in national and international health indices.

This approach has generated two principal strategies for improving the health of human populations. The first is the curative, clinic- and hospital-based strategy (tertiary prevention), which relies on medical technology and services to relieve disease symptoms or to cure individuals of diseases after they have been contracted. This strategy consumes some ninety-five percent of health sector expenditures in Europe and North America, as well as in most other nations around the world.[17] The second strategy is the public health approach, which relies largely on environmental modification, as in protecting water supplies, spraying mosquitoes, or changing the behavior of individuals at risk through such interventions as vaccination and health education. In most nations, the public health strategy receives less than five percent of all health sector expenditures.

Neither the first nor the second strategy attempts to influence the health of human populations by modifying the man-made social environment in which individuals live from birth to death. Attempts to influence health have for the most part been limited to the physical and biological, rather than the sociopolitical and economic dimensions. But, whereas interventions at the biological level may make a difference for the individual (i.e., when a life is saved that would have been lost without medical intervention), they are not a primary determinant of mortality and disease at the level of an entire population. As René Dubos observes:

> The most effective techniques to avoid disease came out of the attempts to correct by social measures the injustices and the ugliness brought about by industrialization. . . the concern with social reforms rapidly evolved into public health practices that brought about spectacular improvements in the sanitary and nutritional state of the Western world. Suffice it to state here that this achievement cannot be credited to the type of laboratory science with which we are familiar today. Rather, it was the expression of an attitude which is almost completely foreign to the modern laboratory scientist. The nineteenth century reformers naively but firmly believed that, since disease always accompanied the want, dirt, pollution, and ugliness so common in the industrial world, health could be restored simply by bringing back to the multitudes pure air, pure water, pure food, and pleasant surroundings—the qualities of life in direct contact

with nature. . . . By preaching the virtues of pure air, pure water, and pure food they had gone far toward eliminating infection and improving nutrition, but *their success had been due more to zeal in the correction of social evils than to understanding of medical problems.* (Emphasis added.)[18]

In fact, particular curative and preventive measures have served to accelerate only slightly the substantial declines in mortality already well under way before either the germ theory or specific causes of disease received wide recognition.[19] Most research on the evolution of mortality trends suggests that improvements in such socioeconomic factors as education, income, nutrition, housing, sanitation, and working conditions are, in combination, the primary determinants of health and mortality, not medical care.

Educational attainment, for example, is an important determinant of mortality differences between socioeconomic classes in the United States.[20] Educational levels appear to influence the extent to which medical as well as disease prevention services are used.[21] Exactly how education influences mortality and health is not yet well understood; but it seems that the most effective preventive health measures are those applied at the individual level on a daily basis (e.g., personal hygiene, treatment of food, storage and use of water, etc.).[22]

In addition to education, improved nutritional status has been an important cause of mortality reductions and improved health. Infectious diseases are the major cause of death among children under five years of age in areas where malnutrition is widespread.[23] In addition, income, employment, housing, and working conditions are all primary determinants of health and mortality levels in human populations. Such findings support the view that the "unnatural," socially constructed environment is the primary determinant of observed patterns of disease and early death.

Efforts to exert control over the physical environment have led to the development of social policies to assist individual members in coping with their environment. Over time, socially designed systems have become more important to individual survival than the natural physical environment, because they control distribution of, and access to, those factors that have an important impact on mortality levels. In many parts of the United States, for example, infant mortality is rising in association with the declining economic situation, and it is projected to deteriorate further because of the lag between economic decline and increases in mortality rates.[24]

To be sure, the physical environment still exacts a toll through such occurrences as earthquakes, tidal waves, floods, and long-term climatic changes. Nevertheless, social policies constitute a kind of natural environment of their own. What is more, the social environment has also begun to affect the natural physical environment in ways that will probably influence health outcomes. In the United States, we have allowed some thirty thousand hazardous toxic waste dumps to exist.[25] Toxic wastes, by-products of industrial production processes, have been targeted as causes of prevalent chronic diseases. The American Public Health Association estimates that eighty to ninety percent of all cancers are environmentally caused.[26] In 1979 the U.S. Department of Health, Education, and Welfare (DHEW) announced that at least twenty percent of all cancers are of occupational origin, and that eight to eleven million workers in the United States have been exposed to asbestos since World War II.[27] DHEW estimates that fifty-eight to seventy-eight thousand of these workers will die "excess deaths" each year—most from lung cancer, a few from abdominal and chest malignancies, and others from asbestosis.[28]

Although the evidence we have presented is partial, the importance of the socially designed environment to disease and mortality cannot be overemphasized. The institutions created within society to mediate between the individual and the physical environment play a central role in determining societal disease and mortality patterns by the ways they function to distribute income and wealth, education, food and food additives, employment, safe working environments, and toxic wastes. These social goods and bads are distributed differentially among groups and individuals according to their place in the socioeconomic system. As noted by Kitagawa and Hauser, "differences in socioeconomic status are responsible for differences in mortality."[29]

Today's disease patterns reflect yesterday's public policies—not just health sector policies, but those political and economic policies that determine the distribution of both social goods (food, income and wealth, employment, education, housing, and safe working conditions) and social liabilities (industrial wastes, pesticides, unemployment, unsafe working conditions, and polluted air, food, water, and soil). Social policy and the public health are inextricably linked. To quote Dubos once again:

> It is to be hoped that social upheavals will never again occasion the physiological misery which allowed the killing epidemics of the nineteenth century, but other social factors may increase the importance of infectious processes. . . . No drug, however potent in antimicrobial activity, can control the infections associated with bronchitis and sinusitis and no vaccine can protect against them, just as it is almost certain that no drug and no vaccine could have controlled the intestinal diseases of filth in the nineteenth century. *It is filth that must be dealt with, or rather a social attitude that must be changed. Each civilization has its own kind of pestilence and can control it only by reforming itself.* (Emphasis added.)[30]

Policymakers and health professionals commonly assume that improvements in the quality of and access to health care services result in concomitant improvements in the health status of human populations. This view implies that increased expenditures for health care will reduce mortality and morbidity rates and increase life expectancy. The evidence we have reviewed fails to support these conclusions. After analyzing the decline in mortality in the United States between 1900 and 1974, the McKinlays conclude that medical measures—the source of most expenditures—have had little impact.[31] The lack of association between health outcomes and expenditures on health care services was also corroborated by Leveson (1979), who found that the rapid decline in mortality rates from the late 1930s to the early 1950s was associated with a slow growth in health care expenditures, whereas the rapid acceleration of health care expenditures following the 1950s was associated with slow improvements in the nation's health.[32]

After reviewing the literature in health economics, Victor Fuchs concludes, "When the state of medical science and other health determining variables are held constant, the marginal contribution of medical care to health is very small in modern nations."[33] And after a thorough analysis of disease trends, Illich concludes that "the specifically medical treatment of people is nowhere and never significantly related to a decline in the compound disease burden or to a rise in life expectancy."[34] Although these conclusions are provocative, they should not be interpreted to mean that medical care is either unimportant or useless. What is necessary, however, is to distinguish between those measures that affect the health of human *populations* and those such as medical care, that do not. The most successful attempts to reduce morbidity and mortality among human populations fall under the category of primary prevention. And the primary prevention strategy that has proven most effective and efficient is health *protection*. The primary prevention strategy that focuses on individuals and groups at high risk, the health *promotion* strategy, has yet to be proven effective.

Exhorting the worker to exercise personal safety in the midst of hazardous working conditions, asking adolescents to exercise mature judgment in the face of sophisticated advertising and social pressures to use (or at least try) government subsidized drugs, imploring poverty stricken mothers to feed their malnourished children a more varied and nutritious diet, and encouraging those who live near toxic waste dumps or nuclear plants to jog, quit smoking, and reduce cholesterol intake have not been demonstrated to be associated with positive health outcomes. Even in those instances where behavior modification techniques have been effective in reducing known risk factors associated with hypertension and cardiovascular disease, improved health outcomes as a consequence of such risk-reducing behavior remain to be demonstrated.[35]

The theoretical orientation that favors the individual lifestyle and behavior change strategy continues to be the dominant approach to primary prevention. Yet there is substantial evidence that personal risk factors interact with the social environment. Harvey Brenner notes that

(1) mortality from heart disease increases during economic downturns and decreases during economic upturns;[36]
(2) infant mortality is inversely related to upturns and downturns in the national economy, and nonwhites carry a greater risk of fetal mortality than whites during economic downturns;[37]
(3) alcohol consumption is inversely related to the state of the national economy, and mortality from cirrhosis of the liver increases substantially during national economic recessions;[38]
(4) there exists an inverse relationship between economic changes and mental disorders; changes in the economy are the single most important factor in mental hospital admissions trends; recessions are associated with substantial increases in both first admissions and readmissions to mental hospitals;[39]
(5) the unemployment rate is directly related to overall mortality rates, suicide rates, homicide rates, and imprisonment rates;[40] with every one percent increase in the national unemployment rate the following effects will occur over a six-year period: 36,887 "excess" deaths; 20,240 cardiovascular failures; 648 additional homicides; 4,227 additional admissions to mental hospitals; and 3,450 additional admissions to state prisons.[41]

Our conclusion is that the health promotion strategy ignores two very important facts: (1) that most of the factors affecting illness and health lie outside the control of individuals; and (2) that life-styles are powerfully influenced, if not fully determined, by the social organization in which they are embedded.

RISK-TAKING VERSUS
RISK-IMPOSING BEHAVIOR

Advocates of the health promotion strategy may respond to these criticisms by noting that, in the final analysis, social change is brought about by individuals or groups of individuals acting together; therefore, there should be no question that the life-styles and behavior patterns of individuals affect the risks of morbidity and early death among the population at large. In this regard, however, it is important to distinguish clearly between *risk-taking* and *risk-imposing* behavior. The former refers to conduct that creates a risk for the individual actor, whereas the latter refers to conduct by an individual or group of individuals which imposes risks on others. In choosing between a strategy of health promotion and one of health protection, the relevant policy question is, In whose life-styles are we going to intervene? Those who may be adversely affected by the risk-imposing behavior of others? Or those who, through enticing others to use harmful drugs or through the dumping of toxins in the environment, willfully expose others to health hazards?

This dilemma is illustrated by the following analogy. Illegal drugs (e.g., heroin, cocaine, marijuana) are considered to be a cause of crime, morbidity and early death in the United States. Millions of dollars are lost each year from crime associated with illegal drug use, enforcement of illegal drug laws, moneys provided to foreign governments to prevent export of raw or processed illegal drugs, and early deaths among users. Although the consumers of such illegal drugs are seen as part of the problem, they are not seen as the whole problem; the dealers of illegal drugs, from the lowliest street-corner pusher to the highest-level Mafia leader, are considered primarily responsible for the extent of the illegal drug problem because they are responsible for creating the demand and the market for these drugs. Because they deliberately market drugs known to generate addiction and illness and to underlie such additional adverse social effects as crime and early death among users, the purveyors are pursued more relentlessly and receive much harsher punishment than the users. The nation's number one woman fugitive, for example, was the alleged leader of a major cocaine ring who jumped $1-million bail several years ago.[42]

Those who consume illegal drugs are seen as the victims of the purveyor. That is, the pusher, for personal gain, deliberately entices those who are susceptible into addiction; therefore the purveyor is viewed as predator and the consumer as prey. Interventions and sanctions aimed at changing the risk-imposing behavior of the drug dealer are seen as having much greater potential impact on the problem than changing the behavior of the risk-taking individuals (the user). In the United States, Attorney General William French Smith said recently that the Reagan administration's drug policy is to emphasize attacking the organized crime networks that control distribution of drugs.[43] This strategy is seen as primary prevention (reducing exposure in the environment); addressing the behavior of the user is generally seen as treatment.

Now let us consider the legal drugs alcohol and tobacco in relation to the above example. Cigarette smoking has been identified by the U.S. Department of Health, Education, and Welfare as the "greatest single risk factor in the U.S.," because tobacco is a carcinogen known to be interactive with other carcinogens.[44] Alcohol addiction makes the illegal drug problem look minor in comparison. The most recent Report of the surgeon general indicated that one in every ten deaths, some 200,000 annually, is associated with alcohol use.[45] Like heroin, alcohol has been shown to be linked closely to crime.[46] Yet, in this not dissimilar situation, the health promotion approach is focused solely on the risk-taking behavior of the addicted individual, while the risk-imposing behavior of those responsible for generating the demand for alcohol and tobacco—the manufacturers, advertisers, and purveyors of these hazardous drugs—is not only systematically ignored but actively supported by government subsidies.

This approach to the major public health problems of alcohol and cigarettes is equivalent to trying to change the behavior of the individual heroin addict while subsidizing the activities of the heroin pusher. Health promotion, at least with respect to the consumers of alcohol and cigarettes, makes no attempt to reduce environmental exposure to these drugs. Instead, the issue is seen as one of choice for the exposed individual. The nonuser is implored to resist marketing enticements, and the user, who may be addicted, is exhorted to stop being addicted. But how is it possible to implore the nonaddict to resist the blandishments of advertisers, who are at least as good at their profession as the health promoters are at theirs, and who, in addition, operate at an incomparably higher level of funding. Almost surely it will be a losing battle. As John McKinlay observes:

> the promoters of disease-inducing behavior are manifestly more effective in their use of behavioral science than are those of us who are concerned with the eradication of such behavior. Indeed, it is somewhat paradoxical that we should be meeting here to consider how behavioral science knowledge and techniques can be effectively employed to reduce or prevent at-risk behavior, when that same body of knowledge *has already* been used to create the at-risk behavior we seek to eliminate. How embarrassingly ineffective are our mass media efforts in the health field (e.g., alcoholism, obesity, drug abuse, safe driving, pollution, etc.) when compared with many of the tax exempt promotional efforts on behalf of the illness-generating activities of large-scale corporations. It is a fact that we are demonstrably more effective in persuading people to purchase items they never dreamt they would need, or to pursue at-risk courses of action than we are in preventing or halting such behavior.[47]

Next, let us consider occupational hazards. The health promotion strategy focuses on "stress management." Although the National Conference on Health Promotion

Programs in Occupational Settings acknowledged a clear association between environmental stress and disease, its recommended interventions are limited to the risk-taking individual:

> It must be recognized that it is a combination of factors within and outside the work situation that interact and contribute to disease. . . . Certain personality, cognitive, and behavior characteristics of an employee interact with characteristics of the environment and influence this association. . . . An occupationally-based stress reduction program could cause people to *change their life-styles for the sake of their health and at the same time reduce absenteeism, enhance productivity, and decrease insurance and medical costs.* (emphasis added.)[48]

The recommended procedures to help workers change their life-styles are "assertiveness training" and the development of "coping" skills such as the relaxation response.

Finally, let us consider how cancer is approached as a major killer of people in industrialized societies. It is ironic that the overwhelming majority of cancer research funds in the United States are provided by the state and by industry, and are allocated to finding a cure for cancer instead of to reducing environmental exposures to carcinogens. Secretary Richard Schweiker of the Department of Health and Human Services praised the National Cancer Institute's "chemo-prevention" program for "focusing more on how we can interfere in the later stages of carcinogenesis to *prevent* cancer, instead of concentrating exclusively on substances which initiate the cancer process." (emphasis added.)[49]

At the same time, Schweiker was involved in drastically curtailing such socially oriented approaches to prevention as hazardous waste control programs, air research programs, and the Centers for Disease Control, to mention only a few.[50]

The evidence we have reviewed suggests that the major public health gains over the last century have resulted from changes in risk-imposing behavior, not risk-taking behavior. The health promotion strategy has little potential for improving the health of at-risk populations. It deals primarily with treatment of those who are already engaged in risk-taking behavior and secondarily with appeals to those who will inevitably be exposed to risks beyond their control or who will be subjected to government subsidized enticements to engage in risk-taking behavior.

The health promotion strategy is based on the assumption that individuals and groups with particular diseases, or who display certain risk-taking behaviors, are responsible for their own situation. They are presumed either to be doing something they shouldn't, or not doing something they should. That is, those displaying risk-taking behavior are considered deviant, and resources are mobilized to bring them into line with what is presumed to be more appropriate behavior, whereas risk-imposing behavior is ignored. For example, the fact that some life insurance companies are now offering reduced premiums for non-smokers and nondrinkers can be viewed from another perspective, as punishing those who have yielded to government subsidized antihealth advertising campaigns.

RECONCEPTUALIZING PREVENTION: ISSUES FOR THE FUTURE

In comparing health promotion and health protection strategies, it is useful to recount this story:

> Imagine a person walking alongside a river who sees some-one drowning. This person jumps in, pulls the victim out, and begins aritificial resuscitation. While this is going on, another drowning person calls for help; the rescuer jumps into the water again and pulls the new victim out. This process repeats itself several times until the rescuer gets up and begins to run upriver. A bystander, surprised to see the rescuer moving away from the victims, calls out, "Where are you going?" The rescuer replies, "I'm going upstream to find out who's pushing all these people in and to see if I can stop it or teach them how to swim."[51]

Health protection, in this instance, is concerned with changing the behavior of the "pusher." Health promotion focuses on teaching the victims of the pusher how to swim—though the river may have become so polluted that it threatens the health of even the best swimmers.

The task of primary prevention is to direct attention upstream, in order to find out why all these people are falling, or being pushed, into the river. When the public health professional looks upstream, it becomes clear that the problem exists on several levels. First, there is the individual who falls or is pushed into the water. If we deal only with those who have already fallen in, this is appropriately called tertiary prevention, or curative medicine. Second, there is the setting or situational environment in which the fall or the push takes place. This includes the individual himself and the physical or social characteristics of the immediate environment which contribute directly to the push or fall. The third level is the broader environment shaped by public policy, which encompasses both the individual and the setting and thus determines whether it is a push or a fall. This level includes rules and regulations set by organizations and institutions with direct or indirect interests in the problem.

The first level of prevention involves educational approaches that seek to empower individuals to make more informed decisions concerning behaviors that effect their health. Although such efforts do not have a record of success, they remain attractive to decision makers. To begin with, they firmly locate the source of the problem in the individual and thus provide a clear causal relationship that can be addressed. Like the slogan at the end of "prevention" advertisements sponsored by the Distilled Spirits Council of the United States—"It's people that [sic] give drinking a bad name"—these programs, whether inadvertently or by design, tend to place the entire responsibility for the problem on the individual. In addition, the premises on which such educational programs are based are consistent with values that support education as a legitimate response to community problems. Finally, such programs allow responsibility for prevention to be assumed with little political threat. By focusing on the individual, attention is diverted from more politically volatile areas, such as the issue of availability.

Educational efforts should continue to be implemented in school and community based programs; however, education should tell the whole story, it should relate the entire chain of causal events leading to at-risk behavior, not just a part. At present, health education typically represents health as a commodity that can be purchased at the physician's office, or as a state that is dependent on one's own behavior patterns; seldom are the risk-imposing behaviors of the manufacturers of illness ever linked to the disease patterns such education is attempting to change.

The second level of prevention involves community approaches to health problems. Problems are no longer defined only at the individual level but are understood within the framework of the larger community. Although education still plays an important role, planning and organizational strategies are emphasized. Since traditional prevention efforts have focused on the individual, the community's power to influence morbidity and mortality has not often been brought into play. Recent studies suggest, however, that there is growing community interest in becoming involved in health issues. This interest needs to be cultivated in order to encourage effort at this level.

One of the major problems in getting communities interested in prevention is the unclear linkage between the intervention and the problem. It is necessary to create bridges to span the gap from the immediate problem to possible levels of intervention. Strategies need to be developed to empower communities to engage in planning processes and organizational relationships relevant to prevention. From the perspective of primary prevention efforts, this means providing education and specific skills to community groups so that decisions about health and health related issues can be made in the interests of the larger community.

The third level of prevention involves public policy issues: the policies of institutions and national organizations in both the private and public sectors, the coordination of agency efforts, funding decisions, and the design of laws and regulations concerning health related matters. This larger institutional environment affects, to a large extent, societal patterns of illness and mortality.

Policies in the workplace, for example, have been slow to recognize the significance of working conditions and safety measures for the occurrence of cancer and related health problems. Yet it is well known that some industries have much higher rates of cancer and other specific diseases than others, and that in some industries such exposures are both common and extremely hazardous. The design and encouragement of company policies that minimize the amount of exposure permitted in the workplace, and alter working conditions and working environments that invite exposure to toxins, noise, and other health hazards, is essential.

Public agencies also have a role in integrating policies that are relevant to health and health related issues. In the United States, at the federal level, at least a dozen agencies with major regulatory impact on alcohol use and related problems have been slow to coordinate their activities with one another. The Department of Transportation's campaigns against drunk driving is a case in point. It has provided messages aimed primarily at individuals (including advertisement campaigns and enforcement activities), without also using its considerable resources to investigate the contributions of automobile design and traffic planning to the occurrence of alcohol related accidents. Similar examples could be provided for the tobacco industry and the major polluters of the environment and those agencies whose regulatory policies could affect the impact of these industries on the public's health.

SUMMARY AND CONCLUSION

It is clear that as a society we have taken a primarily downstream approach to health problems. We wait for people to develop problems that severely affect their lives and then invest enormous resources in attempts to rescue them, after which we send them back into the same human systems that were the source of their problems to begin with. To make the decision to work upstream instead of downstream means that health professionals must accept the challenge to widen their approach from a reactive to a proactive perspective. In this regard, two important steps need to be taken. First, we must begin to question existing definitions of prevention problems and develop broader research methods for addressing those expanded definitions. Second, the values that presently determine how the responsibility for prevention is allocated across the social structure require careful reexamination.

How we determine what is scientific in research and what is ethical and fair in distributing responsibility depends on the basic values we embrace as individuals and as a society. Currently our societal values in this area reinforce a "blaming-the-victim" approach.[52] This means that we understand and react to social problems as failures of the individual to adapt adequately to the larger system. By focusing on the victim we fail to question the conditions outside the individual that give rise to and sustain these problems. We attempt to find causes within the individual to explain the evolution of the problem. This runs counter to the evidence we have reviewed that suggests that even when single causes are apparent they are likely dependent on a range of other contributing factors.

To move toward more effective prevention policies and programs we must broaden the way that a problem is defined. This means deemphasizing individual-level explanations and increasing the emphasis on community or societal-level explanations. With this broader definition of the problem, responsibility for preventing it can be shared more equitably among the various interests that have a stake in the solution. Because problems of disease prevention ultimately affect the well-being of the entire community, the cost of addressing them should be borne collectively.

Once the definition of the problem is broadened, the nature of the research needed to understand it must also change. New questions must be posed even though the complex and value laden nature of these questions makes them ill suited for traditional forms of scientific inquiry. Research into public health issues needs to question rather than accept existing social and economic arrangements. The larger system should be seen as purposeful, rather than neutral, in that the interests of some are served at the expense of others. It is important to ask whose interests are meant to be served, who bears the social and financial costs of alternative social arrangements, and finally, who actually reaps the benefits.

In Western industrialized nations, primary prevention of chronic disease and early death will require embarking on a radically new, "upstream" path in the future. In following this upstream path, four basic principles may serve as guides for action. First, we must realize that human disease cannot be fully understood except within the context of its broader social structure. Second, treatment of sick individuals is an important moral responsibility of our society. We cannot abandon those casualties of the social system who are in need of care and treatment. In addition, however, the moral responsibility for disease prevention is at least as great as the responsibility for treatment. Third, careful research illuminating the social, political, and economic links to health and illness is vitally needed. Finally, social policy is the principal mechanism for instituting upstream primary prevention initiatives. We cannot talk realistically about changing health status without examining the public policies that have resulted in our present status. Only a comprehensive plan of action that begins—but does not end—with treatment of the victim, and moves to a consideration of broader social issues, is likely to provide a reasonable chance for Western societies to prevent unacceptably high levels of chronic disease and early death. Primary prevention entails social as well as individual change. To develop effective and efficient primary prevention programs and policies we must move to meet this challenge.

NOTES

1. K. White, "Prevention as a National Health Goal," editorial, *Preventive Medicine* 4 (1975): 247–251.

2. M. Foucault, preface to *Généalogie des équipements de normalization: les équipments sanitaires* (Paris: Cerfi, 1976).

3. Ibid.

4. Ibid.

5. L. Boltanski, *Prime éducation et morale de classe* (Paris: Mouton, 1969).

6. B. W. Richardson, *Hygeia, a City of Health* (London: MacMillan, 1876).

7. Foucault, *Généalogie*.

8. J. Peter, "Le grand rêve de l'ordre médicale en 1770 et aujourd'hui," *Autrement* 4 (1975).

9. F. Fagnani, *La prévention: example d'intervention hors marché* (Grenoble: Université des Sciences Sociales, Institut de Recherche Economique et de Planification, 1973).

10. E. Morse, "L'avenir de la medécine préventive," in J. de Kervasdoué, J. Kimberly, and V. Rodwin, eds., *La santé rationnée: la fin d'un mirage* (Paris: Economica, 1981).

11. See, e.g., U.S. Department of Health, Education and Welfare, *Healthy People: The Surgeon General's Report on Health Promotion and Disease Prevention*, (Washington, D.C.: U.S. Government Printing Office, 1979); and the consultative document prepared jointly by the health departments of Great Britain and Northern Ireland, *Prevention and Health: Everybody's Business* (London: HMSO, 1976).

12. In France under the new socialist government the minister of health commissioned an important report on prevention: *Propositions pour une politique de prévention* (Paris: Documentation Française, 1982). In Québec, the secretary for social development released a significant report calling for a reorganization of the occupational health system: *Santé et securité au travail* (Québec: Édition officiel du Québec, 1978).

13. J. Knowles, "Responsibility for Health," *Science* 198 (December 16, 1977): 1103.

14. L. Eisenberg, "The Perils of Prevention: A Cautionary Note," *New England Journal of Medicine.* 297 (December 1, 1977): 1231.

15. R. Cooper, M. Steinhauer, W. Miller, R. David, and A. Schatzkin, "Racism, Society and Disease: An Exploration of the Social and Biological Mechanisms of Differential Mortality," *Int. J. Health of Services* 11 (1981): 389–414.

16. V. Navarro, *Medicine Under Capitalism* (New York: Prodist, 1976).

17. World Bank, *Assault on World Poverty: Problems of Rural Development, Education, and Health* (Baltimore: Johns Hopkins University Press, 1975), pp. 374–375. Although this figure is a good indicator of the disproportionate emphasis on medical interventions, we recognize that it does not account for expenditures on health protection by private firms, as well as other government departments outside the health sector. These expenditures can be substantial, particularly in industrially advanced nations.

18. R. Dubos, *Mirage of Health: Utopias, Progress, and Biological Change* (New York: Harper Colophon Books, 1979).

19. T. McKeown, *The Role of Medicine: Dream, Mirage, or Nemesis?* (London: Nuffield Provincial Hospital Trust, 1976). J. Powles, "On the Limitations of Modern Medicine" *Science, Medicine, and Man* 1 (1973): 1–30.

20. E. M. Kitagawa and P. M. Hauser, *Differential Mortality in the United States: A Study in Socioeconomic Epidemiology* (Cambridge, Mass.: Harvard University Press, 1974), p. 23.

21. N. S. Scrimshaw, C. E. Taylor, and J. E. Gordon, *Interaction of Nutrition and Infection* (Geneva: World Health Organization, 1968). W. J. van Zijl, "Studies on Diarrhoeal Disease in Seven Countries by the WHO Diarrhoeal Advisory Team," *Bull. of WHO* 35 (1966): 249–261.

22. G. M. Foster, "Medical Anthropology and International Health Planning," *Med. Anthro. Newsletter* 7 (1976): 14.

23. T. S. Bodenheimer, "The Political Economy of Malnutrition: Generalization from Two Central American Case Studies," *Archivos Latino-Americanos de Nutricion* 22 (1972): 295–305.

24. K. A. Noble, "Are program cuts linked with increased infant deaths?" *New York Times*, 13 February 1983, p. 6; A. Robbins, "An Open Letter to the New Secretary," *Nation's Health*, February 1983.

25. U.S. Congress, *Report to the House Committee on Interstate and Foreign Commerce* (Washington, D.C.: Subcommittee on Oversight and Investigations, 1979).

26. American Public Health Association, "Toxics Group Reports Cancer on Increase," *Nation's Health*, August 1980, p. 1.

27. S. Epstein, *The Politics of Cancer* (San Francisco: Sierra Club, 1978).

28. U.S. Department of Health, Education and Welfare, *Healthy People: The Surgeon General's Report on Health Promotion and Disease Prevention* (Washington, D.C.: U.S. Government Printing Office, 1979).

29. E. M. Kitagawa and P. M. Hauser, *Differential Mortality in the United States: A Study in Socioeconomic Epidemiology* (Cambridge, Mass.: Harvard University Press, 1974).

30. R. Dubos, *Mirage of Health: Utopias, Progress, and Biological Change* (New York: Harper Colophon Books, 1979), pp. 194–195.

31. J. B. McKinlay and S. N. McKinlay, "The Questionable Contribution of Medical Measures to the Decline of Mortality in the United States in the Twentieth Century," *Milbank Memorial Fund Quarterly:* 55 (Summer 1977): 405–428.

32. I. Leveson, "Some Policy Implications of the Relationship Between Health Services and Health," *Inquiry* 16 (Spring, 1979): 9–21.

33. V. Fuchs, "Economics, Health, and Post-Industrial Society, *Milbank Memorial Fund Quarterly:* 57 (Spring 1979): 156.

34. I. Illich, *Medical Nemesis: The Expropriation of Health* (London: Marian Boyars, 1975).

35. L. Yamamoto, K. Yano, and G. G. Rhoads, "Characterisitics of Joggers among Japanese Men in Hawaii," *Amer. J. Pub. Health* 73 no. 2 (February 1983): 147–152; J. M. McKenney et al., "The Effects of Clinical Pharmacy Services on Patients with Essential Hypertension," *Circulation* 48 (November 1973): 1104–1111; A. W. Sedgwick et al., "Long-Term Effects of Physical Training Programme on Risk Factors for Coronary Heart Disease in Otherwise Sedentary Men," *Brit. Med. J.* 281 (July 5, 1980): 7–10; A. McAlister, et al., "Theory and Action for Health Promotion: Illustrations from the North Karelia Project," *Am. J. Pub. Health* 72 (January 1982): 43–50; G. Kolata, "Heart Study Produces a Surprising Result, *Science* 218 (October 1, 1982): 31–32.

36. M. H. Brenner, "Economic Changes and Heart Disease Mortality," *Am. J. Pub. Health* 61 (March 1971): 606–611.

37. M. H. Brenner, "Fetal, Infant, and Maternal Mortality During Periods of Economic Instability," *Int. J. of Health Services* 3 (1973): 145–159.

38. M. H. Brenner, "Trends in Alcohol Consumption and Associated Illnesses: Some Effects of Economic Changes," *Am. J. Pub. Health* 65 (December 1975): 1279–1292.

39. M. H. Brenner, "Effects of Adverse Changes in the National Economy on Health" (Paper presented at the 103rd meeting of the American Public Health Association, Chicago, November 18, 1975).

40. M. H. Brenner, *Estimating the Social Costs of National Economic Policy*

Implications for Mental and Physical Health and Criminal Aggression (Washington, D.C.: U.S. Congress, Joint Economic Committee, USGPO, 1976); M. H. Brenner, "Mortality, Social Stress, and the Modern Economy: Experience of the United States, Britain, and Sweden, 1900—1970" (Paper presented at the annual meeting of the American Association for the Advancement of Science, Boston, Massachusetts, February 21, 1976); M. H. Brenner, "Mortality and the National Economy: A Review and the Experience of England and Wales", *Lancet* 2 (1979): 568—573.

41. M. H. Brenner, "Health Costs and Benefits of Economic Policy," *Int. J. Health Services* 7 (1977): 581—623.

42. *San Francisco Chronicle*, February 14, 1983.

43. *San Francisco Chronicle*, February 8, 1983.

44. U.S. Department of Health, Education and Welfare. *Healthy People: The Surgeon General's Report on Health Promotion and Disease Prevention*, (Washington, D.C.: USGPO, 1979).

45. Ibid.

46. San Francisco *Chronicle*, January 31, 1983.

47. J. B. McKinlay, "A Case for Refocussing Upstream: The Political Economy of Illness," in E. G. Jaco, ed., *Patients, Physicians, and Illness: A Sourcebook in Behavioral Science and Health* (New York: Free Press, 1979), pp. 9—25.

48. A. M. McGill, ed., *Proceedings of the National Conference on Health Promotion Programs in Occupational Settings*. (Washington, D.C.: USDHEW, 1979), p. 18.

49. Drug Research Reports, "Cancer Prevention Cited as Alternative to Environmental Emphasis," *Blue Sheet* 25 (June 2, 1982): 8—9.

50. American Public Health Association, "Supplement: The President's Budget Proposal," *Nation's Health*, March 1982.

51. Adapted McKinlay, "A Case for Refocussing Upstream," p. 9.

52. W. Ryan, *Blaming the Victim* (New York: Vintage, 1976).

4

Technology and the Need for Health Care Rationing

Jean de Kervasdoué, John R. Kimberly, and Jean-François Lacronique

One has only to travel from Hong Kong to New York or from Buenos Aires to Moscow to appreciate the power of technology as a force for standardization in the contemporary world.[1] Similarities in architecture, in mass transit facilities, and in department store wares, are visible reminders that technology transcends political ideology. Public discussions of nuclear arms limitation are psychological reminders of the unforeseeable, anarchistic, and irreversible nature of much technological development.

In this chapter we examine the role of technology and the "technological network" in health care, identifying and discussing questions about the contributions of technology to life and health—questions that are particularly troublesome because they often invoke considerations of morality and economics simultaneously. The questions, though difficult, are real; responding to them with sensible, reasoned policy is one of the challenges for health policymakers in the coming years.

The Technological Network

Our perspective on the subject is a broad one, as we are impressed by the pervasiveness and interconnectedness of technology in health care.[2] In strict definitional terms, the French definition of technology differs slightly from its Anglo-Saxon equivalent: Larousse makes an explicit reference to industry and its processes, while Webster's defines the word as the totality of means employed to procure for man the objects necessary for his subsistence and comfort. *Technology* is a metonymical extension of the word *technique*. Anything that uses or involves technical intervention can be called technological. In the area of health, the consideration of technology should not be limited to the instruments and techniques used by doctors. It extends to the entire spectrum of the work of health care professionals, from the use of the telephone to computer programming. Technology in health care also means documentation, and modern methods in pedagogy and promotion. It includes the vast range of prostheses and instruments that change the lives of handicapped people. Modern management techniques employed by hospitals and health services are included, as is genetic engineering for industrial purposes, because the interaction between living organisms and their environments is beginning to be explained by technological processes (genetic recombination). Technology thus consists of a whole network of sciences that are increasingly interdependent. Modern biology, for example, would not exist without optics, computer science, and solid physics.

A modern hospital is a particularly dense concentration of the technological network. Although the network is more dispersed in private practice, a general practitioner also depends on pharmacists, radiologists, and laboratories for assistance in diagnosis and treatment.

The interdependent character of technology in health care makes evaluation difficult. The example of a new X-ray machine illustrates the problem well. It is certainly possible to evaluate the quality and cost of the prints it makes in comparison with those already on the market. The real question, however, is whether or not the machine can produce new information. It must then be determined if this additional information is useful, if applicable therapies exist, and if trained personnel are available. To evaluate the machine fully one must refer to its necessary complements.

The notion of a network sheds light on the probable nature of future technological developments. Innovations have essentially two sources. They may come from the linear development of a single concept, or from the conjunction of two previously independent branches of technology, which creates new uses and further developments. The former is illustrated by the modern stethoscope, which differs only slightly from Laennec's first model although it is made of materials unknown in the nineteenth century. Telecommunications, a descendent of the telephone and the computer, illustrates the latter. Its proper applications go well beyond the domain of its parent technologies.

What can we expect from this network with regard to the health sector? Can it be controlled? What sorts of choices will confront us in the coming years? These questions are addressed in the following pages.

The End of Empiricism

Since the beginning of this century, life expectancy in Western societies has considerably increased, while morbidity rates have declined. At birth, life expectancy is seventy years for men and seventy-six years for women. Infant mortality has considerably decreased also. The most common illnesses are chronic diseases affecting the elderly.

Technology has contributed measurably to this evolution. Vaccines and antibiotics have made most hospital beds intended for patients with infectious diseases redundant; yellow fever, for example, has almost disappeared. Thanks to insulin, diabetics may now have a normal life span. In certain areas, however, little progress has been made. There are no cures for numerous cardiovascular and cerebrovascular illnesses or for most cancers.[3] Few major discoveries have been made in the last twenty years, and many of those that have been announced and heavily publicized, such as interferon, have not yet lived up to expectations.

The case of interferon is instructive. Many articles were written about this "miracle protein" before conclusive laboratory results were available. The actual substance tested was often impure; control groups were often inappropriate; and dosages varied widely from test to test. In addition, little was known about how interferon functions on the molecular level, nor was it certain whether patients have differential sensitivities to this substance. The considerable fanfare surrounding its development, however, created great expectations, largely in the absence of empirical evidence.

This is not an exceptional case. There are numerous examples of what may be called expectation inflation. At the beginning of this century, no effective treatment for cancer existed. The first positive results of radiation treatment for certain kinds of skin cancer have been extended today to other tumors, even when effectiveness has not been demonstrated. Today, it is not unlikely that a particular cancer therapy regimen is used as much because it is codified and priced as because it is effective. It is difficult to avoid getting caught up in the wave of increased expectations; the only restraint, albeit imperfect, is the ethics of scientists.

For most of us, however, the gaps between promise and performance do not destroy our hopes. And we accept the side effects of potential effectiveness; technology has its risks. If it cures, it can also injure or even kill, particularly where there is negligence, lack of scientific knowledge, or imperfect training of medical personnel.

Health technologies are expensive, not so much because of equipment costs but because of the need for qualified personnel; and they are known to create a "prescribed" demand by practitioners of their widespread use.

Technical Innovation—The Cause of Increased Health Care Costs?

Technical innovations are statistically linked to growing consumption of medical services, and this with growing costs.[4] When the components of medical care are analyzed, it is evident that the sectors showing the most rapid increases in costs are those in which technical advances have recently emerged. Thus in France, in the area of out patient services, laboratory tests and radiology have expanded rapidly, with respective annual growth rates of 22 percent and 7.6 percent, while traditional medical acts such as house calls and general practice consultations have progressed slowly.[5] In the United States, total domestic shipments of X-ray apparatus and electromedical devices increased at an annual rate of approximately 24 percent between 1972 and 1977.[6]

This evolution is most visible in the public hospital sector in France and in university hospitals in the United States, because these are the privileged domains of high technology therapy. The expanding significance of technical services in hospital care is illustrated in table 1 by the growth of radiological procedures and laboratory tests per admission for all categories of hospitals in France. Private practice also reflects the role of technological innovation. In France, radiology accounted for 12.6 percent of medical activity in private practice for the year 1959; in 1976 the figure was 20.2 percent. Technical progress as measured by consumption of technical procedures accounts for about

TABLE 1
PUBLIC GENERAL HOSPITALS (FRANCE)

Year	Number of "Z" *		Number of "B" **	
	By Admission	By Day	By Admission	By Day
1965	22.48	1.0	253	7.3
1970	30.59	1.7	298	16.4
1973	37.54	2.4	394	25.1
Annual Growth Rate in Percentage				
1965–1973	6.6	11.6	12.6	16.7
1970–1973	7.1	12.2	9.8	15.2

*X-ray procedures are evaluated according to "Z". The more complex a procedure, the higher its "Z" number.

**Biological tests are evaluated according to a "B" number.

two-thirds of the increase in volume of medical procedures, independent of price increases.

The causal relation between accelerating technical progress and growing expenses is difficult to determine. Increasing costs can be linked to technological advances in many cases, but in a few instances, costs for individual treatments are reduced. For policy purposes, the direction of causality is of fundamental importance. If one accepts the innovation-push hypothesis, then efforts to improve productivity in the health care system should be aimed at qualitative control, requiring judgments about the future potential of an innovation in the earliest stages of its development.

The alternative hypothesis interprets technical innovation as the response of human genius to legitimate needs. In this view, only excessive use and consumption should be criticized. The eventual control of use would therefore be wholly quantitative; the nature of technical innovation would not be questioned, only its long-term effects. Although these two hypotheses theoretically are not mutually exclusive, differences in the causal priority they assign to technological innovation and the resulting differences in implications for health policy effectively force a choice between them.

THE JUSTIFICATION FOR TECHNICAL PROGRESS

Technical Progress and Quality of Care

The introduction of a technical innovation is normally justified on the basis of an anticipated or demonstrable improvement in the quality of a service rendered by the health care system. Although to contrast qualitative evaluation (subjective) with quantitative measurement (objective) is simplistic, it is possible to analyze the marginal benefits of technical progress by breaking down the notion of quality into five components, each objectively measurable: technical efficacy; cost; comfort; safety; and accessibility. Each of these factors must be evaluated on a different scale and can be analyzed separately; but the overall evaluation of an innovation should be thought of as a complex function of these five independent variables.

TECHNICAL EFFICACY

Efficacy can be evaluated in terms of decreased rates of mortality, morbidity, and illness. Recent examples of technological advances that would rate highly on this dimension include:

The use of chemotherapy in treating hematosarcomas. What was a mortal illness ten years ago is now usually curable.

Artificial prostheses (hip joints in particular), which have transformed prognosis of traumatic and rheumatoid pathology for the elderly.

Dialysis machines and kidney transplants, which have prolonged the lives of renal failure victims.

Intensive care facilities capable of sustaining vital functions. Progress in this area has even led to charges of overuse (artificially prolonging life).

Scientific procedures for evaluating the efficacy of new therapies are generally applied only to innovations in medication, and not to advances in medical instruments. Two explanations are usually advanced to account for this:

Controlled therapeutic tests would be difficult to organize for instruments because of problems of random selection and the composition of test groups.

Progress is more tangible in the area of instrumentation than in that of medication. Thus, strict experimental protocol is not yet needed in instrumentation as it is in the domain of medication, which deals with active molecules so that only marginal improvement over existing products can be expected.

These are questionable arguments that are not based on objective criteria. It should be noted, however, that there is a dearth of methods for determining the efficacy of organizational innovations.

Cost

Many innovations have brought about a reduction in unit costs for treatment. The development of simple tests and instruments (chemically reactive paper tests, enzyme analyses, etc.) exemplifies how automation can reduce unit costs in some instances. Ease of use and the reduction of unit costs, both consequences of automation, also create incentives that may lead to increased consumption, however, and thus to an increase in total costs. Improvements in technology for renal dialysis in the United States is one example. Unit treatment costs were substantially reduced by improved technology; but total costs for dialysis rose dramatically.[7]

Comfort and Safety

Innovations may seek to minimize the following risks and inconveniences which treatment can create for the patient and those around him: accidents and the need for therapy; pain; waiting; violation of privacy; side effects on family or social life.

The current increased effort to develop noninvasive techniques demonstrates how such aims can supersede the technical efficacy of treatment. The following recent innovations are examples of this trend: electrocardiography; isotope scintography; echotomography and echocardiography (ultrasound); thermography; computerized axial tomography (CAT scanning). Research is also being conducted to develop techniques based on magnetism (rheography), nuclear magnetic resonance (eugmatography), and stable isotopes.

These techniques have in common a relative innocuousness. They may be repeated without risk and are usually based on automated procedures that make them simple to use. These two features are particularly favorable because they eliminate the traditional barrier to the diffusion of technical innovations: the need to train highly skilled personnel.

As a consequence of these benefits, there has been a rapid expansion of the applications of these techniques, a phenomenon especially visible in the case of CAT scanners. Another almost caricatural example is the widespread use of thermography. It is generally accepted that this technique is of practically no diagnostic benefit except in the confirmation of breast cancer, a condition that can be precisely diagnosed by histology.

Accessibility

In France and in the United States, the development of home care and "day hospitals" offers the possibility of easy access to quality treatment without traditional hospitalization. In the future, improvements in telecommunications (such as information retrieval, optimal organization of hospital consultations, and long-distance consultation) will facilitate access to health care. The result is sure to be an increase in demand. Unless a substitution effect can be achieved by reducing the capacity of present health care facilities, we can expect an increase in consumption generated by the addition of new services to pre-existing ones.

Any improvement in one of the preceding variables—even if it doesn't improve the efficacy of the whole system—can be considered a contribution to the quality of care. As long as there are positive results in one area, it can be argued that general improvement has been made even if the introduction of an innovation causes a drop in performance in another variable. This is the case, for example, with certain pain relieving therapies for terminal cancer, where a gain in comfort is sometimes achieved against a decrease in life expectancy. In contrast, the higher risks of a difficult operation are sometimes preferred in hopes of a more effective cure.

If one accepts this reasoning, and the possibilty of substituting variables within the notion of "quality of treatment," a classic formula taken from the economics of goods and services can be applied. A demand function can be constructed in which the traditional variable *price* (whose variations determine consumption) can be successively replaced by the variables *discomfort, risk,* and *difficulty of access.* Intuitively we see that any improvement in these factors is capable of increasing demand. This dynamic is well illustrated by any empirical observations that show an increase in consumption of technical procedures.

The Diffusion of Medical Techniques

Patterns of diffusion are not identical from one technique to the next. In some cases the new technique is efficacious, simple to apply, and inexpensive. It thus diffuses rapidly. Frequently, however, the new technique is complex and requires new equipment and a trained medical staff. It is expensive and its effectiveness is not apparent at the time of its introduction but must be determined by studies over several years.

In this case, an innovation added to the arsenal of diagnostic methods and therapies will usually be integrated into the treatment process as a supplemental element. Its marginal cost will not be taken into account (it will rarely be budgeted), and it will only be a question of its marginal benefit, however small this may be. It will be studied (theses, articles, demonstrations, etc.) because it shows the different actors of the health care system in another light, different from the normal market relationship, in which supply and demand are equalized.

A most striking example of a new technology added to the market is the case of echo-tomography. Angiography, the radiological technique for exploring arteries, is several decades old; it is also dangerous, costly, and painful. The necessary equipment is very expensive. In France, there is one such apparatus per million inhabitants. The appearance of the scanner (tomodensitometry) and of echotomography in France around 1975 should have drastically altered treatment patterns since these two techniques permit a reduction in vascular radiography. However, an evaluation of the years following its appearance shows that vascular X-ray installations have maintained a steady level of activity during this time. Nowhere was a significant reduction in the number of arteriographs observed. On the contrary, authorizations for the purchase of vascular X-Ray machines are still relatively easy to obtain in contrast to authorizations for scanners.

An examination of use statistics reveals an important change in the structure and quality of vascular examinations, however. One physician gave the following interpretation of the spectular increases in pathological angiographies: tomodensitometry has created new demands for angiography—to determine the vascular etiology of lesions found by the scanner. Rather than an older technology becoming obsolete in the face of a new technology, new applications have been found for it. Thus, an innovation must entirely replace the former treatment if it is not to simply be added to the list of already existing treatments and so offer only a marginal benefit compared with its cost.

Perhaps in the coming years technology will help reduce the costs of some diagnostic examinations and therapies. It is unrealistic, however, to expect the same kind of overall reductions in health costs as those associated with technical progress in other sectors, where increased productivity means falling prices.

The CAT scanner is a case in point, and its history is intriguing.[18] The idea for the scanner was not new but had never been exploited in the United States, where it was originated. The inventors, a neurologist—W. H. Oldendord—and a physicist—A. M. Cormack—never succeeded in interesting either American doctors or American industry in the idea. The British engineer G. Hounsfield and a firm called Electronic Musical Instruments (EMI) took up the idea, however, and in 1967 succeeded in constructing an instrument capable of producing section images of objects (tomographies) far superior to those produced by conventional radiological techniques. In 1970 an apparatus for medical use derived from this principle was constructed with the aid of the British Ministry of Health. The first prototype was installed in the Atkinson Morley Hospital in London in October 1971.

Clinical experiments quickly demonstrated the potential of the machine, particularly in the diagnosis of brain tumors. It was first published internationally in 1972. In June 1973 the first two commercially functioning units were installed in Massachusetts General Hospital and the Mayo Clinic; they were an immediate success. An improved model capable of examining all regions of the body (not just the skull, as with the English model) was developed at Georgetown University in Washington, D.C. At this point, the larger X-Ray firms showed an interest in this new process. Siemens and Ohio Nuclear brought out machines in 1974. By the end of 1975, there were twenty builders, the largest of them being EMI (Great Britain), Pfizer, and Ohio Nulcear (U.S.).

In August of 1976 a total of 321 machines were functioning in the United States, and by 1978 there were more than 1200. There is now a ratio of one machine per 250,000 inhabitants, of which two-thirds are head-only and the rest full-body machines. The highest concentrations are in Florida and California.

According to most authorities, this is an excessive concentration, even if 80 percent of these machines are located in large university hospitals. They argue that these machines are expensive to buy and also very expensive to operate. The proponents of the technology point to three essential advantages it offers:

The scanner is a noninvasive apparatus and can thus be used for external consultations; hospitalization can thus be avoided or reduced in duration.

The scanner replaces other tests that are more costly and dangerous.

By improving precision in diagnosis the scanner can reduce expenses for unnecessary therapies that are dangerous and expensive.

These are all valid arguments, but an evaluation of this machine after a number of years of experience indicates that the scanner is certainly not an economical instrument. The justification for its use is medical; it improves conditions for the patient being examined (reduced waiting time, risk, and discomfort), while raising the level of technical precision in diagnosis.

Such qualities are, without doubt, sufficient to establish the scanner as a valuable technical advance; but in addition to its purely technical interest, the scanner is also a prestige instrument, a fact that lends it symbolic value. It is thus very attractive to the doctor as well as to the public. It is also a relatively simple instrument to use; it is highly automated, so a trained staff can exploit its full capabilities quite rapidly.

For all these reasons the scanner is a high demand item, and the only present constraint on its use is medical judgment. But should doctors really impose their judgment in this domain? Is this new demand fully justified? Does it lead to an improvement in the general quality of medical care? These three questions are basic to the general problem of technical progress in medicine. The public ultimately pays the price for technical progress and therefore has the right in any particular instance to demand an accounting.[9] But on what criteria will an accounting be based?

The example of the scanner is particularly interesting because it illustrates the clear opposition between the diagnostic efficiency of the apparatus and patient survival rates. It is undeniable that the new technique has completely changed X-ray diagnosis in all intracranial pathology and has considerably improved retroperitoneal and pelvic exploration. One cannot fail to observe, however, that little progress has been made in the last ten years in the treatment of brain and pancreas tumors and most secondary metasteses. Because the medical profession places as much value on the diagnostic as on the therapeutic stages of its activity, it is virtually incapable of judging the ultimate effectiveness of a particular technique. Such questions involve forms of analysis that are foreign to it.

An entirely different problem is that of the geographical distribution of equipment. Given that a certain technique is medically useful, how many machines are necessary to satisfy needs, and where should they be located? Different countries have approached this problem differently. In France, for example, the optimal norm has been defined as one scanner per million inhabitants, according to the directives of the *carte sanitaire*, which governs the distribution of heavy equipment designed for medical use. Yet no one can really say at this time if the French norm conforms more to needs than the American laissez-faire dynamic or the British budgetary system. The economic justification for the norm is that it locates control at the level of supply instead of at the level of demand; but is this justification adequate? This brief discussion of the scanner illustrates many of the difficult questions of social philosophy and policy which must be addressed as new medical technologies are developed and begin to diffuse.

TECHNOLOGY UNDER SURVEILLANCE

Can technology be controlled in its development as it is, to some degree, in its applications? Few today would seriously propose a moratorium on technological research. Many advances are still to be made, and developments that encourage society's fundamental hopes are not likely to be stifled. Progress is the issue and with it, the will to better the human condition. Even if it were desirable, a moratorium would be virtually impossible to carry out. No country, however powerful it may be, has a monopoly on health care research. If any one country halted production of a particular technology, it would risk economic difficulties. What one country did not make, another would, and there would be strong pressure to import new products. The arms race continues despite the dangers and economic hardships it imposes on the nations that participate in it most energetically. How realistic is it, then, to expect a halt in the race for medical progress, a race that is generally considered to have beneficial consequences for humanity?

The demand by patients and doctors for ever more costly, new techniques, techniques whose benefits do not always balance the costs of purchase and operation, seems virtually limitless. Given that moratoriums on research are unlikely and that demand for new technologies is likely to remain strong, what policy options are available? Two alternatives deserve comment. One strategy is to evaluate the quality of techniques as they appear and to develop only the best. This is the aim of technological evaluation. A second strategy is to orient research toward those areas where need is greatest and where potential benefits are largest.

Testing Medical Techniques

Technological evaluation should strive, on the one hand, to verify the actual performance of a technique and, on the other hand, to pass judgment on its total effect, the advantages and the inconveniences it causes the individual and society. Evaluation methods of this sort have long been used in the biomedical field, particularly in the area of pharmaceutical products, where the development and commercial exploitation of new drugs is circumscribed by legislation and a complex controlling apparatus.

Until recently, the instruments and apparatus used in medicine have been much less rigorously controlled, although—like drugs—they may have harmful as well as beneficial effects. Thus, new initiatives in evaluation methods are today chiefly concerned with instrument technology. A specific methodology must be developed to deal with the particular aspects of this field.[10]

The procedure manual of the Office of Technology Assessment created in 1973 by the United States Congress defined four evaluation criteria: (1) the expected benefits, even if multiple, must be identified and measurable; (2) the field of application of the new technique must be rigorously defined; (3) the evaluation must be made in reference to a given population; and (4) application conditions must be precise.

There is, of course, no such thing as an evaluation whose objectivity satisfies everyone. At a certain point it is always necessary to make a value judgment, to ponder advantages and disadvantages. Effectiveness and safety standards, for example, are different for each technology. Effectiveness is defined in terms of benefit, whereas safety is expressed in terms of acceptable risks. Although they are generally measured separately, the qualities are often interdependent. The interrelation between effectivess and safety is illustrated by the case of mammography, or the systematic detection of breast cancer. The potential benefits of this technique are derived from a test that itself subjects the patient to an appreciable risk, radiation. The benefit and risk factors thus cannot be considered separately, and indeed the National Institute of Health's study panel on breast cancer detection recommended that this technique not be used systematically on women under the age of fifty. Each doctor is, of course, free to interpret this ruling in practice.

Many cases are more complicated than this one. For example, there are two methods for treating chronic renal failure: transplantation and dialysis. Dialysis treatment is more expensive, and life expectancy for a patient so treated is less than that for a transplant patient. There is an appreciable risk involved in the transplant operation, however. The transplant patient thus has a longer average life expectancy but a higher mortality risk in the six months following the operation. From the patient's point of view, which is the best choice, assuming there is a choice. The answer varies from individual to individual even though, collectively speaking, transplantation seems better because it is less costly and more effective.

In addition to these difficulties in principle, there are methodological problems in evaluating new technologies.

Side Effects

When the effectiveness of a method is measured, the number of beneficial effects is usually limited. In contrast, the search for undesirable and unexpected side effects cannot be limited to the area of specialized investigation. Surveillance of harmful effects is thus usually more complex and expensive than measuring benefits.

Number of People Concerned

A technology is considered effective to the extent that the potential number of beneficiaries is relatively large; yet the risks involved in the use of a technology should be considered even if they concern only a small proportion of patients. Thus, a comparison of the risks and benefits of a medical technique must depend on an objective appreciation of the importance of the problem for the concerned population.

Delay in Cause and Effect

The beneficial effects of a medical technique are usually noticed before the adverse effects, thus making long-term evaluation necessary. In the case of certain diagnostic and therapeutic methods, this temporal delay may be as long as a generation (as with thalidomide or diethyl stilbestrol).

The Emotional Component

Finally, as in the case of renal failure treatment, the different parties involved may view the situation very differently, primarily because the collective financing of health costs causes each individual to be involved in an infinity of choices. The patient, whose choice is a key element in the system, is especially sensitive to considerations of effectiveness, comfort, and security. Disparities in equipment and access to care seem unjust to the patient, and there is a tendency to accept technology as the guarantee of quality. Health professionals are familiar with this outlook, and they seek to satisfy the constant demand for technical progress. The rapid deployment of scanner equipment in the United States exemplifies the problem. In contrast, the attitude of agencies whose responsibility is to reimburse costs for medical procedures is sometimes characterized as retrograde and restrictive. Nevertheless, it is clear that these agencies cannot always pay for everything for everyone.

The specter of limiting the availability of health care technologies engages emotion. Issues of freedom of choice for the patient and of equality of access to quality treatment—indeed, the foundations of free enterprise in a democratic society—enter the debate. The motivation of those who raise these issues varies. The subject of technical progress is virtually impossible to treat dispassionately; and arguments advanced in any particular case are often buttressed by statistical "evidence" carefully chosen to support a point of view.

APPLICATIONS OF THE TECHNOLOGY

The situation is further complicated by the fact that judgments about the intrinsic value of a technique, its utility and necessity, are not sufficient in themselves; the use of the technique must also be evaluated. When a technology is placed on the market, its evaluators no longer control it and it is not always certain to be used judiciously. Any technique has some applications for which it has been proved useful and other areas in which nothing is gained by employing it; but there is also usually a gray area in between. There is generally a large expanse of ambiguity where effectiveness has not been proved but where potential exists.

Differences in practice from one country to another, from one region to another, or even from one doctor to another can be explained by this ambiguity. Nations with technologically comparable systems of health do not have the same norms and practices, as is illustrated by the fact that at the beginning of the 1970s a U.S. citizen was thirty-eight times more likely than a Swede to undergo a coronary bypass.[11]

A priori evaluation is not sufficient; practices must be controlled and comparisons made between different ideal standards and actual utilization. The way individuals or medical teams use a given technique is thus a matter for serious attention. The methods essential to this type of evaluation are complex, and their impact on health expenditures is uncertain.[12] In fact, in all likelihood, some of these measures will *not* reduce costs and they may even contribute to cost increases. The "demetropolitanization" scenario suggests just such a possibility.

According to this scenario, the oversupply of physicians in industrialized nations will create an impetus for the development of subspecialties and sophisticated technology in hospitals in medium-sized cities. If the criterion for evaluation of the health system is technical medical performance, subspecialists—who are familiar with the use of sophisticated technology—can easily be shown to be more effective. Thus, the quality control system, as it is conceived in the United States and as it tends to develop in Western European countries, has less to do with the overall efficacy of the medical system and its impact on the health of the population than with the efficacy of medicine as measured by doctors. As long as doctors control the premises of evaluation, we can expect increases in the overall costs attributable to technological advances.

Evaluation is difficult, restricted, and often biased, but it does help to reduce abuses, and to define what is known and what is not. The development of technological evaluation methods and quality control of treatment are major innovations in the area of health policy, and their consequences will be felt in the coming years. They are not a panacea, however; they are not sufficient in themselves to control the development of technology and still less to limit health care costs.

Science Policy

Given the difficulty of controlling the utilization of a technique once it has been introduced, an alternative would be to orient research so that only potentially useful techniques are developed. Science policy, in other words, might be used as an instrument for influencing the content of research and hence controlling its products.

How viable might this approach be? Science policy was created at the instigation of men of science, but from the beginning these scientists conceived of participation in policy planning as an evil necessary to their research. In some instances this attitude has now become decidedly noncooperative or even hostile. Although they have willingly accepted support for their work, scientists have been less enthusiastic about control by agencies outside their own community. Nonetheless, in a period of thirty years their autonomy has rapidly eroded.

To illustrate, compare the language regarding biomedical research found in two different French national plans. The second national plan, formulated immediately after World War II, contained the following passage:

> Experience has shown, especially in the case of medicine, that the most productive means of research is to leave initiative absolutely in the hands of researchers in the choice and means of their research programs. Profitable applications usually arise in unpredictable fashion from pure research. It is the role of governing bodies of research to assure them this liberty. [Our translation.]

The basic argument was that, although research structures can be planned, the subjects and methods of research certainly cannot be and should be left entirely to the researcher's initiative. By the seventh national plan (1970–

1975) the language had changed dramatically. "Priority objectives," such as the biology of the brain, were invoked. The socioeconomic importance of each subject was studied, and certain areas, such as the functional organization of the neuron were indicated for development.

Though the difference in perspective between these two plans is striking, the same pattern of evolution occurred in the other industrialized nations. Basically, there have been three phases in the evolution of science policy since World War II. The first phase had its origins in government funding of research. When a laboratory and a few instruments were no longer sufficient, scientists were led to request subsidies from the state. To justify these demands, they alluded to the importance of their work for national defense and the economy. Once the size of the available "pie" had been defined, they were the only arbiters of how it was to be divided. The quote above from the second French national plan is very characteristic of this first phase.

The second phase proceeded naturally from the first. In effect, governments believed the scientists' arguments, according to which scientific research was the driving force behind military independence and social and economic development. This belief was based on an unwarranted generalization derived from a few cases (the atomic bomb, the transistor, etc.). As national investment in scientific research increased, it was no longer just a question of defining the size of the pie to be shared but also the size of the respective pieces. To address these questions, governments developed science policies in the areas of agriculture, health, and the different branches of industry. Restricted at the outset to the creation of institutions and budget allocations, these policies became increasingly precise and gave rise to the third phase.

The third phase was born out of the recognition by governments that not only did science have a social impact but that it might also be actively used to attain certain objectives. The guiding principle of scientific research was no longer simply the desire to solve theoretical problems or further man's understanding of nature. It came to include the deliberate search for solutions to specific economic, political, and social problems. One example was President Nixon's "war on cancer" and the resultant National Cancer Act. In 1971, Nixon declared:

> The time has come for the same type of concentrated effort which smashed the atom and brought man to the moon, to be oriented towards the conquest of this terrible disease. Let us make a national commitment to attain this objective.

The analogy was simple: if we can send a man to the moon, we should be able to find a cure for cancer. Unfortunately, the analogy was seriously flawed. In the words of a scientist at the time, "Could we send a man to the moon if we didn't know Newton's laws?" Apparently not. We still do not know if cancer is a single disease of cellular malfunction or more than a hundred distinct diseases that occur in four general forms. More than ten years after that unprecedented effort, the answer to this fundamental question has not been found.

We would not want to argue, however, that science policy is without benefit. For example, the state must compensate for industry's tendency to finance only what will be profitable in the near term, as this practice is not always consistent with a reduction in social costs. The state must also create openings and points of contact between complimentary disciplines, though in attempting this it is dealing with the unforeseeable. In our view, however, the development of technology will not be controlled by science policy because discoveries are too difficult to predict and because no single country has a monopoly on knowledge.

THE NEED FOR RATIONING

If the development of technology cannot be controlled, what options exist to limit its use? In our view, the most viable option is a system of rationing based on political and ethical criteria. Louise Russell's recent study of the diffusion of new technologies points in this direction. She concludes that it is no longer reasonable to expect societies to pay for all technologies that offer promise—but only for specific, limited kinds.[13] Simple economics dictates the need for a more global view, a frame of reference to arbitrate among various interests.

The word *rationing* is shocking to many. To older people it evokes the period of the Second World War: ration tickets, long lines, and the black market. It is contrary to many deeply rooted social values. And yet it is the simple consequence of two phenomena.

The first we have already considered at length: the proliferation of costly technological innovations in a field where consumer appetite seems insatiable and where manufacturers have no personal interest in limiting costs. The second is simply the fact that values and laws in Western societies make it unthinkable to let the health sector be governed entirely by the dynamics of the market. The inequities that would result would be unacceptable to most people in those societies.

Some form of social security will continue to exist. It cannot, however, continue to pay for everything indefinitely. We have argued that neither the evolution of preventive medicine nor of advanced technology will significantly reduce spiraling health costs, even if notable gains are achieved. Resource allocation will be the prime point of conflict among different professional and political groups.

Some countries, such as Great Britain, are reasonably well equipped to move into rationing of medical resources. Others must profoundly change the organization of their health care systems; this is the case for France and the United States. But before considering each country separately, let us examine the principle of rationing, its necessity and its consequences.

To limit cost increases, a global framework must be defined, and the criteria of definition can only be political in the most noble sense of the term. The synthesis must be based first on moral values and must take into consideration economic, sociological, and technological factors. Cost restrictions lead necessarily to rationing. Rationing itself, however, raises important moral questions, as we will see in the following chapter.

NOTES

1. Public fascination with the promise of technological progress has been analyzed by many people. See, for example, Michel Salamon, *L'avenir de la vie* (Paris: Seghers, 1981).

2. For a broader treatment of this issue, see Jacques Ellul, *Le Système Technicien* (Paris: Éditions Calmann-Lévy, 1977).

3. See Lewis Thomas, *The Lives of a Cell* (New York: Viking Press, 1974).

4. Perspectives on this question have been offered by Jean-François Lacronique: "Technologie et médecine en France contemporaine" (Paper presented at the NIH International Center, April 1976); and by Clifton R. Gaus: "What goes into Technology Must Come Out in Costs" (Testimony by the U.S. Social Security Administration before the President's Biomedical Research Panel, September 1975). Also see S. Altman and R. Blendon, eds., *Medical Technology: The Culprit Behind Health Care Costs?* (Washington D.C.: DHEW publication no. [PHS] 79-3216, 1979).

5. See Simone Sandier and François Tonnelier, "La consommation de soins médicaux dans le cadre de l'assurance maladie du régime général de sécurité sociale," *Evolution 1959–1977* (Paris: CREDOC, 1978).

6. U.S. Department of Commerce, *1978 Industrial Outlook with 5-Year Projections for 200 Industries* (Washington D.C.: U.S. Government Printing Office, 1978).

7. An interesting analysis of the problem can be found in Richard A. Rettig, *Implementing the End Stage Renal Disease Program of Medicare* (Santa Monica, Calif.: Rand Corporation publication no. R-2505-HCFA/HIW, 1980).

8. See Jean-François Lacronique, "La scannographie" *RBM* 1:40–43 (1979); also H. David Banta, "The Diffusion of the Computed Tomography (CT) Scanner in the United States," *International Journal of Health Services* 10:251–269 (1980).

9. For a provocative discussion of some of these issues, see Guido Calabresi and Phillip Bobbitt, *Tragic Choices* (New York: W. W. Norton, 1978).

10. For an excellent review of evaluation policies in a number of countries, see H. David Banta and Louise B. Russell, "Policies Toward Medical Technology: An International Review," *International Journal of Health Services* 11:631–652 (1981).

11. For a discussion of policy differences which may help to explain these and comparable data, see Office of Technology Assessment, *The Implications of Cost-Effectiveness Analysis of Medical Technology*, The Management of Health Care in Ten Countries, Background Paper no. 4 (Washington, D.C.: U.S. Government Printing Office, 1980).

12. Many of these issues are discussed in *Medical Technology and the Health System* (Washington, D.C.: National Academy of Sciences, 1979).

13. Louise B. Russell, *Technology in Hospitals: Medical Advances and Their Diffusion* (Washington, D.C.: Brookings, 1979).

5

The Ethical Challenge of Health Care Rationing

Christopher Robbins

THE MORAL CONTEXT OF HEALTH CARE RATIONING

There are two separate but overlapping areas of moral thought in which the challenge of health care rationing will have to be met. The first is that *public morality*, the area in which principled choices (of policy, planning, and resource allocations) are made by publicly accountable decision makers: politicians, administrators, senior medical personnel, and increasingly, junior medical personnel. It is at this level that the doctrine of the right to health care is at issue. The second area is that of *professional ethics*, which groups together many guidelines, not all of which are, strictly speaking, ethical. Professional ethics may involve the law, rules of etiquette, or procedural recommendations. Nonetheless, many of the principles in this domain *are* moral: they have to do with a patient's life, welfare, dignity, privacy, information, and vulnerability. It is at this level that the question of the service provider's professional autonomy arises.

Because many doctors in the countries considered in this book are state employees, the two areas overlap. In Western Europe, even doctors who remain entrepreneurs are becoming medical civil servants in all but name. The prime example of this is the role of general practitioners in the British National Health Service, but it applies in varying degrees also to countries with highly developed sickness insurance schemes that finance the majority of medical procedures performed. Doctors still cling to the ideal of the autonomous medical practitioner, free to determine his relationship with each patient, to decide what treatment to give, and generally to act in the manner of a monopolistic and technocratic entrepreneur in a conservative or liberal setting. The reality in Western Europe and Canada, however, is that doctors are bound up with a state or semipublic system whose obligations are summed up in the right-to-health doctrine. (In the United States, there is little likelihood that a similar transformation of most doctor's entrepreneurial status will be accomplished in the foreseeable future. Nonetheless, doctors may well find themselves under pressure from health consumer groups or other local committees, and this will reduce their entrepreneurial freedom.)

This context will have to change in order for choices involved in health care rationing to be made; for, of course, rationing x implies that not everyone's "right" to x can be respected and that the distributors of x cannot freely give it to all who are entitled to obtain it from them. The doctrine of health care rights will survive however; it is embedded in Western European modes of life, and it even appeals in a superficial form to medical and paramedical professions in the United States.[1] Most importantly, it can still be useful once the age of health care rationing has dawned: it can form the basis of everyone's legal entitlement to high quality primary and emergency care. Conversely, the illusion of the medical entrepreneur is surely dying, to be replaced by the idea of the "standard" medical practitioner, accountable to the patient, the community, and the taxpayer, with no more (and no less) freedom in his daily tasks than any other skilled worker or civil servant.

Health care rationing requires a new effort of collective moral thought. This may start, as such efforts often have in the past, with an attempt to compute in terms of human happiness the outcomes of various types of rationing procedures and decisions. At the outset this approach encounters grave practical and moral difficulties, however, notably as concerns the nature of the calculations to be made and the requirement that any rationing procedure respect every individual's integrity. Health care planning, resource allocation, and procedures for the provision of care to all involve social choices. They must accord first of all with the human rights context so important to the self-image of Western countries.

The Right to Health Services

This right began as a pious myth; it has enjoyed a vogue among legislators; and current circumstances may well give it concrete value as a guide and protector when rationing is introduced. A right is a moral, political, or legal entitlement. The right to health services arises from the recognition of the moral necessity of helping a sick or dying individual. All persons who need medical care ought to receive it regardless of their financial circumstances. No barriers should exist between the sick, injured, or disabled and appropriate care.

Such a general principle is worth enunciating only if it can be realized in the vast majority of circumstances.[2] It presupposes either that public institutions exist on a sufficiently secure financial and legal foundation to be able to provide medical care and other health services to all who need them, or that some other arrangement (e.g., a mixed public and private medical care system) achieves this result. There are thus two fundamental elements in the notion of the right to health care: first, the principle of equity; second, the existence of collective arrangements guaranteeing the right.

The principle of equity stipulates that relevantly similar cases should be treated similarly in the relevant respects. Thus, "the proper ground of distribution of medical care is ill health."[3] This is not an emergent principle, satisfied when a society's structure merely works toward, or tends to produce, equal access to services for all who need them. The principle requires concrete and precise measures to guarantee open access and to enable utilization. This is why, as a moral principle, the right to health services cannot be realized by the operation of a health care market where services are only available to those who can pay for them but where there is no provision to ensure that everybody is able to pay for them.

The full principle of equity requires a redistribution of health service resources at all levels so that differences between regions or areas within a country are minimized and differences between the rich sick and the poor sick are eliminated, as far as they are relevant to the health service's aims. In this respect, the principle of equity has egalitarian implications (but it does not follow that the principle should be applied in other areas, whereas egalitarianism itself is usually taken to cover a wide range of differences between citizens). The reigning idea is that, however ill health or injury comes about, a just society aims to prevent this harm, or failing this, to remove it and its consequences.

The second dimension of the health care rights doctrine is appropriate institutions to sustain and guarantee them. This is not a utopian requirement: the level at which rights can be realized (in this case, the quality and scope of universally available medical care) is relative to the level of economic development achieved by the state, region, or community concerned. A state is sometimes said to have immediate obligations beyond its financial or other powers, but reason cannot long tolerate this paradox.

Health care rights involve an effective enabling principle (positive opportunity) and not merely a negative principle (the absence of political or social discrimination). They symbolize a form of egalitarianism that goes beyond the minimum form of equality of opportunity (access for those who can pay) to a stronger form (access for all regardless of financial circumstances). This latter requirement entails appropriate government intervention in the health sector, ranging from a mixed market with considerable state intervention (as in France) to a fully nationalized service (as in the USSR; the British system should not be regarded as fully nationalized since the National Health Service does not employ all Britain's health workers or own all its health care facilities).

The right should be to *effective* health services,[4] because the ultimate aim is to reestablish the sick, as far as possible, on the same footing as the healthy and to protect everyone from injury or other ill health. This means that the state is obliged to ensure the availability of effective services. This in turn has consequences for the autonomy of institutions and workers responsible for the delivery of health services: they will no longer be free to set their own standards at every level, and health planners will be drawn into processes of standard setting and evaluation.[5]

It is precisely against the substitution of the market right by a new legal right that the conservative reacts. The state, he would argue, has properly speaking no obligation to provide health services at all; on the contrary, the state or community must limit itself to external defense and upholding the rule of law. Otherwise, it is argued, the individual's right to the enjoyment of his property is sacrificed for collective ends that are better served by voluntarily formed groups within a free market. The individual should, in any event, be responsible for his own health and should be able to enter (either alone or in a group) into free transactions with entrepreneurs offering health services, thus conserving his right to dispose of his possessions and income as he will.

No individual can be entirely responsible for his health, however.[6] In modern conditions as well as in earlier centuries, the state is often the smallest available unit that can act effectively to combat national and international threats to health (e.g., pollution of all kinds, radiation, and infectious diseases, including zoonoses). It has taken an international effort to eradicate smallpox; no state can succeed alone in combating threats to health involving either hard drugs or industrial pollution, particularly where international markets or multinational companies are concerned. Willy-nilly, the state has a very important preventive role;

and if a government wishes to implement a cohesive and fair health strategy, it is natural for it to bow to the considerable public pressure (which has been exerted in most industrialized countries by trade unions and consumer groups) and to attempt to manage all aspects of health services.

It is a short step from this assumption of responsibility to the promulgation of the idea of the right to health services, particularly when it is realized that: (1) the heaviest health service users are not capable of assuming financial or social responsibility for their health (the aged, mentally ill, mentally handicapped, and very young or very poor);[7] and (2) the very development of high technology in medicine has further removed from the individual's grasp (even with private insurance) the possibility of treating every illness without the state's help.[8]

The question follows, however, How can a state that lacks the resources to provide everyone who needs it with, for example, renal dialysis, or a heart transplant, claim to be giving full effect to the right to health services? With the public's seemingly insatiable appetite for health care, how can any state reasonably recognize a universal right to services? Such an act of recognition would mean signing a blank check; it would ruin the national economy.

Faced with this clear limitation, we have to recognize that social welfare rights are not unconditional entitlements but are essentially related to the economic situation of the society concerned (as indeed are human rights). As has been said of the British National Health Service, such an arrangement "offers not a right of access to specified forms of health care, but a right of an equitable share (as measured by relative need. . .) in the available health care resources."[9]

Welfare aims and economic aims are, of course, intertwined, if only in the sense that the promotion of welfare presupposes a certain level of economic activity, and if welfare programs are allowed to grow disproportionately to other sectors, they can threaten the level of economic activity itself. Hence, limits to health service provision can be justified by reference to the need to fulfill other equally desirable social or economic aims.*

Some welfare policies are utilitarian, aiming merely to maximize all citizens' welfare taken as a whole, or to maximize average welfare. In contrast, the right to health services implies, when economic circumstances permit, a guarantee to everyone, and not merely the greatest benefit for the majority. It may be that an individualized service is open to abuse by both providers and consumers; it may be that it is often wasteful; it may be that its effectiveness is doubtful in some cases. Nevertheless, it is the only means whereby the right of the *individual* to health care can be put into effect—at a level where he himself can act to obtain services and can maximize his responsibility for his own health, particularly when these services include an active preventive component. The stipulation that the services be effective entails the further requirement that they be designed to respond to individual and local needs and presumptively implies that the health care system be openly managed by consumers as well as by service providers and administrators.[10]

With priority given to equality of access, questions will arise over how to distribute services within a given budget.[11] These questions will focus especially on resource allocation decisions between regions, between medical specialities (i.e., treatment for types of disease, injury, or disability), and between individuals needing treatment. Rationing in industrialized countries will concentrate on the priorities governing hyperspecialized care, on the assumption that each individual has, at least, an unimpeded right to primary and secondary care.[12]

---

*This is one of the issues implicitly discussed by Rawls in his detailed and extensive reconstruction of the basis of liberal democracy—that is, of a theory of political and social justice. Rawls's *Theory of Justice* centers on the notion that the institutions implementing political and social justice would be implicitly agreed to by a group of rational persons deliberating together under certain well-defined conditions ("the initial contractual situation"). For the purposes of the present discussion, it is not appropriate to review this argument; but Rawls's book is helpful in providing a context for any discussion of the way liberal industrialized and postindustrial societies have developed in the present century.

In sum, the health services right entails eliminating decisive financial barriers between clients and services, ensuring that the services are effective and responsive to needs, and maintaining access to cheaper forms of care should the rationing of a service become necessary. Today, the doctrine of the health services right—in its human rights context—can continue to guide policy choices and protect individuals.

Professional Ethics

To study professional ethics—the second aspect of the moral context of health care rationing—our focus shifts to the centers of authority that, in all the countries under study, have laid down rules of discipline for certain professions in return for public respectability and legal recognition. The supreme professional body for doctors in France is the *Ordre des Médecins*; in the United Kingdom it is the British Medical Association (BMA) and in the United States the American Medical Association (AMA). Their respective statutory positions and other functions differ, yet they are all sources of decisions on questions of medical ethics. For example, the BMA has produced a *Handbook of Medical Ethics*.[13] Publications of this sort reveal that, in this context, *ethics* includes legal obligations and matters of etiquette as well as moral advice. The last is clearly the most important, covering the duty to treat emergencies, avoidance of outside pressures when making medical decisions, confidentiality, research, screening, abortion, severely malformed infants, AID, euthanasia, brain health, tissue transplantation, suicide, and so forth. The *Handbook* also includes a short section on "Allocation of Resources," which gives useful guidance to doctors on their duty to explain that National Health Service resources "can never be infinite," adding that, "As the resources available within the NHS are limited, the doctor has a general duty to advise on their equitable allocation and efficient utilisation" (p. 35).

This, as the text itself recognizes, represents a considerable development away from the traditional doctrine of the special doctor-patient relationship (the "entente"), in which treatment was advised, offered, and paid for entirely within that relationship. The practice of medicine is no longer entirely determined by the profession itself, working in a medical care market; parliaments, planners, managers, and various boards and committees all influence the volume and nature of medical care—even in general practice—in Western European countries, especially where each act of service is separately accounted for.

Nonetheless, the independence of the medical profession is as vehemently protected in Europe as it is in the United States.[14] It is an old principle that a doctor's acts may only be judged by other members of his profession.[15] Such control measures as exist (e.g., measures controlling prescribing by general practitioners) tend to be carried out by medically qualified persons (designated by the *Ordre des Médecins* in France[16] and Health Ministry employees in the United Kingdom). In the future it will be vital for each health care system to deal further with the explosive issue of who is to sit in judgment of health care professionals.

Another important element of the medical profession's self-image is the sanctity of clinical freedom. This now somewhat mythical doctrine has, after all, an element of reality, for any skilled worker must be given the responsibility to exercise his skill and be accountable for the results. Still, there cannot be absolute clinical freedom in a rationally and explicitly managed health service,[17] for there has to be at the very least, some intervention from management (acting on behalf of the community) to allocate resources, encourage fairness, and discourage wasteful or ineffective forms of treatment. This applies particularly to the hospital sector, where rationing measures would—in a fair health care system—most often be applied.

It is essential for the medical and paramedical professions to recognize that the linked doctrines of the doctor-patient "entente," of professional independence, and of clinical freedom cannot, in their traditional form, continue to determine the relationship between doctors and other parts of the health care system. Not only will rationing impose de facto constraints but the advent of consumer organizations in the health field will also increase doctors' awareness of their potential accountability to the community at large as well as to individual patients.

The period of transition in which doctors find themselves is indeed extremely complex. The emergence of a "Lalonde generation" of health care subsystems emphasizing preventive measures including education for health, serves only to accentuate this complexity. In recognizing that curative medicine can only deal with a fraction of today's health problems, and that the factors behind the problems are a complex set of psychosocial and economic factors,[18] doctors face a multiple challenge.

In facing this challenge, the first need is to *transform the doctor-patient relationship*, which, at present, is often an uneasy mixture of friendly encounter and technological intervention.[19] As a friend, a doctor can give preventive advice, even moral counsel;[20] as a technocrat, he is inclined to treat the patient as an object, as if his condition were determined not (at least in part) by his behavior but (predominantly) by a series of physical, chemical, or biological factors. When the general practitioner adopts this attitude—particularly toward "difficult" patients whose health problems have a significant social element—he reaches for his prescription pad without giving advice or taking other more appropriate measures. Frequently, a passive patient and a hard-pressed doctor will connive in treating the patient purely technically. In today's highly technological hospitals, the technical process reaches its apogee; doctors play the role of infallible technocrats while patients simply lie there; this happens even though the effectiveness of much acute hospital treatment has not been evaluated.[21]

Instead of retaining a technological monopoly in medicine, doctors need to return to encouraging the patient's self-knowledge, as concerns both his life-style and the effect medical treatment may have.[22]

The second need is to *change the structure of health care delivery* by giving new importance to community based primary care (including education for health), which must operate on the basis of multidisciplinary teams. The *BMA Handbook* does not yet fully accept the principle of team-work. On nurses, it says that they "are conscious of their own professional status and nursing expertise. It is essential for the well-being of the patient, however, that the doctor be accepted as the leader of the health care team" (p. 39). Though this may be true in many situations, there are certain types of health problems for which social factors, for example, may be predominantly important and curative medicine correspondingly less to the fore. For these sorts of problems doctors will no longer be independent entrepreneurs awaiting requests for their services but will encourage consultation with a member of the medical team *before* a health need arises so that patients can develop responsibility for their own health.[23]

Depending on the degree to which a political system emphasizes equality of results as well as equality of access, the primary care provider's role could expand to embrace active promotion of prevention. Some middle-class groups may already see the virtues of prevention, but other people—those in the direst need—must be sought in the highways and hedges. If service providers seriously assume primary preventive responsibilities, they cannot sit back and wait for their clients to ask for services but must enter their communities as active promoters of health.

The third need is to create *new managerial structures for health care*, structures in which service providers participate alongside administrators and community representatives. At the outset, some distinctions will have to be made concerning the various managerial functions and the bodies appropriate to perform them. First, there is a policymaking and regular financial planning function, for which an integrated cycle on the British model would be a possibility. The idea would be to devolve responsibilities as far as possible onto regions and districts, making the former accountable directly to the national parliament,[24] or to regional assemblies (as in Italy). Second, the function of national supervision over changing roles within the medical and paramedical professions—and over ethical dilemmas that arise—would need to be carried out independently of government and of health care managers. In the countries under discussion, this supervision has mainly been the responsibility of supreme professional bodies (ethical committees), and some quite extraordinary decisions have sometimes emerged.[25] There is a clear need, however, to widen awareness of these ethical discussions, to publicize the problems, and to open up the debate. If this does not happen, ethical decisions made by individual doctors may be publicly examined only in retrospect, damaging both the principle of confidentiality and the doctor's own confidence in his judgment. Of course, doctors will be subject in the future to the usual controls as regards negligence; but they need the support of the whole community in making ethical decisions, particularly those resulting from the need to ration health care resources.[26] Third, each health care system needs community bodies to identify particular problems and points of conflict or tension; such bodies should only look at resource allocation in the broadest terms and should not discuss particular cases. And fourth, there is a role for regional or local health service "ombudsmen" (they now exist in the United Kingdom and in Italy) to review particular cases about which complaints are made; such reviews should normally be confidential and final results made known only when it serves the public interest.

Since medical ethics involves the whole range of doctors' obligations, it cannot fail to be changed by progress in each of the three areas sketched above. The BMA *Handbook* well illustrates a transitional—and in some respects positive— response to the advent of new roles for doctors. There is no reason that a shift in resources toward community and family medicine should not involve increasing the number of general practitioners and—as they become more open toward (and more accountable to) the rest of the health care system—increasing their rewards commensurate with their increased responsibilities. There is no other way to ensure that a widened and reinforced medical ethic will emerge from the process of change, although, given the widespread mistrust of the political arena in industrialized countries, one can sympathize with the medical profession for wishing to slow this process down.

RATIONING: UTILITY AND EQUITY

We have examined the moral context of health care rationing. What practical consequences may flow, in the present economic climate, from applying the refined doctrine of the right to health services to health planning and health services delivery? What aspects of medical ethics will come into play?

Before rationing can even be considered, there is much to be done. Health care systems must get a clear picture of health needs region by region, and regions must do the same district by district. Needs are hard to define, and data based only on service uptake will not suffice.

In addition, each must carry out evaluations of the effectiveness of the most expensive types of service (candidates for rationing), comparing them where possible with cheaper forms of care and comparing inpatient with outpatient or domiciliary services.[27] The expansion of services of unproven effectiveness will be unjustifiable (e.g., current treatment for alcoholism and for certain cancers).[28] The attitude that health is a priceless asset that justifies any expenditure with the smallest probability of success,[29] prevalent until now, can no longer be sustained.[30] Perhaps medical research and health services delivery research could be expanded using the money currently spent on dubiously effective or inefficient diagnostic and therapeutic procedures. At present only a very small fraction of health expenditure is devoted to research,[31] and research on the delivery of health services, in particular, is said to be starved of resources in many countries.[32]

Finally, doctors must be able to benefit from ethical guidance: not from within the medical profession only, and not solely on the basis of the current state of the law.

Independent, representative public bodies are needed to discuss the moral issues and formulate policy that can be followed by the medical and paramedical profession.

Such bodies could consider, for example, a situation in which, because of limited resources, there are only fifty renal dialysis facilities in a district where 100 patients need them (there is no possibility of renal transplants), and the clinical prognosis is the same for each patient (this means that the rationing decision is no longer a purely clinical matter).

One response by a national, independent, and pluralist body discussing this issue might be to leave the matter to each individual doctor, on the grounds that no general guidelines could ever adequately anticipate the special qualities of the cases to be dealt with. This refusal to make decisions at a corporate level would tend to make the problem a matter of the doctor's private morality, his own intuition. This would not be acceptable, however, for in a pluralist society a doctor has no right to impose his personal moral decisions on others, even if they come to him as patients, reposing their trust in him.[33] No person working in a public service has the right to ignore what public context of morality already exists, or to ignore the broader consequences of his acts.[34] To account for—and, if necessary, defend—his actions, a doctor needs to be able to appeal to wider and more authoritative principles than his own moral intuition.

A national ethical body can discuss—independently of the pressures of day-to-day medical practice—the non-clinical criteria to be employed in rationing decisions, so as to guide doctors (and be fair to them). The following criteria might be considered:

the patient's chances of leading a full life (relative to his age and situation) once the treatment has been given;

the patient's probable life expectancy once the treatment has been given;

the patient's attitude to the treatment (cooperative, passive, etc.);

the patient's value to his or her family (as breadwinner, housekeeper, parent, nurse, etc.);

the patient's contribution to the community (the value of the job he or she does, the importance of any voluntary work undertaken).

These initially plausible criteria are illustrative of a common approach that is nonetheless highly problematic. The approach has two kinds of defects: practical and moral. Practically, the allocation method relies on too many subjective or imponderable criteria. Whereas the purely physiological facts may be relatively clear in each case, the psychological or social facts are neither readily quantifiable nor easy to agree on. A patient may appear noncooperative or psychologically below average to one observer but not to another; the consequences to a family of the loss of the breadwinner—or to a firm of the loss of a managing director—may be largely unpredictable. The approach presupposes a kind of utilitarian comparative calculus of outcomes: for example, that two years of relatively contented life for an elderly patient are less valuable than a longer period in more difficult circumstances for a more active person in his or her fifties. Individuals' conceptions of the good life, and their goals, differ widely and fundamentally in Western countries. A rational utilitarian calculus seems out of the question. How can a professional violinist's satisfactions be compared with a policeman's, either generally or in particular cases? How can a family's reaction to the loss of its main provider be compared with the reaction of parents to the loss of a young adult son or daughter who has, in formal terms, no dependents? Clearly, applying these criteria can have little pretense to objectivity; it will very likely fail to appear fair to the community as a whole.

The first moral objection to this allocation method is that the utilitarian approach does not respect each individual's autonomy; that is, each person's choice of his goals, his way of life, his ultimate values. Instead, it imposes on individuals a general calculus of social benefit, treating each person only as a bearer of a certain quantity of utility, whose goals are in themselves without importance. For our purposes, the objection may be even more sharply put: a health service that allocates resources according to strictly utilitarian principles is intervening in an area for which it should have no responsibility—the individual ways of life, aims, and aspirations of persons in a free society. Western societies lay down a certain widely defined moral orthodoxy, but it would be illegitimate to use health services to enforce this orthodoxy; an open society tries to create institutions that facilitate their own, and society's, overall development in new as well as traditional ethical directions.

A second moral objection is that the utilitarian approach involves decisions to use individuals to serve welfare ends without their consent. Discrimination against the old, the weak, the mentally below average, depressives, and those without dependents entails that the community is prepared to sacrifice some individuals in the cause of overall welfare. Yet it is impossible to genuinely obtain the consent of those discriminated against to this arrangement, for they have no obligation to accept—and no conclusive reason to believe—that they are wholly useless and to be cast aside. The utilitarian criteria imply a deep lack of respect for the rejected, a respect that is fundamental to the basic structure of a liberal-democratic society and its public institutions.*

This situation is different from a context in which people have accepted a certain risk and have agreed that they will be used in certain ways for a limited period, and that moreover, health services will be subordinated to the overall goal. In time of war, medications may be rationed in favor of those members of the armed forces who, on recovery, will

---

*Since the acceptance of treatment by the "lucky" patients involves a tacit recognition of their social or financial responsibilities, some of them may also be, in effect, used by the rationing system to serve welfare objectives that they do not wholeheartedly support.

be able to fight again, as happened during the Second World War.[35] In contrast, the renal dialysis example does not involve the survival of society as a whole, so it cannot imply the subordination of the individual's rights to a higher goal.

If the utilitarian formula is rejected for practical and moral reasons, what other criteria can be identified for the allocation of the renal dialysis machines? One possibility would be simply to rank patients according to age, on the grounds that this provides a clear criterion related to the length of time each individual will probably benefit from the treatment in question. It is not self-evident why the elderly should be discriminated against, however, and the principle would be subject to great strain when dealing with, for example, eminent elderly people who are still active in their chosen careers. This approach is likely to turn out to be a way of using the value-to-the-community criterion without admitting to it.

Another alternative might be to operate on the first-come-first-served principle, which, after all, applies to nonurgent treatment in health services with waiting lists (e.g., the British NHS and some health maintenance organizations in the United States). A major doubt must be expressed about this principle too, however. In some countries certain disadvantaged social groups do not readily apply for medical treatment, or need encouragement to do so, or wait until a condition is very serious before doing so. Health care firms and individual doctors would need to rely on the community as a whole to ensure that health care rationing was as fair as possible—by minimizing barriers between certain social groups and services. Measures to accomplish this would have to include adjusting the financial structure of the health care system, individualized preventive programs, and widespread health education designed to reach non-health-conscious and disadvantaged groups.

The alternative to the waiting list criterion would be the random allocation of renal dialysis machines—for example, by lottery—to persons who could benefit from them. An objection to a random procedure of this sort might be that arbitrariness is no substitute for fairness; however, if waiting lists are considered very unfair, this objection to random allocation is less forceful. Another objection to random allocation would be that its explicit use undermines the authority of public services generally and medical workers in particular. A deliberate (as opposed to unwanted but recognized) chance mechanism is a dangerous thing in a public administration because it undermines the social acceptance of collective action. The health service would need considerable support from the rest of the community in weighing this against other considerations, aiming—as it must—to produce a maximally fair result that is also generally acceptable.

In considering these issues, two typical cases may be examined to demonstrate some of the pitfalls that have already been observed. The first case is that of a renal dialysis unit in Seattle that used criteria concerning an individual's future and usefulness, along the lines of those listed above. What had happened elsewhere in the United States during the initial period when a new technology was scarce was that:

> The patients who were rejected died—perhaps for having too little money, or because of having been judged uncooperative, or even because of being a prostitute and thus judged less valuable than other patients.[36]

The results at Seattle, however, were that women were discriminated against (two-thirds of the "lucky" patients were men), and other rejects were drawn disproportionately from among the old, the weak, the mentally subnormal, depressives, and others with no dependents.

The second case occurred in 1981–82 in the United Kingdom, and it has aroused much interest in care policy for newborn babies who are very severely handicapped both mentally and physically. In a celebrated court case a pediatrician was charged with the attempted murder of a handicapped newborn infant who died a few days after birth. It was alleged that, where such children are rejected by their parents and consequently will have to be cared for in a public institution, it is relatively common practice to withdraw food and/or some forms of medical treatment from them; their death inevitably supervenes within a few days. One of the criteria apparently applied in such cases is whether a worthwhile quality of life would be enjoyed by the child in question. Another criterion applied is a measure of the resources to be provided by the community to care for the child. This constitutes an implicit rationing decision, for the only reason to apply these criteria is the possibility that a better quality of life could be bought for someone else using the same resources. British public opinion seems by no means unanimous on this, until recently little publicized, policy.[37] There is no national body by which the public is represented that could discuss the present treatment policy and alternatives to it (on the basis of evidence received in confidence if necessary). For this reason, no adequate effort has been made to separate discussion of principles from discussion of particular cases.

These examples illustrate some important points:

1. Rationing of resources at the national or regional level is (in at least two of the countries described in this book) being translated into choices between individual patients at the point of service delivery;[38]
2. Post factum decision procedures that make use of criminal or civil liability damage the medical profession and health services, put untold strain on individual doctors, and contribute nothing to a calm consideration of the issues of principle; health services must not await litigation before collectively reviewing policy in a pluralistic setting apart from the arena in which individual decisions are made;
3. Reviews of rationing criteria and treatment policy should be carried out at the national level, because local reviews

and decision making tend to embrace narrow criteria and ignore wider social consequences;

4. Decisions made according to utilitarian criteria are likely to have unforeseen and grave secondary social consequences (and so it remains unclear whether a random allocation method might be less unacceptable socially).

CONCLUSION

Current doctrines about the right to health, and the medical profession's traditional assertion of its total freedom in clinical matters, are changing and must go on doing so. The former never could be interpreted as a right to any and every service however costly; it is a right of access to free or inexpensive health services, which for reasons of equity and efficiency should use readily available primary care facilities for the treatment of the vast majority of health problems. As regards medical ethics, doctors will more and more come to recognize that they must work in teams accountable to the publicly managed health services as a whole, as well as to their own profession and individual patients.

These issues are especially important when health care rationing arises: resources are scarce, and we urgently need criteria for their allocation. The right to health brings into focus the whole set of human and social rights of which the observance constitutes liberal democracy. Rationing procedures that do not respect every individual's life prospects and values must be dropped or radically modified. In particular, the utilitarian approach may result in the exploitation of individuals for unclarified social ends. The doctor's role is not to make isolated personal decisions case by case but to participate openly in a public discussion of the principles to be applied in medical rationing. This discussion should look for principles that respect human rights, give clear guidance to doctors, and are, as regards their consequences, socially acceptable. In regularly reviewing the working of these principles, an independent national ethical body may move away from the currently plausible utilitarian approach to the use of waiting lists or random allocations. The social consequences of these methods deserve the most careful evaluation.

NOTES

1. "It is the basic right of every citizen to have available to him adequate health care" (AMA House of Delegates Resolution, 17 July 1969). See also the American Nurses' Association's "*Code for Nurses*: Quality health care is mandated as a right to all citizens," reprinted in *The Nurse's Dilemma* (Geneva: International Council of Nurses, 1977).

Health care rights are more concretely enshrined in some national laws, especially the national health service legislations in the United Kingdom (1948) and in Italy (1978); on the former, see B. B. Abel-Smith, *National Health Service: The first 30 years* (London: HMSO, 1978).

As regards the Italian National Health Service Law (no. 833 of 1978), see the first article:

La Repubblicatutela la salute come fondamentale diritto dell' individuo e interesse della collettivita mediante il servizio sanitario nazionale.

La tutela della salute fisica e psichica deve avvenire nel rispettoo della dignita e della liberta della persona umana.

As regards Canada, it is noteworthy that the "Bible" of its health care system—the *Health Charter for Canadians*—makes no such explicit provision, referring instead to the availability of all services to all Canadians. There is useful discussion of the precise import of this, and of its practical effect, in M. Trahan, *Health Insurance in France, Australia and Canada* (Ottawa: Department of National Health and Welfare, 1981), especially pp. 212, 218, and 225–227.

On the international defense of rights to health, see, for example, the *European Social Charter* (1961), Article 11 (the right to protection of health); the *International Covenant of Economic, Social and Cultural Rights* (1966), Article 12; and the *Alma-Ata Declaration* (1973), Section I, (contained in *Primary Health Care* [Geneva: WHO, 1978]).

Pithy criticisms of universal welfare rights promoted under the aegis of the United Nations have been made by M. Cranston in his *What are Human Rights?* (London: The Bodley Head, 1973), pp. 65 ff. He argues that, applied to the whole world, social and welfare rights are neither practicable (because not all countries have the resources to put them into effect), nor universal (a right to a holiday with pay can only apply to employees), nor of paramount importance. But he says (p. 69): "To claim economic and social rights for the members of a given community is a reasonable exercise." The doctrine which I shall refer to is precisely about claims made within given countries in relation to their economic situation, and not claims made on behalf of humanity as a whole.

2. On this principle, see Cranston, *Human Rights*.

3. B. Williams, *Problems of the Self* (Cambridge: Cambridge University Press, 1973), p. 240. The essay in question, "The Idea of Equality", is reprinted from its original source, P. Laslett and W. Runciman, eds, *Politics, Philosophy and Society*, vol. 2 (Oxford: Blackwell, 1962).

4. For "effectiveness" see A. Cochrane, *Effectiveness and Efficiency* (London: the Nuffield Provincial Hospitals Trust, 1972), p. 2 and passim.

5. World Health Organisation (Europe), *Guidelines for Health Care Practice in Relation to Cost-Effectiveness* (Copenhagen: WHO, Europe, 1981).

6. For arguments against the minimum state, see, for example, J. Lucas, *The Principles of Politics*, section 67, esp. pp. 294–295.

7. See, for example, the *Report of the Royal Commission on the National Health Service* (London: HMSO, 1979), par. 2.12.

8. I have not tried to argue that the defense of health service rights is essential to a liberal democracy once it has reached a given stage of economic development. No doubt this could be attempted from either of the following two starting points:

> The "free rider" problem. It would be unjust to allow a person paying nothing towards health protection to benefit indirectly from the schemes set up by others; even if the free rider enjoyed no entitlement to medical care, he would, for example, benefit from the lower level of infectious disease in his environment and from any other social or economic improvements made possible by the health services paid for by others (on this, see J. Rawls, *A Theory of Justice* [Oxford: Oxford University Press, 1972], pp. 267–270);

> The principle of "self-respect." If this is essential to a liberal democracy (as will be discussed further in this chapter), then every individual should be enabled as far as economic circumstances permit to fulfil his aspirations and ambitious: health care clearly can help individuals to avoid or to be cured from potentially disabling diseases (on this approach, see F. Michelman, "Constitutional Welfare Rights and a Theory of Justice," in N. Daniels, ed., *Reading Rawls* [Oxford: Blackwells, 1975]).

9. R. Klein: "Costs and Benefits of Complexity: The British National Health Service" in R. Rose, ed., *Challenge to Governance* (Beverly Hills: Sage Publications, 1980), p. 113.

10. See the *Alma-Ata Declaration*, Sections IV and VII (5).

11. For a discussion of the various modes of rationing, see D. Mechanic, "Rationing Medical Care," *The Center Magazine*, September/October 1978.

12. See the *Alma-Ata Declaration*, Section V, which the WHO is now following up with an intensified campaign.

13. London: British Medical Association (1980). The statutory body governing medical practice in the United Kingdom—the General Medical Council—has published a booklet entitled *Professional Conduct and Discipline*.

14. BMA, *Handbook*, p. 43. On Canada, see Trahan, *Health Insurance*, pp. 213, 234, 239.

15. Aristotle, *Politics* III, trans. Sinclair (Harmondsworth: Penguin, 1962) 2:124.

16. On the relationship between the state, social security, and the medical profession in France, see V. Rodwin, "The Marriage of National Health Insurance and La Médecine Libérale in France: A Costly Union," *Milbank Memorial Fund Q.* 59, 1 (1981): 16–43.

17. M. Cooper, "Economics of Need: The Experience of the British Health Service," in M. Perlman, ed., *The Economics of Health and Medical Care* (London: Macmillan, 1974).

18. World Health Organization (Europe), *Primary Health Care* (Copenhagen: WHO, 1979).

19. J. P. Dupuy, "On the Social Rationality of Health Policies," in Perlman, *Economics of Health*.

20. Seneca valued his doctor as much for the gift of friendship as for the healing art: *De beneficiis* VI. xvi.

21. On the lack of evaluation, see, for example, T. McKeown, *The Role of Medicine* (London: The Nuffield Provincial Hospitals Trust, 1976), p. 116. On technology in medicine, see R. Taylor, *Medicine Out of Control* (Melbourne: Sun Books, 1979).

22. Descartes agreed with Tiberius that "everyone over thirty had enough experience of what was harmful or beneficial to be his own doctor," *Oeuvres* (Paris: Vrin, 1972), 4:329–330.

23. See note 18.

24. A suggestion made by the British Royal Commission in chapter 19 of its report (see note 10).

25. For example, as late as 1966 in France the Conseil de l'Ordre des Médecins declared formally that contraception was none of a doctor's business. See J. Ardagh, *The New France* (Harmondsworth: Penguin, 1970), p. 377.

26. See K. M. Boyd, *The Ethics of Resource Allocation and Health Care*

(Edinburgh: Edinburgh University Press, 1979), especially pp. 52–53 and 94–95.

27. For remarks on the classic ischaemic heart disease comparisons, see Cochrane, *Effectiveness*, pp. 50–54. For other problems, see Council of Europe, *The Comparative Costs of Health Care given Inside and Outside Hospitals* (Strasbourg: Council of Europe, 1981).

28. See R. Maxwell, *Health Care: The Growing Dilemma* (New York: McKinsey, 1974), p. 42; and K. M. Boyd, *Ethics*, pp. 52–55.

29. For a sixteenth century version of this view, see Montaigne, *Essais*, Bk. II, chap. 37: "Toute voye qui nous meneroit a la sante ne se peut dire pour moi ny aspre, ny chere."

30. Doctors "often aim at treating people they can't treat" (Boyd, *Ethics*, p. 51).

31. In the mid-seventies expenditure on publicly financed medical research represented on average share of 0.04% of GDP in OECD countries, whereas the average share for public expenditure on health stood at 4.4% (OECD, *Public Expenditure on Health* [Paris: OECD, 1977], pp. 10 and 23).

32. See World Health Organization (Europe), *Health Services in Europe*, 3d ed. vol. 1 (Copenhagen: WHO, 1981), chaps. 8, 11.

33. See, for example, the BMA's approach: "A doctor must not allow his decision as to what is in the patient's best interests to be influenced by his own personal beliefs" (*Handbook*, p. 17).

34. See S. Hampshire, "Public and Private Morality," in S. Hampshire, ed., *Public and Private Morality* (Cambridge: Cambridge University Press, 1978).

35. Example cited by I. Kennedy in "Unmasking Medicine" (1980 Reith Lectures), *The Listener* 104, no. 2687 (13 November 1980): 644; now in book form under the same title (London: Allen and Unwin, 1981). See also S. Bok, "The relevance of moral philosophy to medicine," in H. P. Gleason, ed., *Getting Bigger* (Cambridge, Mass.: Oelgeschlager, Gunn and Hain, 1981).

36. Bok, "Relevance of Moral Philosophy," p. 27.

37. See, for example, the *Times* (London) of 26 March 1982. The BMA *Handbook* does not discuss the current care policy in detail, except to say that "for an infant the parents must ultimately decide" (p. 29), not a perspicuously helpful suggestion.

38. Renal dialysis or transplant is now available in the U.S. for nearly all patients, but the cost for 1984 is estimated at $3 billion (1980 prices). See Bok, "Relevance of Moral Philosophy," p. 27. It is difficult to see how this arrangement is either fair or practicable in the long term.

Part III
CASE STUDIES

6

France: Contemporary Problems and Future Scenarios

Jean de Kervasdoué, Victor G. Rodwin, and Jean-Claude Stephan

The French health system is characterized by three distinguishing features: a strong central state; a quasi-public national health insurance (NHI) system; and a powerful medical profession that has tenaciously demanded respect for four principles: free choice of the physician by the patient; freedom of prescription by the doctor; mutual agreement by the physician and patient on the price of services; and fee-for-service payment. Since the Medical Charter of 1927, when these principles were first promulgated, they have been widely accepted even though they are often violated in practice.

The organization of health care in France rests on an uneasy truce, which periodically explodes into conflict, between the state, NHI funds, and medical trade unions.[1] The conflicts grow out of two contradictory ideologies: solidarity and liberal-pluralism. On the one hand, the French state has assured its citizens the right of access to health services and pays most of the bill through the *Caisse Nationale d'Assurance Maladie des Travailleurs Salariés* (CNAMTS), the principal NHI fund; on the other hand, medical trade unions have demanded, and so far obtained, the preservation of a health system that is both liberal and pluralist.[2] *Liberal* refers to the four principles mentioned above—what the French call *la médecine libérale*. And *pluralist* refers to the presence of institutional diversity; for example, the existence of powerful private proprietary hospitals—*cliniques*.

Since these ideologies are not always compatible, the French health system in many ways appears to be the outcome of contradictory policies.[3] In the name of solidarity, the state has intervened actively in the health sector. As a result, France is presently endowed with a network of modernized public hospitals and numerous public health programs in areas ranging from maternal and child health to deinstitutionalization programs for psychiatric hospitals. In the name of liberalism, however, since NHI is financed to a large extent on the basis of payroll taxes below a wage ceiling, the system is rather regressive; and, in the name of pluralism, differences between occupational groups both in levels of coverage and in premiums paid, result in inequities. What is more, since World War II, there is no other European country in which the private practice of medicine—both ambulatory and hospital care—has become so established.

The marriage of NHI and la médecine libérale in France constitutes a costly union. It has been costly in the economic sense for the rate of growth of France's health expenditures has been one of the highest among OECD countries. It has also been costly in a political sense because political debate has focused more on the structure of the entire social security system than on the social organization of medicine, the objectives of the health system, or alternative means of achieving them.[4] In the future, it will be interesting to see if the fundamental policy issues will be identified and explicitly confronted or if they will be avoided, and how. These issues revolve around the following questions: What kinds of political and institutional mechanisms will be established to decide what proportion of the gross domestic product (GDP) to devote to health? By what criteria should health and social expenditures be allocated? How can revenues and expenditures be kept in balance? Who should finance these expenditures and how (e.g., income taxes or payroll taxes)? How can France move from the present system of administrative centralization and rigid controls to a system more open to local initiatives and more adaptable to the evolution of new medical technologies and management methods, and to emergent risk factors? What mechanisms will be devised to monitor the quality of medical care and to evaluate its impact on health status? Finally, how will health care be rationed, and will the procedures for health care rationing be explicit or implicit?

To answer these questions, a crystal ball is of little use. The futurologist can only analyze the past, discern some critical elements in recent trends, and extrapolate, venturing into an unknown and turbulent ocean in which there is a high probability of drowning. Contrary to what we are often told, the utility of forecasting lies not in predicting the future but in tracing alternative futures on the basis of which we can try to avoid disasters and to ensure that what appears possible becomes probable. Thus, we begin this chapter by tracing the evolution of the French health system. Next, we analyze the present predicament. Finally, we outline some possible scenarios whose probability will depend, of course, on the evolution of the economic and political situation in France.

A BRIEF HISTORY OF FRENCH HEALTH POLICY

Following World War II and until the beginning of the 1970s, the French health system grew without any apparant constraints. This expansion phase coincided with a period of triumphant success in the medical and biological sciences. Politicians, citizens, and health professionals believed that more was better: more pharmaceutical products, more hospitals, more personnel, more innovation, and more expenditures. There was a broad consensus on this approach to health policy; to such an extent, in fact, that there was no political debate about priorities in the health sector—a sure sign of tacit agreement between major interest groups.

In the early seventies, the economic crisis struck and the situation changed. Signs of this change came as early as 1965 when the *patronat* (association of employers) released its report on the future of French social security.[5] Two years later, President de Gaulle centralized the formerly more autonomous social security funds to tighten control over social expenditures. It was not until several years later, however, that the exponential growth of health expenditures was widely perceived and policymakers began pointing out that this growth was not accompanied by a significant increase in life expectancy.

By the mid-seventies, questions were raised about the quality of medical care, the role of hospitals within the health system, the prevailing method of fee-for-service reimbursement, the relative efficiency of private versus public hospitals, and the effects of the CNAMTS's reimbursement policies on the structure and evolution of the health sector. At the present time, these issues remain central to regulatory policy and day-to-day management. Before considering them in more detail, let us first highlight several turning points in the evolution of French health policy from 1945 to 1980.

Negotiations and Contracts with the Medical Profession

Since the first health insurance law of 1928, there have been a series of explosive conflicts between health insurance funds and physician trade unions.[6] The controversy was repeatedly over the issue of fee setting. The physician trade unions refused to abide by negotiated fees and sign contracts with local health insurance funds because they did not want the state to be in a position to monitor and potentially control their income. Until 1960, the law that was supposed to establish a negotiated fee was not enforced. The physician trade unions even refused the "Gazier plan" proposed in 1956, despite the fact that it would have adjusted their fees to a cost of living index.

In 1960, two years after de Gaulle's rise to power, the government imposed a system of individual contracts on physicians. This forced them to accept nationally set fees if they wished to be reimbursed for their services. In giving physicians individual choice in deciding whether to abide by national fes, a severe blow was struck at the collective power of trade unions. The government's strategic move produced irreconcilable disagreements between physicians and divided the formerly unique trade union, the *Confédération des Syndicats Médicaux Français* (CSMF). It also spurred the creation of a second national physician trade union, the *Fédération des medécins de France* (FMF).[7] The system of individual physician contracts functioned for a decade, and by 1970 eighty percent of physicians in private practice had signed individual contracts with the government, thus agreeing in principle to abide by the nationally set fees.

In 1971, largely in response to the rising costs of medical care and to ideas promoted by the Seventh Plan's Commission on Health and Social Transfers,[8] a national collective contract was finally accepted by the government, the CNAMTS, and the physician trade unions.[9] The contract was good for four years and applied to all physicians except those who individually took the initiative to opt out. National fees were negotiated annually on the basis of a relative value scale—the *nomenclature*; and a system of statistical profiles on the procedures performed by each physician was established to monitor the volume of medical care provision. Until 1975, for the most part, the physicians abided by the fee schedule while increasing the volume of their procedures; however, during this period, the system of physician profiles was not operational and health care costs continued to grow. In 1976, a new national collective contract almost identical to the preceding one was signed, but it functioned with difficulty—especially during the annual fee negotiations.

Within two years the difficulties had grown into open conflict between the state and the largest physician trade union, the CSMF, which represents roughly forty-five percent of all physicians in private practice. In July of 1979, the government blocked the previously agreed upon increases in physician fees, urged self-discipline in controlling the volume of medical procedures, and threatened to link future increases in fees to effective control of volume such that the rate of increase of health expenditures not exceed the rate of increase of the GNP. The CSMF called three strikes between October 1979 and June 1980. The final strike resulted in violence between demonstrators and the police, and so in June, when it came time to renew the collective contract, the president of the CSMF refused to sign.

A new collective contract was signed on July 1 between the state and the FMF, which represents only thirteen percent of physicians in private practice. The innovation in this latest round of negotiations is that the collective contract applies to all physicians and that those who do not wish to abide by the national fees can sign a special agreement, thereby joining a "second sector" in which they are free to determine their own fees "with tact and reasonableness" so long as they indicate the fee on the patient's reimbursement form.[10] The patient remains reimbursed on the basis of a national fee schedule unless the physician has altogether opted out of the system, in which case the patient is hardly reimbursed at all.

Significant as it was, the crisis of 1980 was but the most recent one in a history of conflict between physician trade unions and the state.

The Hospital Reform Act

In 1958, the Hospital Reform Act was passed. Its purpose was to modernize the French hospital system by linking regional specialty hospitals to university medical schools[11] and to restore the reputation of French biomedical science, which had progressively lagged behind since the beginning of the century. The principal provision of the reform was a shift in the reimbursement of hospital based physicians from fee-for-service to salary payment. In the French tradition of reform by decree, the Hospital Reform Act took advantage of Article 92 of the Fifth Republic's constitution, which allowed the prime minister to pass an ordinance and thereby circumvent normal parliamentary control. Since the architect of the reform, Robert Debré, was not only a distinguished pediatrician but also the prime minister's father, implementation of this reform was closely monitored by the government. Not surprisingly, it succeeded incompletely reorganizing the hospital system in spite of vigorous resistance by physicians, who were hostile to the principle of being paid like civil servants by the state.

Although there were measures taken to facilitate the transition, the Hospital Reform Act soon made salaried payment in hospitals the rule and encouraged full-time salaried work. In addition, it encouraged physicians to engage in research and teaching as well as in clinical work. Perhaps the principal innovation following the act was the emergence of new scientific, as opposed to clinical, disciplines within the large teaching hospital. Professors hired in such fields as biochemistry and biophysics began establishing research laboratories as well.

Despite these changes, the Hospital Reform Act preserved some of the financial interests of the highest ranking clinical professors—*les grands patrons*. It conserved their right to hospitalize their private patients in "private" beds in their *service* at the public hospital; they were allowed to use up to four percent of their beds in this capacity (this privilege was recently revoked). In addition, new investment funds accompanied the act and thereby increased the hospital centered focus of the French health system. The development of new medical technology and specialization contributed to the rising costs of hospitals and eventually to the reform of social security.

The Reform of Social Security

In 1967, the ordinances of August 21, subsequently ratified by the law of July 31, produced a major reform. The reasons for the reform were largely owing to a "structural deficit" in health insurance financing: health care costs were rising faster than the wage base on which payroll taxes were levied. Having come out of a social democratic tradition, in

1945 the original founders of the social security system believed that the individual regional and local funds should be managed by elected representatives; but this did not provide the government with the degree of control that it wanted over the funds. Consequently, the 1967 ordinances divided the responsibility for managing the system between representatives of workers (trade unions) and of employers (the *patronat*). Since the trade union movement is split and the patronat is unified, however, power actually rests with the partnership between the patronat and the state.

The main theme of the 1967 ordinances was to coordinate the administrative and financial branches of the entire social security system: health insurance—including maternity, invalidity, and industrial accidents; family benefits; and pensions. Each branch was given some autonomy to manage its funds and the responsibility for keeping its financial flows in balance. In addition, local and regional funds were placed under the administrative authority of national funds, which are responsible for maintaining overall budgetary balance. On the health side of the social security system, the CNAMTS became the central banker for the entire health system.

Despite the 1967 reform, the CNAMTS has failed to eliminate frequent and growing deficits, and consequently the Ministry of Finance and the prime minister have repeatedly intervened to increase the level of payroll taxes and raise issues about more fundamental reforms, none of which have yet been implemented.

The Hospital Law and Health Planning, 1970–1980

The Hospital Law of 1970 represents a new stage in the evolution of French health policy—one of increased planning and regulation. The idea of medical progress was not questioned, but all new hospital construction as well as capital expenditures were supposed to conform to a national, as well as a detailed regional, plan elaborated on the basis of national standards. This procedure is known as the *carte sanitaire*.[12] Whereas previous regulatory measures emanating from the Ministry of Health aimed to encourage hospital modernization and better management, the 1970 reform was far broader in scope. It proposed to rationalize the French hospital system by creating a new "public hospital service," to which all private hospitals could become associated.

Above all, the Hospital Law aimed to control the growth of the private sector. It established regulatory commissions charged with authorizing hospital expansion and capital expenditure programs in the private sector. Also, the Hospital Law encouraged cooperation between hospitals within a region and sought to establish a "harmonious distribution" of facilities based on identification of health needs. France's twenty-one administrative regions were divided into 284 health service areas (*secteurs sanitaires*), and each area was required to conform to national standards.

Despite the passage of the Hospital Law, however, the number of hospital beds in the private sector continued to increase—at least until 1979.[13] The "public hospital service" has still not succeeded in coordinating public and private sector growth, and health care expenditures continue to soar.

THE PRESENT PREDICAMENT: THE COST EXPLOSION AND STRATEGIES TO CONTROL IT

Between 1960 and 1980, the total consumption of medical services in France as a percent of GDP, soared from 4 to 7.5.[14] That represents an average annual rate of increase of 15.3 percent in current prices and 7.9 percent in 1970 constant prices.[15] The explosion of health care costs is exacerbated by the economic situation, for growing unemployment as well as slow economic growth have reduced the revenues of the CNAMTS, thereby increasing its deficit.

What can be done to balance the structural deficit in health care financing? The state has two principal options: to increase revenues or to control expenditures.

Methods to Increase Revenues

INCREASE PAYROLL TAXES

Payroll taxes for health insurance provided by the CNAMTS are currently equal to 18.95 percent of the taxable wage base. Employees pay 5.5 percent on their full wage; employers pay 8 percent on the full wage and 5.45 percent on the wage below a monthly ceiling of Fr 7,080 ($1,770). Over the past eight years, payroll taxes for employers as well as for employees have been raised on six occasions as part of financial salvage operations to balance the social security budget.

RAISE WAGE CEILINGS

To raise or even to eliminate the ceiling under which employer payroll taxes are assessed would increase revenues while simultaneously reducing inequalities, since employers with employees earnings wages above the current ceiling pay proportionately less than those with employees earning wages below the ceiling.

EXTEND THE TAXABLE BASE

Another method to raise health insurance revenues would be to tax capital in addition to labor or move toward a value-added tax. The main argument for a move in this direction is that the present tax burden penalizes labor-intensive industries and favors capital-intensive ones.[16] Moreover, during periods of recession the present mechanisms encourage employers to reward overtime work rather than increase the number of employees. One might reasonably ask, however, whether it makes sense to tax new investments when these are all the more necessary to restructure the present economy.

"Fiscalize" the Entire System

Raising the wage ceiling and extending the tax base represent methods by which to redistribute the tax burden of firms within the parafiscal system. Financing social expenditures out of the government budget (through the fiscal system) is another option—one with very different economic and political implications.[17] Such a reform would eliminate the concept of contributory insurance schemes. Firms would be relieved of the tax burden they now bear but the state would be forced to increase taxes in order to finance the present level of social expenditures. Politically, this would shift power away from a corporatist social security organization managed by trade unions, and the patronat, to the state. Consequently, the social security system would fall under the public sector and be bound by its administrative procedures. Parliament would have to approve its annual budget; all health personnel including physicians would become civil servants; and the degree of administrative centralization would most likely increase.

Increase Private Financing

Roughly eighty percent of French health expenditures are collectively financed by the CNAMTS and the Ministry of Health. That leaves twenty percent in the form of private financing by individual out-of-pocket payments. One way to finance the growth of health expenditures is simply to increase the share of private financing through copayments or deductibles. This method would probably result in individuals subscribing to private health insurance to protect themselves against their increased risk.

Methods to Reduce Expenditures

Price Controls

In France regulation of prices is a well-established tradition, and the health sector is no exception to the imposition of administrative pricing. On the demand side, policymakers can attempt to reduce utilization of services by adjusting the level of copayments and deductibles. On the supply side, policymakers can manipulate reimbursement rates for physicians in private practice as well as for private and public hospitals.

Demand-side policies are strictly limited in a society that has grown accustomed to NHI. Nevertheless, a number of minor measures can be taken whose effectiveness depends on the price elasticity of demand with respect to the service in question. In 1977, for example, the Council of Ministers reduced reimbursement rates for certain "nonessential" drugs from seventy to forty percent of the controlled prices. In 1980, the government imposed a copayment as well as a deductible for long-term hospitalization: copayments above Fr 80 a month for six months or above a total of Fr 480 were assumed by the CNAMTS.[18]

On the supply side, regulation of physician fees is one of the cornerstones of French health policy. As we have seen, negotiations with the medical profession have resulted in agreement by a large majority of physicians to accept nationally set fees. The problem, however, is that the *nomenclature* of professional procedures is more of an instrument for purposes of billing the NHI funds than an instrument for giving price signals to physicians so as to encourage them to behave in ways that are cost effective. Since the *nomenclature* is the result of negotiations between professional medical associations, the CNAMTS, and the government, it also reflects the relative power of medical specialty groups to negotiate advantageous fees for the procedures controlled by their disciplines.[19] Thus, although negotiation of the *nomenclature* is a critical institutional mechanism for controlling reimbursement rates of physicians in private practice, it is not necessarily an effective instrument of price control.

In addition to physician reimbursement rates, French policymakers also control reimbursement rates to proprietary hospitals (cliniques) and to public hospitals. Both are reimbursed largely on the basis of costs incurred, the principal unit of reimbursement being the patient day (*prix de journée*). In the public sector, the value of the patient day for year $n + 1$ is calculated by dividing total operating costs—including teaching, research, and administrative costs, other ancillary costs, plus the institution's deficit for year n—by the total number of patient days. In the private sector, the patient day is less of a catch-all category for, in contrast to the public hospital, operating room costs, expensive drugs, laboratory costs, blood transfusions, and prostheses are all billed separately on a fee-for-service basis.

From the point of view of price control over hospitals, coordination is exceedingly difficulty to achieve because the CNAMTS negotiates the rate of the patient day for cliniques, whereas the department prefect, on instructions from the Ministry of Health as well as the Ministry of the Budget, sets the rate of the patient day for public hospitals.[20]

VOLUME CONTROLS

In an open-ended system characterized by fee-for-service payment under NHI, the problem with price controls is that the volume of services can often be adjusted to compensate for rigid price regulation. This is true for private practice in the ambulatory sector as well as for cliniques and public hospitals. Thus, policymakers in France have attempted to control the volume of services provided.

In the ambulatory care sector, since the collective contract of 1976, the system of statistical profiles on the procedures performed by each physician was computerized. The rationale has been to control the quality of medical care and to sensitize physicians to the financial implications of their activities. The system is based on finding irregularities in medical practice and issuing sanctions to doctors who overprescribe tests and drugs. This is exceedingly difficult, however, because criteria on proper workloads have not yet been agreed on. If the entire medical profession is influenced by reimbursement incentives to increase medical procedures, particularly specialty services and high technology medicine, or if it is influenced by cultural norms to overprescribe drugs, the effect of the profiles will be negligible.

Since 1980, all French physicians receive periodic statements summarizing the consultations and procedures for which they have billed the CNAMTS through the intermediary of their patients. Enormous amounts of data have been collected on patterns of physician activity. Information is currently being collected by the CNAMTS on the sociodemographic characteristics of physician clientele populations. This is critical, for it will one day enable the CNAMTS to go one step beyond pointing up disparities in the procedures performed by physicians; it will enable the CNAMTS to ignore disparities easily explained by such factors as age and sex and to investigate selectively the seemingly less justifiable disparities.

In the hospital sector there have been isolated attempts to control volume and regulate quality of care. However, there has been no systematic effort comparable to the physician profiles either in the cliniques or in the public hospitals. When volume controls have been imposed in the hospital sector, they have been largely procedural methods to reinforce price controls; for example, the attempt to put limits on allowable rates of expenditure increase and to regulate administrative procedures such as hospital budget reviews.[21] Although French hospitals are not financed on the basis of closed budgets, estimated budgets may be inferred indirectly once one knows the allowable patient day rates and the estimated number of patient days.

With respect to cliniques, more refined classification schemes have been devised within which to regulate expenditure increases of like groups of institutions. With respect to public hospitals, every year a circular is issued by the Ministry of Health—after consultation with the Ministry of the Budget and the Ministry of Social Security (now part of the Ministry of Social Affairs)—which sets the allowable rate of increase for all hospital budgets. In addition, entire categories of expenditure within hospitals have been strictly limited, and new positions for full-time staff have been denied by the Ministry of Health.[22]

CAPITAL CONTROLS

In contrast to price controls and volume controls, which are short-run methods to contain expenditures, capital controls are designed to contain long-run health expenditures. They aim to limit expenditures for hospital expansion and modernization, new medical technologies, and new "human capital"—doctors. Although controls on hospital investment have been a part of national economic planning in France since 1946, controls on the supply of medical manpower are relatively new.

With respect to hospital facilities and capital expenditures, the carte sanitaire procedure originally aimed to promote redistribution of health resources. At the national level, areas of need were explicitly identified and standards were devised in terms of hospital bed/population ratios for specific medical services. At the regional level, resource inventories were carried out for each of the 284 new health sectors. The level of existing resources was compared to the national standards and public issues were made on the basis of the observed disparities. The result of this exercise was to identify substandard regions and to legitimate new investments there. There was no corresponding decrease of hospital beds, however, in regions that were above standard.

Since 1976, the carte sanitaire procedure has served as an instrument for the planning of retrenchment. Over a period of ten years (1970–1980), the rejection rate on hospital investment requests (in the private sector) increased from fifty-five percent to over eighty percent.[23] As for the public sector, a series of new circulars as well as a new law have increased the Ministry of Health's authority over the growth of public sector hospitals.[24] In 1976 the government decided to stabilize the aggregate number of hospital beds in France. In 1979, the law of December 29 granted the minister of health authority to close down hospital beds in the public sector. So far, no beds have yet been closed by ministerial decree. Under the previous regime, the carte sanitaire standards served as criteria for assessing where to cut. Under the present regime, however, policymakers are talking of expanding hospital personnel, not reducing beds.

Along with the December 1979 law granting the minister of health power to close down hospital beds, as part of a long-term cost control policy, the French government passed legislation reducing the number of physicians by cutting enrollments in the medical schools. In effect, since 1971 the ministers of health and education were granted the authority to control indirectly the supply of physicians by controlling entry into the medical school pipeline. The criteria for controlling entry were supposed to reflect the university's capacity for training physicians; however, in 1979, when it was declared that the number of medical students accepted into their second year of training would drop over a few years from nine thousand to five thousand, there was no longer any doubt about the fact that France had imposed a *numerus clausus*. One may speculate about the reasons for this; no doubt it was partly to control long-run health care costs but also to conserve the prestige of the medical profession—or at least its income.

STRUCTURAL CHANGE

Price controls, volume controls, and capital controls have one thing in common: they assume that the way the health system is presently organized will stay the same. If we relax that assumption, however, there may be other cost-control strategies—ones that make use of structural change, for example, reinforcing prevention programs. In March 1982, Minister of Health Ralite received the report of an urgent task force he had appointed to make recommendations in the field of prevention.[25] Thus far, his first measure has been to designate four regions to receive starting budgets for a range of prevention programs.

If these programs remain a political priority and function effectively, they could significantly reduce the burden of disability and disease associated with alcoholism, smoking addiction, and poor working conditions; however, all of these achievements would not eliminate deaths from cancer, degeneration of the circulatory system, or other diseases that require costly medical technology and prolonged hospitalization. We do not mean to argue against disease prevention programs; for one would have to distinguish between alternative levels—primary, secondary, and tertiary (see chap. 3)—and alternative probabilities of success. The effectiveness of prevention programs is hardly certain, however. For example, a century of antialcohol campaigns have hardly made alcoholism in France disappear, owing largely to the importance of the wine industry. Moreover, structural change provokes vigorous reactions from vested interests: hospital associations, physicians, and industry.

Taking account of the recent history of French health policy as well as the present predicament and various strategies to control health care costs, what alternative futures can one envision for the French health system?

SCENARIOS FOR THE FUTURE

In most of Western industrialized nations, either the state or emergent consumer organizations, or both, have been important forces for questioning existing arrangements for financing and organizing medical care—and for promoting structural change. In France, the government has not had sufficient legitimacy to significantly reform the financing of health expenditures and reorganize the health sector. As for consumer organizations, they are inconspicuous compared with those of other Western nations. There are several reasons for this.

First, in France great respect is accorded to distinguished citizens, particularly scientists. Why criticize those who know? Doctors have both social status and expertise and it is still considered in bad taste to challenge the authority of this most respected profession.

Second, the French administrative system is vertical and extends from the center to the periphery. Three centuries of political centralization have had an impact on the country and its people; it is therefore not surprising that there is a virtual absence of grass roots movements and a reluctance on the part of local government to innovate or to promote community based experiments to solve local problems.

Finally, individualism is a distinguishing feature of French character; and it is reinforced today by the failure of collectivist ideologies. The dream of a utopian society has lost currency. The events of May 1968 had no political repercussions and the ideas have eroded. The things that were violently condemned—centralization, hierarchy, elitism, unemployment, political inertia—still exist and have even intensified. The temptation is therefore to turn inward, to live one's own life rather than attempt to improve the lives of others.

For all of these reasons, it seems likely that modifications in the organization of health services are likely to be influenced more by the state of the economy and, possibly, by the French government, than by consumer movements. Of course, such movements will exist, but they will remain a pale replica of foreign movements and more of an outlet for protest than an active force for change.

Given these assumptions about French society, we can imagine four alternative scenarios for the future of the health sector in France.

Scenario One: Extrapolation of Present Trends

This scenario assumes the continuation of present trends, with neither health professionals nor consumers modifying their behavior: fee-for-service payment is maintained without strict regulation of fees or control over the volume of medical procedures prescribed; patients continue to exercise free choice of their physicians; and doctors are free to prescribe as they please. Within the hospital, the per diem mode of reimbursement is maintained, there is no systematic control of patient admissions or of lengths of stay, and excess capacity of hospital beds in certain regions continues.

In this scenario, national health insurance, public hospitals, and la médecine libérale continue to coexist in the absence of a unitary administrative authority. The payer (CNAMTS) neither plans nor decides about the allocation of health resources.[26] There are no stringent regulatory controls. In short, this scenario is characterized by the uncontrolled growth of health expenditures.

HOSPITAL EXPENDITURES

Based on the evolution of French hospitals between 1965 and 1977, linear trend extrapolations indicate a stabilization in the aggregate number of hospital-bed days. The number of hospital beds has already stabilized, admission rates are rising, and lengths of stay will become shorter. At the same time, however, one can also expect growth in hospitalization of the elderly as well as growth of skilled hospital personnel. The intensity of medical care will increase, and new complex therapy as well as diagnostic procedures will require highly qualified personnel (biomedical technicians, computer specialists, skilled nurses; and so forth).

Such changes are likely to increase the volume of medical care per hospitalized patient as well as the unit costs. Thus, the rate of growth of hospital expenditures is not likely to decrease despite government efforts to contain costs. We would therefore project a continued rate of increase of seven percent (in constant prices) over the next fifteen years.

EXPENDITURES FOR AMBULATORY CARE

The number of physicians in France has increased rapidly and will continue to do so. In 1980 there were already more than 100,000 physicians, of whom 70,000 worked in private practice. Recent projections suggest that 150,000 physicians will work in private practice in the year 2000.[27] A recent study by CREDOC suggests that the demand for medical care from general practitioners is no longer completely elastic in areas with high physician populaton ratios;[28] but this phenomenon of relative saturation does not appear to apply to specialists.

To predict changes in the way physicians are remunerated is much more difficult. It is probable that physician reimbursement mechanisms will change considerably, but it is hard to say how rapidly these changes will occur. It is also difficult to know if the pluralism of medical care organization will be maintained or if there will be shift toward public sector control and salaried payment for all physicians. Whatever happens, it is likely that the level of renumeration of physicians will remain high—well above the average income in France.

HEALTH EXPENDITURES AS A PROPORTION OF GDP

The following projections assume that expenditures (in constant prices) on hospitalization and ambulatory care will continue to grow at an average annual rate of seven and eight percent, respectively. Assuming a four percent rate of growth for the gross domestic product (GDP)—a very optimistic hypothesis—health care expenditures in 1995 would represent 12.3 percent of GDP. If instead of a 4 percent growth rate of GDP we assume a 3.5% rate, health care expenditures would be equal to 14 percent of GDP in 1995.

These results may appear surprising; yet they are based on reasonable assumptions. Less than two years ago a rate of 10 percent of GDP devoted to health care expenditures seemed unthinkable. In order to maintain health care expenditures under 10 percent of GDP in 1995, however, the rate of increase, in constant prices, would have to exceed the rate of GDP by no more than 2.17 percent over the entire period. Since the Eighth National Plan predicts that health care expenditures will represent 10 percent of GDP as early as 1985, we are inclined to consider our trend extrapolations conservative.

The health care system does not exist in a political-economic vacuum; it is part of a whole, and in the long run, external factors and general economic conditions may have a more decisive influence than the internal factors we have just discussed. Will they restrain the growth we anticipate?

Over the next ten years, most experts would agree that we can expect a continuation of international tensions; a persistence of instability in international money markets; a decline in the rate of growth of developed countries; a price increase in energy and raw materials; and a decline in industrial and agricultural employment. One might conclude that the lower rate of economic growth would limit the increase of health care expenditures. This is possible, but two factors are likely to counteract this effect: the price increase of energy and raw materials, which is reflected in health care expenditures; and the scarcity of employment opportunities in the industrial and agricultural sectors, which creates pressure for job creation in the service sector. Given rising rates of unemployment, it is hard to imagine the government limiting the growth of a labor-intensive sector such as health care.

The preliminary studies for the Eighth National Economic Plan showed that a one percentage point change in the GDP would result in a Fr 25 billion change in the social budget (all social security and state welfare expenditures). Only an annual growth rate of 6 percent for GDP would make it possible to finance a level of health expenditures equal to our trend extrapolations. Since the GDP is predicted to grow at an annual rate of 2.5 percent from now to 1985, and since the longer term does not look better, this first scenario based on a policy of laissez faire appears economically unrealistic. In the future, it seems more probable that the state will intervene in the health sector along the lines of one of the next three scenarios.

Scenario Two: Encouragement of the Market Mechanism

This scenario is characterized by a progressive reduction of national health insurance benefits and by the growth of private insurance to finance a larger share of total health care expenditures. The aim of such a policy is to assure financial balance of the social security system without increasing payroll taxes and cumbersome supply-side regulations. The health system becomes regulated on the demand side. While the idea of health insurance is not questioned, such reform appeals to the principle of maximizing free choice of subscribers and forcing them to make their own trade-offs between the level of premiums paid and the amount of coverage and benefits received. In theory, this will moderate the level of health care consumption.

An extreme version of this scenario would eliminate the accomplishments of the French social security system. It would reduce health insurance coverage and eliminate payroll taxes. State intervention would be limited to preventive measures such as traditional public health or assistance programs for the unemployed and for low-income and high-risk populations. All the rest would be taken care of through the private sector or by nonprofit associations. Under the government of Prime Minister Raymond Barre, there was serious interest in such a scenario; but even then it seemed unrealistic, for no one believed that French trade unions would ever accept the erosion of their acquired privileges.

A milder version of this scenario would recognize that there are limits beyond which the state cannot easily withdraw. After all, seventy percent of health expenditures are incurred by only ten percent of potential beneficiaries.[29] Such concentration of health expenditures on a relatively small population makes it difficult to imagine the private sector underwriting these costs. Other limits have to do with the perverse incentive effects of the reimbursement system, which tends to encourage hospital centered care. If the CNAMTS were to reduce coverage of *minor risks*, it could lead to substitution of hospital care for ambulatory care rather than the other way around. If the CNAMTS were to reduce benefit levels significantly and let the private sector underwrite minor risks entirely, there would be per-verse incentives to increase the number of cases covered under *major risks*.

Despite these drawbacks, the milder version of this scenario is a serious option for reform; it could conceivably involve the following measures:

INCREASE THE LEVEL OF COPAYMENTS

This kind of measure would disproportionately penalize low-income households, which are those most often without supplementary insurance coverage.

TRANSFER MINOR RISK INSURANCE TO THE PRIVATE SECTOR AND ESTABLISH COMPENSATING SOCIAL GUARANTEES

The provision of special health care programs for low-income groups financed on the basis of taxes on private insurance premiums is an example of one such measure. Another example is the design of rules regulating competition between private insurance companies, for example, the prohibition of exclusion clauses that eliminate high-risk groups from coverage; or the requirement of minimum benefit levels. Such compensating mechanisms, while indispensable to limit inequities in private insurance, would diminish the effect of reducing the scope of national health insurance and the anticipated moderation of health care consumption.

IMPOSE DEDUCTIBLES RELATED TO INCOME

This mechanism would impose a deductible on family health care expenditures before reimbursement under national health insurance. The deductible would be set in proportion to income and vary according to the size of the family. Health care expenditures would be entirely covered for that portion above the threshold—in contrast to the copayment mechanism, which requires families to contribute a percentage of the expenses whatever their income or level of health care consumption.

In comparison with the other measures outlined above, this mechanism has several advantages. It is easier to understand and more equitable. Furthermore, the possibility of injustice or error due to the ambiguity of the term *minor risk* is eliminated; there is only a minimum threshold of relevant expenditures whatever the nature of the risk may be. There is no need to fear gaps in coverage; nor is there reason to expect negative effects such as the establishment of a two-tiered medical system or a shift of medical care to hospitals. The only danger might be the increase of elective health care once the threshold has been exceeded.

Scenario two falls on the conservative side of the political spectrum, but as we have seen, it allows for various policy options—ranging from the growth of private health insurance to the imposition of a deductible directly related to income. The latter option is politically unrealistic because the middle classes would be opposed to turning health insurance into a social redistribution program. The former option is most unlikely because labor unions would be unanimously opposed. As for the more basic notion of encouraging the market mechanism in the health sector, it is likely to encounter substantial opposition. The existence of national health insurance in France is widely accepted and it is therefore difficult to rally support for attempts to dismantle it.

Scenario Three: Increased Regulation

This scenario assumes that the French will want to preserve the major characteristics of their present health care system while containing health expenditures and achieving more control over the health system. As we have already noted, cost containment may be achieved by a variety of controls. The challenge for the government is to make them acceptable to major interest groups.

Proponents of increased regulation and planning recommend the design of improved information systems and the development of epidemiology, preventive medicine, and health education. In addition, they advocate ongoing evaluation of the health care system so as to improve the efficiency of medical care and of health institutions. Also, they urge the development of continuing education programs for general practitioners, tighter controls over their power to prescribe, an incomes policy to guide annual fee negotiations, and the imposition of limits on the number of students admitted to medical schools.

In this scenario, the present cost-based per diem reimbursement system for hospitals is replaced by prospectively set, closed budgets. In addition, a strict program for all future hospital development is established; and the CNAMTS is given more authority to manage the entire health care system. This will result in a decrease of hospital admission rates as well as lengths of stay, a redeployment of personnel, and the elimination of excess capacity (estimated at seventy thousand beds in the spring of 1980).[30]

In summary, these measures attempt to increase the range of public health programs while tightening control over the supply of health services. They will work effectively only if the power of key actors is restricted—in particular, the medical profession's clinical freedom to prescribe and the hospitals' carte blanche to bill the CNAMTS on the basis of per diem costs. Both physicians and hospitals will have to accept the principle of a closed budget and explicitly confront alternative criteria for rationing scarce health resources.

Although there is already an implicit system of health care rationing at present, it is hard to imagine how such a scenario could come about since the very term *rationing* causes fear and reminds the older generation of World War II. It may be necessary for the economic situation to deteriorate further before any government gains sufficient support to impose such reforms. Perhaps only then will the key actors in the health sector be persuaded that control mechanisms may be the least of all possible evils.

Scenario Four: A Unitary National Health Service

Scenario four would create a British National Health Service (NHS) à la française. The state would administer the entire health care system, a single ministry would be created to combine planning and financing functions, and a limit would be imposed on the total budget allocated to health care. It is not difficult to imagine a French adaptation of this model. Hospitals would function much like public enterprises in the nationalized sector. All physicians would be remunerated on the basis of salaries and acquire civil servant status. Several categories of hospitals would persist: university hospitals, general community hospitals, local rural hospitals, and hospitals specializing in long-term care. All hospitals would receive an annual budget that could be revised if necessary during the year, and they would have precise objectives set in advance on the basis of national and regional health plans.

For the most part, general practitioners would be responsible for ambulatory care; specialists would be based in hospitals. Whether in individual or group practice, general practitioners would have a monopoly over primary care. They would also be responsible for preventive medicine (e.g., maternal and child care and school health programs) and participate in health education and occupational health programs. As for physician remuneration, it would most likely be based on salary payment in combination with capitation payments and fee-for-service reimbursement for such services as house calls and various twenty-four-hour coverage duties.

The advantage of such a system is that it resolves one of the major difficulties of rationalizing health care systems: it links planning and decision making to financing and reimbursement mechanisms and thereby reduces the potential for contradictory policies.[31] The central instruments to guide resource allocation under a national health service would be the national and regional health plans. The object of these plans would be to promote an equitable and efficient distribution of health resources. Clearly, this would require dismantling the present national health insurance system and thus entering into conflict with the patronat as well as with professional organizations (medical and hospital associations). Moreover, such a system would require substantial centralization and would therefore be difficult to reconcile with regional autonomy.

The idea of an NHS reflects a socialist ideology, but the diversity of institutional possibilities that exist actually means that an NHS à la française defies ideological labels. In addition to the British NHS organized around fourteen regions and financed essentially through general revenue funds, one can imagine a system of health insurance funds providing services in kind to their insured population. Another possibility is a regionalized health system that maintains the pluralism of multiple actors (regions, health insurance funds, mutual aid societies) with major financing based on payroll taxes.

Whatever the final model may be, the idea of organizing health care around the concept of a public service provokes strong resistance, in France, from health professionals who fear imminent restrictions of clinical freedom and anticipate deleterious effects on the quality of care. Although attitudes are slowly changing, this scenario is not likely to be implemented even if the Left comes to power under conditions of economic recession. Without a recession, there would be no urgency for major reforms that challenge the existing status quo. And without the Left in power the probability of scenario two or three would far surpass that of scenario four.

Conclusion

The preceding scenarios do not exhaust the range of possibilities for the future of French health policy. We have examined only those options that seem most probable under conditions of slow economic growth and political centralization. More attractive than any of these scenarios, we think, would be the development of regional initiatives in order to avoid the rigidities of excessive centralization. In this regard, the election of President Mitterand in May 1981 gave reason for hope. Effective decentralization would require such cultural and political transformation, however, that it is not likely to occur. Nevertheless, the cost-control strategies we have described and the scenarios we have outlined cannot be avoided for long.

NOTES

1. V. Rodwin, "Health Planning under French National Health Insurance," in H. Blum, *Planning for Health*, 2d ed. (New York: Human Sciences Press, 1981), chap. 13.

2. V. Rodwin, "The Marriage of National Health Insurance and *la Méde--cine Libérale* in France: A Costly Union," *Milbank Memorial Fund Quarterly* 59 (Winter 1981).

3. J. de Kervasdoué, "La politique de l'Etat en matière d'hospitalisation privée, 1962–1978," *Annales Economiques de Clermont-Ferrand*, no. 16 (1980).

4. Rodwin, "The Marriage of National Health Insurance and *la Médecine Libérale*." For good comparative data on health expenditures, see *Public Expenditure on Health* (Paris: OECD, July 1977).

5. "La securité sociale et son avenir," *Patronat Français*, supplement to no. 253 (June 1965).

6. H. Hatzfeld, *Le grand tournant de la médecine libérale* (Paris: Éditions Ouvrières, 1956).

7. J. C. Stephan, *Economie et pouvoir médical* (Paris: Economica, 1978).

8. Sixième Plan, *Santé et prestations sociales* (Paris: Documentation Française, 1971).

9. L. Thorsen, "How can the U.S. Government Control Physicians' Fees under National Health Insurance? A Lesson from the French System," *Int. J. Health Services* 4, no. 1 (1974).

10. *Convention nationale destinée à organiser les rapports entre le corps médical et les caisses d'assurance maladie* (Paris: CNAMTS, May 1980).

11. H. Jamous, *Sociologie de la décision: la réforme des études médicales et des structures hospitalières* (Paris: Éditions du CNRS, 1969).

12. G. Moreau, "La planification dans le domaine de la santé: les hommes et les équipements," *Revue Française des Affaires Sociales*, special no. 4 (October–December 1980).

13. Kervasdoué, "La politique de l'Etat."

14. *Comptes nationaux de la santé.* (Paris: CREDOC, 1982).

15. Ibid. For an analysis of long-cycle changes in French health care expenditures see V. Rodwin, "Management Without Objectives: The French Health Policy Gamble," in G. McLachlan and A. Maynard, eds., *The Private-Public Sector Mix for Health: The Relevance and Effects of Change* (London: Nuffield Provincial Hospitals Trust, 1982).

16. C. Rollet, "Pourquoi modifier l'assiette des cotisations sociales?" *Droit Social,* Septembre/Octobre 1978.

17. A. Euseby, "Faut-il fiscaliser la sécurite sociale?" *Droit Social* 5 (1978).

18. Decree No. 180-8 January 8, 1980. *Journal Officiel,* 8-1, p. 65.

19. G. de Pouvourville, "La nomenclature des actes professionels, un outil pour une politique de santé?" *Revue Française des Affaires Sociales.* 1981.

20. The mechanics of hospital reimbursement in France are clearly summarized by W. Glaser, *Paying the Hospital in France* (New York: Center for the Social Sciences, Columbia University, 1980).

21. These regulatory mechanisms are discussed in more detail by R. Launois and D. LeTouzé, "Analyse économique des mesures prises en France afin de maîtriser la croissance des dépenses sanitaires," in D. Truchet, ed., *Etudes de droit et d'économie de la santé* (Paris: Economica, 1981).

22. Ibid.

23. Moreau, "Planification dans le domaine de la santé," p. 22.

24. The two circulars date from August 1, 1977 (BOSP 77-34, no. 13315), and from March 3, 1978 (Circular no. 536, BOSP 78-14, no. 14658). Law no. 79-1140.

25. *Propositions pour une politique de prévention,* Rapport rédigé sur sa demande, à l'intention de Monsieur le Ministre de la Santé (Paris: Documentation Française, March 1980).

26. For more detail on the separation of planning and financing in France as well as in the U.S., see V. Rodwin, "On the Separation of Health Planning and Provider Reimbursement: The U.S. and France," *Inquiry* 18 (Summer 1981).

27. Conseil Economique et Social, Report by P. Magnin, "L'Adaptation des professions médicales et paramédicales aux besoins de santé de la population française," March 1979.

28. H. Faure, A. Thauront, and F. Tonnellier, *La Médecine Libérale—Densité, Activité, Consommation de Soins dans les Régions et les Départements, 1972–1980* (Paris: CREDOC, April 1982).

29. A. Mizrahi and A. Mizrahi, "Concentration and Influences of Socioeconomic Factors" (Presentation to the International Symposium on

Health and Economics, University of Instelling, Antwerp, Belgium, April 1980). Recent data from a regional survey indicate that 4 percent of beneficiaries consume 50 percent of health expenditures (*Qui Consomme Quoi?* [Paris: Caisse Nationale d'Assurance Maladie, March 1982]).

30. Commission de la Protection Sociale et de la Famille, *Eighth National Economic Plan* (Paris: Documentation Française, 1980).

31. Although the combination of health planning and financing under a single ministry may be necessary to achieve greater control over the health sector, we do not mean to imply that it is sufficient. The case of England suggests that it is not. See, V. Rodwin, *The Health Planning Predicament: France, Québec, England, and the United States* (Berkeley, Los Angeles, London: University of California Press, 1984) chap. 7.

7

Québec: The Adventures of a Narcissistic State

Marc Renaud

Québec is a striking example of what some have described as the growing subordination of civil society to the state.[1] In Québec this phenomenon has assumed a magnitude and visibility without parallel in North America. During the last two decades the Québec state has encroached upon the market and become itself the center of social praxis and the principal manager and arbiter of social crises. In essence, during the sixties and seventies, the state attempted to mobilize and subordinate society to the imperatives of economic growth, to assume responsibility for social needs such as education, culture, and health care, and to acquire a stabilizing role in the quest for national sovereignty and the regulation of class conflicts. As a corollary, the state has became the champion of modernist values.

These changes were promoted under the banner of social democratic ideals: greater distributive justice and increased social solidarity. The displacement of the private by the public sector and of the market by the state manifested itself simultaneously in two contradictory trends. On the one hand, authority and initiative for change were centralized and bureaucratized; on the other, the state extended its support to social movements that demanded local and per-

I would like to thank the following for their criticisms and comments: L. Bozzini, A. Chauvenet, D. Friedman, G. Gagnon, D. Gaucher, V. Rodwin, M. Sfia, L. H. Trottier, and the members of the Research Group on the Sociology of Health at the University of Montreal.

sonal autonomy—citizen participation in the power structure, a redefinition of male-female relations, improvement
in the quality of public services and so forth. It seems as
though the state sought to subordinate or even absorb the
private sector from above as well as from below: from
above, by increasing bureaucracy and civil servants; from
below, by coopting consumer movements, social activists,
and feminists, whose objective was to stop the absorption
of civil society by the state. Much like the notion of narcissism in psychoanalysis, Québec's government seems to
have overinvested in its own ego while disinvesting in
society. The history of Québec over the last two decades is
largely the history of the emergence of a state perpetually
preoccupied with mobilizing the energies of civil society
around its own growth and toward the extension of its own
legitimacy.

The importance of this "narcissism" of the state in Québec is the result of a dynamic specific to Québec society: the
context of an aging economic structure—in which the
upper echelons of the richest private firms were inaccessible
to an increasingly educated francophone population—
what has been called Québec's "quiet revolution" took
place in the early sixties. The revolution was achieved by
modernization and expansion of the governmental apparatus until it rapidly became, directly or indirectly, the
principal employer of the new francophone middle class.
The emergence of this class is probably the single most
important social force in Québec's recent development.
Unable to find work in the private sector, this new francophone middle class found, and still finds, its interest in
increasing the government's employees and extending its
legitimacy.[2] In this pursuit the middle class has often allied
itself with the less privileged classes. Despite its own internal divisions, the middle class has sought local hegemony in areas where the provincial government operates
autonomously in relation to the federal government; this is
especially so in health, education, and cultural affairs. In so
doing, the midde class has promoted the development of a

political culture that tends to reinforce the growth of the public sector and to value a two-sided strategy for the governance of civil society—one that is both bureaucratizing and debureaucratizing.

Québec's health care reforms must be understood in this context. What is most remarkable about them is not the desire to rationalize the system of health services, or is it the sweeping reforms themselves—many of which have been attempted by other Canadian provinces and by other countries; rather, it is the speed, the visibility, and the magnitude of the proposed institutional changes. In short, what is surprising is the *style* of the reforms.[3] In an apparently paradoxical effort of support for both the development of medicine and demedicalization, both professionalization and deprofessionalization, both centralization and decentralization, and both central direction and self-management, the Québec state turned its health sector into a laboratory for social experimentation without parallel in other Western industrialized countries. In an attempt to accelerate history, starting from farther back than other Canadian provinces or most other countries, the Québec state attempted to go as far as possible as fast as possible, coopting along the way various social movements and new social practices.

In this sense, the Québec experiment in reforming the health and welfare sector permits a view in microcosm, and across a reduced time scale, of phenomena that appear or will appear in a slower or more diffused manner elsewhere. These are the phenomena which I should like to highlight in this essay. From the ideological and organizational turbulance that these reforms have generated, I shall attempt to disentangle the changes that have in fact been introduced and that are often in conflict with the ideals of the first reformers. In addition I shall analyze these changes as the outcome of social and economic forces that have constrained the state to submit society to the imperatives of economic growth. First, however, let us briefly review the history of Québec's health care reforms.

HISTORICAL OVERVIEW

Just as the Canadian federal government was the instigator of a series of social security measures after World War II, it also became the agent of reform of the health care system through its programs of matching funds. Although health care is the constitutional responsibility of the provincial governments, during the fifties and sixties several provinces reacted to these federal initiatives largely in response to electoral pressures: they only provided services in the traditional areas of public health and mental health.[4]

In the years following the war, as in the United States, the federal government subsidized hospital construction, biomedical research, education of personnel, and various other programs, such as the antituberculosis campaigns and maternal and child health care. At the end of the fifties, after years of conflict between the federal and provincial governments, and in the face of mounting hospital deficits, the federal government followed the lead of the social-democratic governments of the western provinces and achieved a consensus on the necessity of a national, universal, and compulsory health insurance program for all hospital services in Canada. Between 1957 and 1961 all the provincial governments agreed to participate in this program. Consequently, the late fifties and sixties were characterized by a phenomenal expansion of hospitals[5] and of the use of medical services.[6] During this period, the federal government exercised relatively weak controls over the health sector. What was perceived as good by the medical profession, which was becoming increasingly specialized at this time was automatically looked upon favorably by the public. As a result, Canada found itself in the mid-sixties, and still finds itself today, with a higher ratio of short-term hospital beds per thousand inhabitants (5.6 in 1966, 5.4 in 1973) and a higher average length of stay (10.1 days in 1966, 9.4 in 1973) than the United States. In other words, national hospital insurance in Canada created incentives that favored development in the most expensive sector of health care: hospitals.

In the same spirit of unconditional support for the development of medicine without concern to rationalize the organization of medical services or to reduce costs, in 1966 the federal government passed a universal, public, and compulsory health insurance program to make free ambulatory care available to consumers. This program was accepted and introduced by the provincial governments between 1968 and 1971.

At the end of the sixties perception about these programs changed radically. It was suddenly realized that the transfer of expenses from the private to the public sector had produced an increase in public spending on health care which was twice the rate of increase of the gross national product.[7] This was caused largely by substantial salary increases for hospital employees and by the growth in range, and use, of medical services. No longer subject to the laws of the market, these expenditures not only grew more rapidly than the GNP but also became directly visible in the national accounts, competing with other areas of public expenditure. Simultaneously, the so-called paramedical professions began to demand better wages. These professions had multiplied and the number of people working in them had grown in conjunction with technological development and medical specialization. Citizen movements appeared in the working-class districts of large cities; tensions between the government and the medical profession began to develop. Finally, at the beginning of the seventies, the economic situation deteriorated, leaving public authorities only a thin margin to maneuver for expenditure increases related to health care.

In this context the initiative for reform went from the federal government to provincial governments. Unable to control rising costs—since the provinces exercise management responsibility over the health care system—the federal government ceased introducing major reforms[8] This transfer in leadership was decisively confirmed in 1977 when the federal government changed its methods of financing the hospital and medical care insurance programs. The entire responsibility for introducing necessary reforms in the organization and administration of services was left in the hands of the provinces.[9]

Paradoxically, though of all the provinces Québec had been the most hesitant to introduce federal programs, and had the reputation of being one of the most reactionary provinces as far as redistributive programs, it was the Québec government which took the limelight during the seventies and gained the reputation of being avant-garde in the area of health and social welfare reform.

In 1966 the Québec government named a commission of inquiry on health and social welfare (the Castonguay-Nepveu Commission) whose mission was to investigate the system of health and social services as well as income security. Several members of this commission, including its president, Claude Castonguay, became members of the government about the same time that the most important part of their work was published. Their authority was thus well established and the social climate was very favorable to them when they began to implement the multiple recommendations they elaborated during their four years of work on the commission.[10]

The Castonguay-Nepveu Commission wanted to offer a whole range of quality health and social services to all and to develop an efficient administrative apparatus. Free services was not the commission's only aim—this was already imposed by the federal plan. There was also a desire to integrate, to systematize, and to plan the roles and functions of the health care and welfare system so as to reduce costs and offer better services to the whole population, without regard to income or place of residence. As was the case in reports of similar commissions in other provinces, several ground rules were redefined; and there was a proposal to rationalize the health care system by an increased role for public authorities in the administration and organization of health services.

In contrast to the reports developed elsewhere, however, in Québec the goal of rationalization was accompanied by a set of ideals that gave to the Québec reforms a social democratic coloration. These ideals provided visibility and were attractive to groups opposing the established order. Inspired by a whole series of new social movements and social practices of the sixties, the commission supported the need to (1) create a new, more holistic medicine in opposition to a mechanical, hospital centered medicine; (2) develop a more community based and preventive approach to health care; (3) decentralize the decision making process and incorporate consumer and workers participation in the decision making process; and (4) equalize somewhat the rights and privileges of those health workers who have a technical and university education and who have direct responsibility for the patient (i.e., those we loosely call health care professionals).

Castonguay and his team instituted these reforms in the typical ambitious, coercive, and authoritative style of Québec governmental reforms since 1960. In less than four years they passed legislation on the health care professions, the organization of health care, and the administration of health services on a scale without parallel in North America. Some organizations were abolished: local health units; others were created: local health and social service centers (CLSCs), departments of community health (DSCS), regional councils for health and social services (CRSSSs), the Québec Professions Board (OPQ), and the Québec Health Insurance Board (RAMQ); and others had their roles and functions redefined: the Ministry of Social Affairs (MAS) and the professional corporations. Several administrative procedures were modified, and management responsibilities were given to persons hitherto unfamiliar with such work. Finally, the entire structure was clarified on paper by distinguishing operational management tasks from conceptual tasks, and by a reclassification of all organizations into a few well-defined categories. In short, a significant administrative reshuffling took place. As Dr. Sidney Lee, Vice-Dean of the McGill faculty of medicine wrote:

> Overall, . . Québec has accomplished a major reorientation of its health system in a relatively brief time frame. The

extraordinary opportunity presented to a small group of
dedicated individuals to study the problems, devise proposed solutions and then endeavor to implement them
from positions of power is probably without parallel elsewhere in the world.[11]

As we will see, however, the logic of social development
that inspired the reformers and mobilized groups in favor of
the reforms slowly gave way to a much more coercive and
narrow logic, that of economic development. The reforms
led to a restructuring of power relations between dominant
elites, to a modernization intent on pursuing productivity,
and to the introduction of new moral values in health care.
These changes are certainly important; but they are not
truly comparable to the grand social designs which had
inspired a degree of popular support undreamed of by most
politicians.

THE REAL IMPACT OF THE REFORMS

It is certainly too early to evaluate in a decisive manner the
impact and social significance of the reforms that resulted
from the recommendations of the Castonguay-Nepveu
Commission. Foreign observers have remarked that in
Canada—and this seems more true for Québec, though
official statistics are not yet available[12]—the result of the
state's financing health care expenditures has been an almost unbelievable stabilization in cost increases. Table 1
provides a comparison of health care expenditures in Canada and the United States:

Such figures are only the most visible and measurable
indication of what has actually occurred in Québec in the
seventies. One must consider far less superficial (some
might say more questionable) indicators to understand the
precise nature of the social dynamics at work behind the
rhetoric of the debates and struggles, and behind the prom-
ises of social laws and regulations. State intervention in
the area of health seems to have contributed to the produc-

TABLE 1

TOTAL HEALTH CARE EXPENDITURES IN CANADA AND THE UNITED STATES

	Percent of GNP	
Year	Canada	United States
1960	5.62	5.32
1965	6.07	5.88
1970	7.10	7.43
1973	6.84	7.68
1975	7.10	8.63
1976	7.08	8.79

Source: Santé et Bien-Être Social Canada, *Indicateurs du domaine de la santé: Canada et provinces* (September 1979), p. 87.

tion of three major changes, which we will consider successively.

A Profound Change in the Power Structure

Anyone observing the Québec scene in the last twenty years from the standpoint of political sociology would be surprised by the massive entry into the governmental apparatus of new social actors often referred to as technocrats or planners. It would be more sociologically exact to call them by the term coined by Robert Alford—"bureaucratic rationalizers."[13] They seek to reorganize society according to a managerial logic and, in the area of services, to extend their power over the organization of these services by placing suppliers—professionals, institutions, and others—under the control of administrative councils, regional councils, and above all, governmental bureaucracies.

This phenomenon has characterized all major interventions of the Québec government since the beginning of the sixties (reforms in education, culture, and the economy); but it was even more apparent in the reshuffling of the health and social welfare sector. One reason was the exceptional strength of the old powers (in particular the medical profession and religious communities) the government came up against. Another factor was the exceptional legitimacy and authority Claude Castonguay and his team enjoyed. As André Lajoie, former researcher from the commission and director of the Center for Research in Public Law at the University of Montreal, noted:

> The health reform was a project promoted essentially in the name of its beneficiaries and an ideology of accessibility and rationalization. But it was advanced by technocrats, that is, and with no pejorative connotation intended, by a group whose power lies in the expertise they possess. It was a project which favored the emerging classes of the sixties in Québec: (1) new graduates seeking jobs in the public sector, who would become the new administrators and the new personnel to the relative detriment of the old religious property owners and the dominant professional groups; and (2) doctors and nurses.[14]

Without necessarily attributing a Machiavellian intent to anyone, it would seem that the objectives of holistic medicine, decentralization, citizen and worker participation in decision making, and a degree of deprofessionalization served first and foremost to reinforce the position—even to assure the dominance—of the bureaucratic rationalizers and, as a corollary, the new center of power: the state.

As a result, to accommodate this new reality, the former uncontested monopolies—in particular the medical profession, the nursing profession, and the hospital industry—were obliged to commence a process, as yet unfinished, of internal reorganization. In creating organizations such as CLSCs, DSCs, CRSSSs, and the OPQ, the state, in the words of Frédéric Lesemann, "had knocked a billiard ball at the old powers," destabilizing them and forcing them to realign.[15]

For example, in creating the local health and social service centers (CLSCs), a new organizational model was formed which was inspired by the people's clinics of the late sixties radical movement. This introduced some potential competition between public sector medicine (the CLSCs) and private practice and accelerated the tendency for general practitioners to form group practices. Many doctors abandoned traditional private, office based practice and joined together in *polycliniques*, often with twenty-four-hour service seven days a week. Likewise, the creation in the CLSCs of multidisciplinary teams of salaried doctors, which were administrated democratically by client councils, must have stimulated some new thinking on the part of the medical profession concerning primary care. The concrete effects of such new thinking are not yet apparent, although the development of family medicine and community nursing indicate perhaps that it is now beginning to provoke some innovation in existing modes of professional practice.

It is important to emphasize, however, that once the medical profession had reorganized itself and reestablished its alliance with the governmental bureaucracy on a new basis, that is, when the CLSCs had ceased to be useful in the realignment of power between the medical profession and the bureaucratic rationalizers, the CLSCs were more or less put aside by the Ministry of Social Affairs. Fewer and fewer CLSCs were created and their role was redefined; they became functional units to fill the gaps left by other institutions responsible for providing health and welfare services. This led many people to believe, despite indications to the contrary, and even if the game is not yet over,[16] that the quest for a renewal in medical practice and in the organization of health and social services had failed.[17]

The departments of community health (DSCs) represented an upgrading of the roles and functions of community health. Specialists in public health, who formerly had very little prestige within the medical profession, saw their authority and salaries increase considerably. They became the medical spokespersons for the state, with the tasks of public information, health education, community service, and disease prevention.

The regional councils for health and social services (CRSSSs) started a dialogue between hospital administrators and the public. Directors of the different health and social service institutions were forced to sit around the same table and negotiate the allocation of resources among institutions in a given region. For the first time, the "éminences grises" were obliged to present themselves in public, partly because the central bureaucracy simply can no longer handle such problems alone.

Finally, with the creation of the Québec Professions Board (OPQ) and the new Code of Professions, the professional corporations, which have responsibility for managing their respective professions, were forced to argue among themselves the domains of their professional procedures and thus to hammer out definitions of their professional territories. In addition, in forcing the professions to clearly distinguish between public protection (a function theoretically assigned to the professional corporations) and the defense of the economic interests of the profession (a function theoretically assigned to the professional associations), many disagreements between the associations and the corporations were forced out into the open.

In short, the creation of these diverse organizations constituted, in a manner of speaking, the introduction of a Trojan horse into the battle over the organization and administration of medical practice. Though the battle is not yet over, if there is one reasonably certain impact of the reforms it is the establishment of a new power alignment in the area of health care. A new center of power has emerged, the state, and it now defines many of the rules of the game.

The Introduction of a Productivist Logic

Until the end of the sixties the health care sector had evolved almost entirely in response to market forces. It responded to changes in medical technology, to the population's growing demand for medical care, and to the interests of the principal entrepreneurs in the health sector: doctors, the hospital industry, and manufacturers of pharmaceutical as well as medical equipment. Even the government's program of hospital insurance (established in 1960 in Québec) did not change this situation.

By 1970, however, when the medical care insurance program was implemented, the economic climate had changed. The federal as well as provincial governments were more aware of spiraling increases in health care costs. A few years later the economic crisis exacerbated the problem. Quite independently of political opinion, the state was forced to assume a central role in the allocation of health resources. It tried to change significantly the traditional model of private entrepreneurship that had always governed medical practice. The state replaced the market. Traditional laissez faire was replaced by a logic of economic efficiency.

Indicators of this new logic of economic efficiency can be seen first of all in the administrative vocabulary that, with the arrival to power of Castonguay and his team, replaced the references to "quality of care," "excellence," and "devotion" that had dominated in the preceding era. Instead, there are new "objectives," "programs" to accomplish them, and "evaluations" of these programs. These are conceived in relation to "geographic territories" and "target populations." Attempts are now made in health care as well as in social services to distinguish between "primary" services, specialized "secondary" services, and ultraspecialized "tertiary" services. In short, a new vocabulary has emerged, a technocrat's vocabulary, whose common denominator is the realization that the health care system is an industry and should in consequence be run like an efficient industry, that is, according to administrative decisions based on statistical criteria of rates of return and productivity. Popular usage has not lagged far behind in this change. The newspapers recycle the industrial vocabulary without delay. Articles appear in the press about "budget cuts" in the hospitals; "fiscal budgetary constraints" in institutions, and resulting layoffs; the "merger" of various services or the change in "vocation" of various hospitals or services.

This new, industrial logic has become evident also in the socioeconomic composition of the administrative personnel. Whereas at the end of the sixties, doctors, nurses, and religious communities had, for all practical purposes, control of health care institutions, since then it is the economists, accountants, demographers, epidemiologists, operations researchers, certified administrators, and sociologists who staff the growing number of research institutes, as well as the ministry and the regional centers. They are the ones who set the tone of governmental policies, to the great chagrin of the former power brokers.[18]

Finally, this logic can be found in governmental policies, rules, and directives. In effect, since the reforms, the same basic principle has always been at work: deliver the required services to those needing them with a minimum of delay and with the least expenditure. Thus, hospitals have tried and continue to try—not without problems—to restructure themselves. Functional hierarchies of services are generally established. There are efforts to achieve greater complementarity between institutions and between types of institutions, as well as precise contractual ties when this is possible. In addition, strict controls are being developed concerning the length of hospital stays, and programs such as one-day surgery and home care are being developed to reduce length of stays to a minimum. Finally, there is now a proliferation of rules governing the purchase of high technology equipment and the recruitment of additional personnel.

Similarly, there are efforts to modify methods and criteria for hospital finance. Previously, budgets were most often approved on a line item basis, with no general overview of the hospital sector and its growth. Today, with increasingly rigid constraints, new incentives, new methods for setting hospital budgets (for example, budgetary base review), and new techniques for financial management, administrators are forced to produce the same amount with fewer financial resources.

This, according to the labor unions, leads inevitably to a quest for maximum efficiency in personnel management, to the detriment of the human side of care and of job satisfaction. Thus, the most specialized personnel are assigned to those tasks requiring the greatest expertise. When work can be done by less skilled or lower paid employees, the division of labor is reorganized if local conditions permit it. Following the enactment of the Professional Code (1973), the professional corporations sought to define the specific areas of expertise for each of the twenty professional groups. This is supposed to insure that the jurisdictional confines of each profession are specified and that expectations, and levels of responsibility, productivity, and eventually remuneration, are carefully defined. The wage scales for the different categories of workers, including doctors, are now the object of formal negotiations between government representatives and worker and professional trade unions. Admission requirements to professional schools and licensing practices have also become the object of negotiations between the professional corporations, the universities, and the ministries concerned. In addition, records are kept of medical procedures performed by each doctor in order to eliminate procedures defined as unnecessary. These records are monitored by the committees of professional corporations as well as hospital and government agencies. In certain hospitals this data is even stored in information retrieval systems to insure, on a daily basis, the optimum utilization of nurses' work. Some characterize this as the beginning of taylorism in professional hospital work.[19]

All in all, and this is certainly not a phenomenon unique to Québec, what has characterized state intervention is a break with the artisanal past and the ushering of the health care system into the modern era. In being forced to pass from "feudalism" to "capitalism," the health sector has been subjected to the productivist logic that underlies the development of other sectors of industrial production. By a reversal of perspectives, which history has witnessed time and again, we see that, in the quest to achieve a more just and more equal society, the objectives of economic efficiency can prevail sometimes at the expense of justice and equality.[20]

A New Morality in Health

Since the twenties there has been a social movement that has demanded equal access for all to the fruits of discoveries in medicine. It is in response to this movement that the Canadian provinces introduced hospital and medical care insurance during the sixties and seventies and has gradually extended coverage. The movement has never questioned the intrinsic value of contemporary medicine. Quite the opposite, it has considered medicine one of the great accomplishments of humanity. What it has desired is benefit for all without distinction by income, age, or place of residence.

During the seventies, however, at least in North America, another fundamental movement began to take shape. The issue was no longer just improper distribution or inequitable access to health care. The legitimacy of medicine itself came to be questioned. What had been unanimously praised since the beginning of the century now came under scrutiny. A number of consumer groups as well as numerous studies began to expose prejudices in medical diagnosis and therapy based on class and sex.[21] The growing medicalization of social problems and the technology-intensive and dehumanized nature of health care were denounced. Also, health professionals were criticized for eroding the autonomy of their patients and for the negative effects of therapeutic labeling. The incapacity of modern medicine to cure people of the major killer diseases despite ever increasing expenditures was also pointed out. Finally the basic etiological principles of medicine were questioned from the perspective of their scientific and ideological foundations.

In a curious coalition, scientists, workers' movements, and business interests began to express their disillusionment with the dominant hospital and technology based medicine. Using different arguments and despite their sometimes diametrically opposed interests, consumer groups, critics of psychiatry, feminists, epidemiologists, ecologists, defenders of nonconventional kinds of medicine, groups of doctors and nurses, and even upper-level executive, as well as some government bodies, joined together to provoke a veritable "cultural crisis of medicine."[22] What was in question was less the fact that medicine had not made itself accessible to all, as was the case in previous decades. The accusation was aimed at the scientific foundations of medicine itself, its paradigm, its view of the body, and its vision of sickness and health. The medical perception of the causes of mental and physical health and sickness were found to be too narrow. Therapy and the approach to illness was considered too technical. The values and the behavior models advanced by medicine were seen as biased.

It was in this ideological climate that the Castonguay-Nepveu Commission delivered its report in 1970. Although it could not have been foreseen at the time, the appearance of this new social movement gave a different significance to the recommendations of the commission and its subsequent reforms than that orginally intended by the reformers. Whereas the reformers had wished simply to rationalize the health care system on the basis of new broad principles, the ideological context was such that the concept of holistic medicine and, in particular, the issue of prevention came to have a social relevance that no one could have foreseen. For example, several CLSCs, modeling themselves on the early "people's clinics," tried to improvise diverse forms of social and political action to act upon the largely social causes of illness. As a result, public authorities felt their position threatened and saw the need to impose stricter controls and directives.

With the reform, diverse professions came to define themselves as the champions of disease prevention. Thus, social workers, general practitioners, and nurses redoubled their efforts to develop new models of intervention (e.g., community organization, family medicine, community nursing) and gave themselves new roles and tasks. More and more conscious that living conditions were as important as viruses and bacteria in the etiology of illness, and aware of the limits of their therapeutic arsenal (medication and surgery), a growing number of general practitioners began to inform their patients of the risks associated with living conditions and the danger of overconsumption of medication. State reformers, professional groups, and protest groups began to talk more of prevention and to praise the reforms that sought to change the approach to health and illness.

The emergence of this prevention ideology played indirectly into the hands of those who were faced with rising costs and who wanted to impose a productivist logic based on criteria such as costs and benefits. Thanks to the emphasis on prevention, it became legitimate to defend a more limited idea of the hospital. Originally the principal line of defense against illness, the hospital was now to be seen as the last and ultimate barricade society erects to protect itself against illness. In this context the federal ministry of Health published a widely known document, whose central ideas were to be taken up somewhat later in other countries: *A New Perspective on the Health of Canadians*, commonly known as the Lalonde report. The report maintains:

> For these environmental and behavioral threats to health, the organized health care system can do little more than serve as a catchment net for the victims. Physicians, surgeons, nurses and hospitals together spend much of their time in treating ills caused by adverse environmental factors and behavioral risks. It is evident now that further improvements in the environment, reductions in self-imposed risks, and a greater knowledge of human biology are necessary if more Canadians are to live a full, happy, long and illness-

free life. . . . These problems cannot be solved solely by providing health services but rather must be attacked by offering the Canadian people protection, information and services through which they will themselves become partners with health professionals in the preservation and enhancement of their vitality.[23]

What underlies the report is the desire to widen the dominant etiological model of illness. The new notion includes not only internal metabolic variables but also psychic and somatic variables, as well as factors related to individual behavior and the external environment. Although new laws established ways of better protecting the public against pathogenic agents in the environment and in working conditions, what is striking is that despite all of these provisions, it is still necessary to devote an incredible amount of human energy and financial resources on measures to change individual pathogenic life-styles. The antituberculosis campaign has been succeeded by a veritable crusade against tobacco, alcohol, obesity, and all other individual behavior shown by research in epidemiology to be potentially dangerous to health.

If one is to believe government publicity and the practices of the professional groups who have now become the champions of prevention, the good citizen of the eighties is defined according to health criteria. He gets up in the morning, weighs himself, and eats a balanced breakfast following the guidelines of a nutritionist. At work he avoids tension and refuses cigarettes offered him by his colleagues (or better yet becomes a militant antismoker). He takes at least an hour lunch break at noon and eats a proper meal containing the right amount of calories and no alcohol; and if he has a hunger attack in the afternoon, he eats some fruit instead of buying the fat and sugar rich products available from vending machines. Returning from work, and taking care to fasten his seat belt and not to lose patience in traffic jams, he stops off at a fitness club at least every other day to do some jogging. His evening meal is a balance of meat, fish, vegetables, and fresh fruit. Before retiring for his minimum eight-hour sleep he listens to soft music and does relaxation exercises. On weekends he tries to exercise and relax more. From time to time he undergoes tests appropriate to his age and condition following orders from his doctors, who keeps a complete medical record on his family history.

A French journalist intrigued by this phenomenon in Québec, where "one must keep fit," wrote:

> Take care of yourself, work on your health, don't count on state aid, return to the good old principles of hygiene—could Orwell be wrong? Contrary to what the author of 1984 imagined, in the West Big Brother seems to have a tendency to abandon his bothersome solicitude and to put down his arms: "Sorry boys I just don't have the means. . . " Very well. Except that perhaps one sees in Québec more clearly than in France the first symptoms of a new ideology. Will the ascetic ideal, which the priest has given up on in the name of God, now be preached to us by professional hygienists in the name of Health? No drinking, no smoking, no overindulgence in food. The rude discipline of physical effort for the body. . . It is as if eternal damnation was a less fearful prospect than high cholesterol or high blood pressure.[24]

This new morality in health has led some to say that in Québec, by a happy combination of circumstances, health policy has replaced illness policy. There is a tendency to forget, however, that an important semantic shift is taking place regarding the vision of health. Ten or fifteen years ago one spoke of the "right to health" in demanding a collective plan of redistribution of revenues to achieve quality care available to all. Now this slogan takes on a different meaning. "Right" has become "duty"; each individual must maintain his health by exercise, abstention from tobacco, moderate consumption of alcohol, proper eating, wearing a seat belt, periodic medical tests, and a series of other measures that the individual must always initiate. Whereas the "right to health" derived from the principle that people have the right to be sick and to be properly treated, now people suddenly have the "duty to be healthy."

Ten years ago the state was practically encouraging its citizens to increase their consumption of medical services through the development of hospital and medical care insurance programs. Now it seems to be saying the opposite: they must reduce consumption. This impression is reinforced by the following developments: the policy of rationalization applied to the organization of health care; budget cuts in hospitals; and health promotion campaigns. The new order is, "Take care of yourself"—with the help of a vast series of new experts (physical education specialists, nutritionists, gerontologists, behavior modification and relaxation specialists, etc.). In other words, the notion of risk itself seems to have changed meaning. Whereas the Castonguay-Nepveu Commission and the social movements that backed it invoked "risks" and said that we must be protected against them by a policy of collective solidarity (i.e., insurance programs), the ideological context and the financial constraints of the state seem now to have given this notion the meaning of "risk factors." Moral responsibility is imputed to the individual, that is, as some American sociologists say, the victim is blamed.[25]

WHAT HAPPENED?

What is remarkable in the process of change in Québec's health care sector are the shifts and displacements in the goals and stakes, as well as the fluctuations in alliances and ideologies. From the time of the Castonguay-Nepveu Commission report to the present, there has been a transformation that no one could have foreseen. Whereas the issue of health costs was formerly perceived as intrinsically linked to the principle of redistributive justice, cost control is now becoming the standard criterion for making decisions, with too little reference made to justice and equity. Administrative decentralization was advocated to permit an optimum adjustment of the health care system to local conditions; but now the governmental bureaucracy attempts to centralize everything, except in those increasingly numerous cases where it admits its inability to act without the participation of the local population. Whereas participation by beneficiaries and workers in the decision making process of administrative councils was to be desired and encouraged, now the bureaucratic rationalizers are monopolizing the largest share of power and discouraging popular participation. Whereas it was hoped that the obligations and privileges of the diverse professional health care groups would be equalized somewhat, there is now an increase of professionalism in public aid programs and a race for acquisition of higher professional status. The rules of the game have been rationalized, but no real change has occurred in the respective status of the different professional groups concerned. And whereas it was hoped that prevention would become an instrument of the collective fight against illness, victim blaming has now become almost state policy.

What is important is this mutation, which could be illustrated by further examples, is that a new social contract is now being negotiated in the field of health care, a contract whose terms are beginning to appear clearly. To properly understand these terms, the evaluation of the health care sector must be placed in the context of the general evolution of capitalism as a mode of economic organization in Québec.

An effort must be made to place these changes in context in order to understand why health problems have become problems of administrative management and politics; why the state, in seeking to absorb civil society and its attendant social dynamics has intervened complacently, even narcissistically, to establish a new balance of power in decision making; why the state has sought to submit the organization of health care to a productivist logic; and why, trying to shift health problems to a different domain, it is imposing new norms and new values on the relationships of individuals to their bodies.

It can be said that the evolution of capitalism in the last century has been characterized by the extension of market relations to more and more diverse aspects of human behavior—including, since the Second World War, health care. Another trend has been the gradual introduction of these relations into the logic of development of big capital. Finally, there is a qualitative change in the way the state manages a society in which such relations establish themselves. Let us examine, in turn, the impact on health care of these different aspects of the evolution of capitalism.

The Extension of Market Relations to Health Care

Industrial capitalism started with the production of a limited number of common consumer goods (food, clothing, and other domestic products). Then, capitalism gradually affected an ever increasing number of aspects of life. People left domestic industry to become paid workers for companies whose size did not stop growing. More and more goods were produced by industry, and the intended market for these goods has grown to a global scale. Increasingly, relations between individuals and between groups no longer operate as direct human relations of reciprocal exchange, but, by the intermediary of the market, they are indirect, mediated by buying and selling. Market relations are substituted for more personal and communal relations. As Harry Braverman has said:

> Thus the population no longer relies on social organizations like the family, friends, neighbors, the community, elders, or children, but with few exceptions, it must have recourse to the market not only for food, clothing, and housing, but also for its leisure, security, childcare, and care for the aged, sick, and handicapped. Gradually, it is not only the satisfaction of material needs and services which come from the market, but also the more intimate structures of life.[26]

Since they are occupied with working far from home, people have less and less time to take care of others. Thus, institutions that deliver services have emerged to define and respond to human needs. Gradually these institutions have been transformed. For example, hospitals were once asylums for the indigent but now are vital centers of mod-

ern technology; charitable institutions have been transformed into highly professionalized firms delivering social
services; and hospices for the aged, once very unpopular,
have become desirable living quarters for a growing number of senior citizens. As the service market organizes and
extends itself everywhere, entire sections of the population
find themselves dependent on it for survival—the sick, the
handicapped, the poor, and the aged.

After the war, with the prodigious development of medical technology, pharmacology, and specialized medical as
well as paramedical practice, the "health care sector" entered massively into the era of industrial capitalism. In the
last few decades, health care problems have been transformed almost completely into specific consumer problems
involving a whole line of commodities and services for
specific economic markets. Good health, as well as recovery
from illness, has come to mean good consumerism.[27]
Michel Bosquet has eloquently pointed out the implications
of this transformation.

> We are surrounded by a material environment and a system
> of social relations which rob us of our identities and reduce
> to a minimum our powers of self-determination, expres-
> sion, and growth. All aspects of our life are subject to the
> same unifying, standardizing, and depersonalizing force.
> Our needs, the products we buy, and how we spend our
> leisure time are all imposed upon us from the outside. Our
> thoughts are dictated by an unending stream of propo-
> ganda, and we mouth words that are not our own.
> Hundreds of counselors besiege us with their stereotyped
> messages and teach us what is good for us.
>
> And when our bodies (that is to say our selves) have been
> lashed about like a cork in the sea by an incoherent and
> disordered life, they give out; but we are soon snatched up
> by another unifying and standardizing apparatus: the
> medical-hospital machine.
>
> In the hospital we are again, for our welfare (of course),
> forbidden to think, to express ourselves, or to exist by
> ourselves. For the system, we are illnesses and not patients,
> not a body that enjoys, gives birth, protests, or suffers, but

an assembly of organs that is examined to find the infection, the precise disorder that must be remedied. (This is the price of efficiency.) Leave it to the specialist, he can fix it. Like any broken machine returned to the factory, our body will be moved from station to station, passed before different machines, and finally fixed by an operation we do not understand so it can resume its "normal operation" as a part of the great social machine.[28]

Like other human activities in the past, after the war, people's health entered the orbit of production, distribution, and consumption. This circuit is not called "the health market"—that would disturb our humanist values—but instead "the health care sector," or the "health care system." People are confronted in their intimacy by a group of professionals whom they have learned to trust; and they are subjected to a cognitive despotism. Their lives have become more and more subject to the order and the particular vision of the medical elites, whose therapeutic efficacy is much less evident than at the time of the struggle against infectious disease.[29]

The Insertion of Market Relations in the Logic of Capital Development

Having become an economic sector for production and consumption like any other sector, the health sector has become industrialized in the strictest sense. It has become a vast industry that must respond to the logic of capital development and to the needs of large firms producing medical equipment and pharmaceuticals. As has been documented for the economy in general by S. A. Marglin[30] and H. Gintis,[31] and for health care by V. Navarro,[32] J. B. McKinlay,[33] S. Reverby,[34] M. Sarfatti-Larson,[35] and others, this industrialization of health care provision has very specific consequences: the logic of capital accumulation entails—almost inevitably—a growing bureaucratization of management and, eventually, some degree of proletarianization of the work force.

As medical care has been provided with the aid of increasingly sophisticated machines, instruments, and medications, and as the biomedical sciences have improved in a symbiotic fashion, there have been higher production costs; an increased concentration and development of administrative and regulatory agencies; and a division and specialization of labor. In North America, rising health care costs for consumers have led to strong public demands for subsidized medicine (i.e., tax-supported medical programs). This is what the Canadian government responded to by subsidizing some health programs and enacting health insurance programs. This has allowed the new coordinators of "progress"—the bureaucratic rationalizers—to appear. Faced with a crisis created by the perception of runaway costs, they first had to concentrate on the task of containing and rationalizing the growth of the health sector, despite their initial desire for change and their ideals. Since labor amounts to seventy percent of hospital costs, their first effort was an attempt to codify and systematize—in short to rationalize—human labor.

As a consequence, as was the case in other industrial sectors at the beginning of the century, there has been a process of labor equalization, dequalification, and taylorization. In short, the work force has been to some degree proletarianized. Even doctors are subject to this process. When one considers the reduction of their professional autonomy (with regard to the object, the tools, the means, and the remuneration of their work), the growing controls imposed over physicians (upon admission to medical school, in the course of their training, as well as later on, in hospital and government bureaucracies), and the transfer of their tasks to lower-paid professionals, one is forced to admit that doctors, in spite of their privileges, are following, in part, the same route as artisans of the previous century. As for other categories of workers, the fact that they are so desperately seeking the symbolic attributes of professional status is perhaps an indication of the advanced degree of dequalification in their line of work.

Health care workers constitute a well-educated section of the population which knows how to use slogans, mobilize energies, and manipulate political parties to its advantage. Perhaps the process of proletarianization will cease the day that some of these workers, doctors in particular, will have lost those attributes that appear feudal to a better educated, well informed population and that seem to camouflage deep inequalities to those who are less well paid than doctors. One thing is certain: although the class rank of professionals may not visibly change, the insertion of the health sector into the logic of capital development—and the consequent bureaucratization—will lead to a sharp reduction in the privileges professionals have cherished over the last century. The assembly line, perhaps, will not be their fate, but further division of labor will occur, and they will become no more than pawns on a vast chessboard over which they are increasingly losing control.

The New Role of the State

When recovery from illness as well as good health became linked with the buying and selling of commodities and services, the state, whose traditional role was to manage society and assure social harmony and economic growth, was forced to intervene from time to time. On occasion it was necessary for the state to protect the market (e.g., by defining what was legitimate professional practice and what was not). It was also necessary for the state to subsidize the market (e.g., through hospital construction programs); to replace it entirely (e.g., through public health programs); or to protect citizens from the dangers of the market (e.g., through laws on working conditions in hospitals). But overall these interventions were only temporary or punctual. They did not lead to a replacement of the market by the state.

As the costs of providing health care became increasingly socialized through the major insurance programs, and as the administration of the health sector became increasingly bureaucratized, the state began to assume a predominant role. In Québec, because of the particular nature of class relations (described earlier in this essay), and in contrast to what happened in the other provinces and the United States, the state clearly relegated the market to a secondary role and became itself the principal allocator of resources. For all intents and purposes it is the state that dictates to hospitals, social service agencies, hospices, and a whole series of service organizations, how they should be organized, whom they should treat, and in what numbers. With its reimbursement policies the state establishes a hierarchy of medical procedures. With its insurance programs for the aged and needy, it influences the choice of pharmaceutical products. The state submits the health care sector to a logic of efficiency and productivity. In like manner the state demands of its citizens, in the name of a new health morality, that they maintain their health so as not to drive up costs in the medical sector to the detriment of other sectors of the economy. Social order is thus maintained.

The first chapter of this book, as well as the work of O'Connor,[36] Habermas,[37] Offe,[38] and others has supported the view that there has been a qualitative change in the role of the state in the industrialized nations. This has occurred in different manners and at different rates according to the country concerned. Overall, however, we see a shift in the role of the public sector. Whereas, initially its role was to manage and prevent crises originating in the private sector, the public sector, itself, has gradually become the site in which crises erupt and have to be resolved or prevented. From its traditional role of regulator of social tensions, the state has become the leader in the imposition of a new social order.

This is what seems to have happened in Quebéc. We have traced the historical movement by which health problems have become problems of consumption, and subsequently, problems of administrative and political management. In this process the Québec state intervened so that service institutions, as well as the populaton could adjust to the new industrial era. Like Narcissus investing all his libido in himself, the state employed all the means at its disposal. It manipulated ideals and progressive ideologies, coopted new social practices, and defined new rules of the game for various groups (always ready to abandon them later). In so doing, the state imposed its presence and initiated changes on a scale perhaps without parallel in other industrialized countries. By an incredible tour de force the Québec state succeeded in pushing back the market and in subordinating civil society so as to make the organization of the health care system compatible with the exigencies for expansion of a dependent and fluctuating economy. This was accomplished without creating too much disturbance at a time when technocratic control had become irreversible and when support for protest groups had begun to weaken.

CONCLUSION

Up until now we have spoken of the state as if it were a monolithic block suffering despite itself the constraints of its environment and manipulating ideologies and social movements whenever it wishes. If it is true that during the last two decades the relations between the Left and the Right, to speak in simplistic terms, were structured in a way to allow state intervention, then in the years to come the structure of these relations will probably involve a reversal or, at the least, a slowing down of this tendency.

In the sixties and at the beginning of the seventies, the social democratic vision of a welfare state that was both generous and strong was shared by several groups. Among them were the labor movement, whose base was increasing in numbers and militancy; consumer organizations which demanded stricter state control in product quality and services; and the feminist movement, which demanded equality for women in the job market. There were also many intellectuals who had undertaken the mission of mobilizing and organizing working-class districts or even developing new social designs for society. Finally, the "peace-and-love" generation shared in this vision of a more just and equal society.

In Québec, these movements took on a larger meaning and importance because an entire social class, the new French-speaking middle class, aspired to prestigious and well-paid jobs, which only the state could supply. In this context, most political parties could only encourage state interventionism. With the exception, perhaps, of the government led by the Union Nationale party between 1966 and 1970, we can say that every party in power since 1960 has had pretensions of embarking upon grand reforms and has proclaimed innovative social programs all based on the premise that the state should assume greater importance in the administration of civil society. Faced with this unusual alliance, the Right, usually hesitant before policies inspired by social democratic ideals, could not but agree to the growth in state interventionism, which was necessary in any case to maintain social harmony.

Today, the situation has significantly changed. The Right, acquiescent as it was, has become aggressively reactionary due to the prolonged economic crisis. It has become the champion of a return to the market as allocator of resources. The Right hopes, with a certain nostalgia, that a return to the apparently natural laws of supply and demand wil recreate the social dynamics that have been smothered somewhat by the various social programs of the state.

As for a good part of the contemporary Left in Québec, it has little interest in playing the bureaucratic games necessary to gain the resources for the realization of its goals. What is more, it is disillusioned by the failure of socialism and communism in the world. It realizes that its former leaders, who now hold the reins of power, have retained few of the principles of the various social movements. These movements were coopted, and the only demands deemed acceptable were those that led to an increased role for the state. The notion of destroying all forms of hierarchy including the power of the state, was largely ignored. The Left now has a tendency toward introspection, toward the rekindling of traditional struggles, and toward the kinds of state narcissism that such struggles have provoked. Its present program is to increase individual autonomy and create for itself a new world, not by revolting against the state but by achieving independence from it and from civil society as it is presently structured. Among certain social groups there is now a tendency to explain in personal terms what in an earlier period was explained according to impersonal principles. Support for traditional community struggles is disintegrating. Contrary to the philosophy of the sixties, it is no longer thought that collective solutions (which evoke state intervention) can resolve individual problems. Among less disillusioned or more deprived social groups, new social networks are being created. Self-governing production units proliferate and consumer co-operatives are being established. But whether the traditional Left or Right gains power, no one cares; in either case, nothing will change.

These phenomena are nowhere more evident than in the health sector, whose very nature has changed profoundly. As L. K. Zola argues with much insight, since the Second World War medicine has been in the process of replacing religion and law as the principal mechanism of social control.[39] A social worker described this phenomenon in an exceptionally concise manner.

A woman at the beginning of the century admits to her confessor that she isn't happy. The latter replies that she isn't on earth to be happy but to earn a place in heaven by the sweat of her brow and. . . by the steady functioning of her uterus. Today, the same woman wil be told by a health professional, to whom she goes to "confess," that to be happy she has only to know herself better, communicate better, find her place better, and in short, *Be herself*. While waiting to *become herself*, a small prescription: three valium a day, today and forever. If she follows this advice—and she probably will—it is EST, Inc., Marriage Encounter, Inc., Editions de l'Homme, Roche, Inc., and many therapists who will reap the greatest benefit. The confessional kneeling-stool makes way for the therapist's couch, and the imposed penitence is endless self-examination.[40]

Although, as a gift of God, health has never been more than one of the pillars of life, we see that it is now defined by the World Health Organization as a "complete state of physical, mental, and social well-being." In other words, it has come to mean happiness and life itself. At one time the health sector was limited to the hospital, to medical care organizations, and to the conquest of disease. Now a growing number of human problems are explained in terms of sickness and health and are submitted to examination by an apparently neutral and benevolent medical system whose boundaries are becoming impossible to define.

In this context of profound change in the mechanisms of social control and of excessive cooptation by the state, a New Left is being constructed. This New Left is somewhat reminiscent of its sixties counterpart in the United States. The community movements (people's clinics, citizen's committees, etc.) have—with a few rare exceptions—been eclipsed; and union struggles, especially in the hospitals, have lost the popular support they enjoyed not long ago. There is still an extreme Left that tries, for better or for worse, to breathe new life into them, but it has, at the most, only a limited success. What appears to be gaining momentum are those movements (gay rights, environmental, holistic health, new psychotherapeutic, etc.) whose common denominator resides in searching for the self, affirming an identity, and planning for a new society based on radically different premises than our contemporary one.

According to this New Left there can never be a truly different society without the appearance of a new culture and new forms of revolutionary consciousness. What seems to have happened is that the state has emptied society of its substance; the public sector has increasingly policed, even invaded, and controlled the private sector; and life has become increasingly medicalized. As a result, a deeply rooted movement has emerged in society which declares traditional collective struggles illusory. In contrast, this movement proposes that Small is beautiful, and we must destroy hierarchies, reject power struggles—and the ambitions so inevitably associated with them—and return to a state of nature where technology will no longer invade us.

Although it is organized, this New Left still refuses to place itself in the domain of traditional political struggle. Although ecologists, homosexuals, advocates of autosuggestion and alternative therapies, and others are beginning to regroup, their institutions remain outside the mainstream of society. Quite the opposite is happening with the Right in the early eighties. As defensive as it was during the last two decades, it is now becoming militant. In health care, it demands an expansion of private fee-for-service practice, an increase in fees, a reduction of public services, greater professional autonomy, and an increased role for the market mechanism in the allocation of health resources. With the general upsurge in conservatism and a New Left that has temporarily abandoned the idea of political struggle, it is the Right that now is beginning to define the frame of reference for debates.

What will the future bring? The multiplicity of social forces at play, the rapidity and the sometimes unexpected character of change, the complexity of organizational and other structures that condition and limit change—all complicate the picture. Prediction, a fascinating intellectual endeavor, is also a perilous and illusory one. In any event, one thing is certain: it is in the dialectic of a strong Right and a restructured Left that the history of the coming years in Québec will be written. And, whatever groups impose themselves, whatever political parties take power, we will most likely remember the beginning of the eighties as a vast collective therapy to cure ourselves of the narcissism of the state.[41]

NOTES

1. See, for example, Jean-Pierre Garnier and Denis Goldschmidt, "L'Etat, c'est vous," *Le Monde Diplomatique*, February 1979, p. 28; and Alain Bihr, "L'inavouable compromis," *Le Monde Diplomatique*, January 1980, p. 32.

2. Marc Renaud, "Quebec's New Middle Class in Search of a Local Hegemony," *International Review of Community Development*, no. 39–40 (1978), pp. 1–36. What characterizes this new francophone middle class (or in other terms the new *petite bourgeoisie*) is that it suffers systematic discrimination because of the symbolic capital its members bring to the job market. In the economic context peculiar to Québec (a weak economy largely controlled by anglophone interests, lack of geographic mobility to areas outside the province, forced social mobility of Québec's francophone population in the fifties, and since then massive education of the baby boom generation), the Québec francophones who have university educations have identical job capabilities on the job market. In a sense they have a forced vocation toward the public sector and an interest in having the state create interesting and diverse jobs for them.

3. See my, "Reform or Ilusion: An Analysis of the Québec State Intervention in Health," in D. Coburn, et al., *Health and Canadian Society: Sociological Perspectives* (Toronto: Fitzheures & Whitside, 1981) pp. 369–392.

4. For analyses of the Canadian experience, see, among others, Andrew Allentuck, *The Crisis in Canadian Health Care: Who Speaks for the Patient?* (Toronto: Burns & MacEachern, 1978); R. F. Badgley and S. Wolfe, *Doctors' Strike: Medical Care and Conflict in Saskatchewan* (Toronto: MacMillan, 1967) and "The Impact of Canadian Health Insurance and Unresolved Issues of Inequality" (unpublished, 1979); B. R. Blishen, *Doctors and Doctrines: The Ideology of Medical Care in Canada* (Toronto: University of Toronto Press, 1969); Ake Blomquist, *The Health Care Business* (Vancouver: The Fraser Institute, 1979); S. Andreapoulos, ed., *National Health Insurance: Can We Learn from Canada?* (New York: John Wiley and Sons, 1975); *Commission royale d'enquête sur les services de santé*, Hall Commission (Ottawa: Éditeur de la Reine, 1964); Robert Kohn et Susan Radius, "Two Roads to Health Care: U.S. and Canadian Policies, 1945–1965," *Medical Care* 12, no. 3 (1974): 189–201; H. E. MacDermot, *One Hundred Years of Medicine in Canada (1867–1967)* (Toronto: McClelland and Stewart, 1967); J. E. F. Hastings, "Federal-Provincial Insurance for Hospital and Physician's Care in Canada," *Int. J. of Health Services* 1, no. 4 (1971): 398–414; C. H. Shillington, *The Road to Medicare in Canada* (Toronto: Del Graphics, 1972); Lee Soderstrom, *The Canadian Health System* (London: Croom Helm, 1978); Malcolm G. Taylor, *Health Insurance and Canadian Public Policy* (Montreal: McGill-Queens University Press, 1978).

For an analysis of the Québec experience, see, among others: Andreapoulos, *National Health Insurance*; Françoise Boudreau, "Changes in the System for the Delivery of Psychiatric Care in Québec" (Ph.D. dissertation, University of Toronto, 1978); Colloque Jean-Yves Rivard, *La réforme des affaires sociales au Québec: 1970–1980* (Montreal: Éditions Administration et Santé, 1980); Joan Hoffmann, *The Democratization of the Boards of Directors of Anglophone Hospitals in Quebec* (Ph.D. dissertation, McGill University, 1979); Sidney S. Lee, *Québec's Health System: A Decade of Change, 1967–1977* (L'Institut d'Administration Publique du Canada, 1979); Frédéric Lesemann, "Classes dirigeantes et gestion des rapports sociaux: la réforme des services de santé et des services sociaux au Québec" (Ph.D. dissertation, École des Hautes Études, Paris, 1978); Marc Renaud, The Political Economy of the Québec State Interventions in Health" (Ph.D. dissertation, University of Wisconsin, 1976); Jean-Yves Rivard et al., *L'évolution des services de santé et des modes de distribution de soins au Québec* (Gouvernement du Québec, 1970); Yanick Villedieu, *Demain la santé* (Montreal: Québec-Science, 1977).

5. In Québec, for example, while there were only 79 hospitals in 1932 (not including mental institutions) with a ratio of 3.26 beds per 1,000 population, by 1955 there were 122 hospitals with a bed population ratio of 5.2 and in 1970, 187 hospitals with a ratio of 5.96.

6. In Québec for example, whereas in 1932 there were 37.4 admissions per 1,000 inhabitants, in 1955 there were 99.1 per 1,000, and by 1970 the ratio was 123.3. In 1948 only 41.2% of births occurred in hospitals. By 1962 this number passed 95%. Similarly, the number of persons working in the health sector increased: 2.6% of the work force was employed by this sector in 1931, 5.2% in 1961, and 6.0% in 1971. The number of doctors per 1,000 inhabitants also increased from less than one in 1931 to 1.2 in 1961 and 1.8 in 1976; these figures were much higher than the optimum number recommended by the Royal Commission on Health Services for 1991. It must be added that, contrary to the case of the United States more than 50% of Canadian doctors are general practitioners or specialists in family medicine. The number of nurses has also increased from 1.5 per 1,000 in 1931 to 2.4 in 1964, 4.1 in 1971, and 4.5 in 1976.

7. An important element in this change of perception was the publication of the seventh report of the Canadian Economic Council, entitled: *Les diverses formes de la croissance* (Ottawa: Éditeur officiel, 1970).

8. Since the end of the sixties, the federal government has been satisfied with advancing certain ideas. See, in particular, the reports published by the federal government since that time: *Rapport des comités d'étude sur le coût des services sanitaires au Canada*, Willard Report (Ottawa: Government of Canada, 1969); *Le centre de soins communautaires au Canada*, Hastings Report (Ottawa: Éditeur officiel, 1972); *A New Perspective on the Health of Canadians*, Lalonde Report (Ottawa: Government of Canada, 1974).

9. Whereas in 1977 the Federal government paid for about one-half of the expenses for these programs in each province, following a policy favorable to the poorest provinces, in 1977 certain taxes were transferred to the provinces and direct contributions were limited to a percentage based on

the growth of the GNP. Thus, the provinces were left with the entire administrative and financial responsibility for the health care system. See Soderstrom, *The Canadian Health System*.

10. *Rapport de la Commission d'Enquête sur la Santé et le Bien-Etre Social*, Castonguay-Nepveu Report (Québec: Government of Canada, 1967–1973).

11. Sidney, S. Lee, *Québec's Health System: A Decade of Change, 1967–1977* (Montreal: L'Institut d'administration publique du Canada, 1979), p. 52.

12. See, on this subject, Nicole Martin, "Les instruments économiques," in Rivard, *La réforme des Affaires Sociales*, pp. 31–38.

13. Robert R. Alford, *Health Care Politics: Ideological and Interest Group Barriers to Reform* (Chicago and London: The University of Chicago Press, 1975).

14. André Lajoie, "Les instruments juridiques," *La réforme des Affaires Sociales*, p. 15.

15. Frédéric Lesemann, "Qu'est-ce que les CLSC ont produit depuis 5 ans?," *Les CLSC, cinq ans après* (Féderation des CLSC, 1978), p. 9.

16. See on this subject, Marc Renaud et al., "Practice Settings and Prescribing Profiles: The Simulation of Tension Headaches to General Practitioners Working in Different Practice Settings in the Montreal Area," *American Journal of Public Health* 70, no. 10 (October 1980): 1068–1073; Frédéric Lesemann, ed., *La prise en charge communautaire de la santé*, special issue of *Revue Internationale d'Action Communautaire* 1, no. 41 (1979); and Yanick Villedieu, "Les petits pas: des idées et des pratiques nouvelles qui font péniblement leur petit bonhomme de chemin," *Québec-Science* 19, no. 2 (October 1980): 44–49.

17. Several texts have been published on this subject: Denise Couture, "La division du travail en CLSC, *Recherches Sociographiques* 19, no. 2 (1978): 271–280 and "Les médecins et la médecine dans les CLSC," *Recherches Sociographiques* 19, no. 1 (1975): 119–124; Michel Brunet, "Le professionnalisme, obstacle au changement," *Recherches Sociographiques* 19, no. 2 (1978): 251–260; Jean-Louis Gendron, "La structuration du pouvoir dans l'implantation des CLSC en Estrie" (Ph.D. dissertation, Laval University, 1979); G. Divay and J. Godbout, *La décentralisation en pratique* (Montreal: INRS-Urbanisation, 1979); Lesemann, *La Prise en charge communautaire de la santé*; Marc Renaud, "Les CLSC: une utopie nécessaire," *Administration Hospitalière et Sociale* 23, no. 6 (1977): 26–29.

18. Thus one of the most prestigious doctors in Québec wrote:

> Since the economists and sociologists have imposed their concept that medical care is an industry, the fabled health care industry, and have made the economic factor and the cost benefit relation a major concern in the organization and distribution of medical care, "Castongism" has displaced

considerably the essential factors of comprehension, compassion and motivation so important for the quality of health care [*La Presse*, 4 Dec. 1978]. . . . I have never understood how economists, politicians, and sociologists could advance with such assurance into the complex domain of medical care or bio-medical research without even asking themselves if they have the required expertise or knowledge [*La Presse*, 7 Dec. 1978].

It is difficult to accurately measure the number of these directors because of their diffusion in the various institutions of the social service system. As an example, consider these figures. In 1968 the ministry staffs were composed of 32.9% doctors and 13.9% economists and accountants. In 1974, excluding the RAMQ created in 1970, we have 7.4% doctors and 32.6% accountants and economists.

19. François Lamarche and Michel Dore, "L'organisation du travail et les travailleurs," in *La crise et les travailleurs* (Montreal: 1980), pp. 83—91.

20. This reversal in perspectives is especially evident in the anglophone provinces of Canada. In contrast to Québec, they did not negotiate with doctors the conditions for opting out of the health insurance program. Consequently, as a result of budget constraints, a considerable number of doctors have chosen to opt out of the medical care insurance program. In Ontario, for example, the rate of opting out is around 20% and even 100% in certain specialties. In Québec, however, there are few cases of physicians who opt out. Opting out calls into question the redistributive nature of the program because once again the lowest income groups experience the greatest difficulty in receiving health services. See the Hall Commission, *Le programme de santé national et provincial du Canada pour les années '80: engagement ou renouveau?* (Ottawa: Éditeur officiel, 1980).

21. To mention a few: John S. Bradshaw, *Doctors on Trial* (London: Wildwood House, 1979); Rick Carlson, *The End of Medicine* (New York: Wiley, 1975); Ivan Illich, *Nemesis Medicale* (Paris: Seuil, 1975); Thomas Mckeown, *The Role of Medicine: Dream, Mirage or Nemesis?* (Nuffield Provincial Hospitals Trust: Londres, 1976); John B. McKinlay and Sonja McKinlay, "The Questionable Effect of Medical Measures on the Decline of Mortality in the USA in the 20th Century," *Health and Socity* 53, no.3 (1977): 405—428; Vicente Navarro, *Medicine Under Capitalism* (New York: Prodist, 1978); John Powles, "On the Limitations of Modern Medicine," *Science, Medicine and Man* 1, no. 1 (1973): 1—30.

22. This expression belongs to John Ehrenreich, ed., *The Cultural Crisis of Modern Medicine* (New York: Monthly Review Press, 1978).

23. Marc Lalonde, *La nouvelle perspective de la santé des Canadiens* (Ottawa: Editeur Officiel, 1974), p. 6.

24. Huguette Debaisieux, "Québec: tant qu'on a la santé. . .", *L'Express*, 15 December 1979, p. 68.

25. Robert Crawford, "You Are Dangerous to Your Health: The Ideology

and Politics of Victim-Blaming," *Int. J. Health Services* 7, no. 4 (1977): 663–680; Antoinette Chauvenet, *Médecines au choix, médecine de classes* (Paris: PUF, 1978) especially, pp. 213–235.

26. Harry Braverman, *Labor and Monopoly Capital: The Degradation of Work in the Twentieth Century* (New York: Monthly Review Press, 1974).

27. See on this subject, René Dubos, *Man Adapting* (Paris: Payot, 1973).

28. Michel Bosquet, "Plaidoyer pour les médecines douces," *Le Nouvel Observateur* 7, no. 4 (1980): 33.

29. With industrialization, improved living conditions and hygiene as well as discoveries in the field of bacteriology brought about, for all intents and purposes, an end to fatal infectious diseases. At the same time there have been increasing mortality rates from complex diseases. These illnesses, especially cerebro-vascular disorders and cancer, are called "diseases of civilization," because they are not simply degenerative illnesses associated with age but problems created by industrialization and pathogenic life-styles. Despite gigantic resources invested in research and despite specialization, contemporary medicine is largely ineffective in curing these illnesses. In addition, we have seen an increase in number and intensity of a whole series of minor chronic problems— colds, migraines, stomach ailments, backaches, anxiety, insomnia— which, although not mortal and not debilitating, make life miserable. Here again, despite the problems they inflict on society, medicine is really powerless to cure them except perhaps by heavy doses of medicine which may have side effects, or at least further weaken an already fragile organism.

30. S. A. Marlin, "What do bosses do? The Origins and Functions of Hierarchy in Capitalist Production," in Andre Gorz, *The Division of Labour* (Atlantic Highlands, N.J.: Humanities Press, 1976), pp. 13–54.

31. H. Gintis, "Alienation in Capitalist Society," in R. C. Edwards et al., ed, *The Capitalist System* (Englewood Cliffs, N.J.: Prentice-Hall, 1972), pp. 274–284.

32. Vicente Navarro, "The Crisis of the Western System of Medicine in Contemporary Capitalism," *Int. J. Health Services* 8, no. 2 (1978): 179–211.

33. John B. McKinlay, "Towards the Proletarianization of Physicians," Mimeographed (Boston: Boston University, 1980).

34. Susan Reverby, "The Search for the Hospital Yardstick: Nursing and the Rationalization of Hospital Work," in S. Reverby and D. Rosner, ed., *Health Care in America: Essays in Social History* (Philadelphia: Temple University Press, 1979) pp. 206–225.

35. Magali Sarfatti-Larson, *The Rise of Professionalism: A Sociological Analysis* (Berkeley: University of California Press, 1977).

36. James O'Connor, *The Fiscal Crisis of the State* (New York: St. Martins

Press, 1973); and *The Corporations and the State* (New York: Harper and Row, 1974).

37. Jurgen Habermas, *Legitimation Crisis* (Boston: Beacon Press, 1973).

38. Clauss Offe, "The Theories of the Capitalist State and the Problem of Policy Formulation," in Leon Lindberg et al., eds., *Stress and Contradictions in Advanced Capitalism* (Lexington, Mass.: Lexington Books, 1975).

39. Irving Kenneth Zola, "Healthism and Disabling Medicalization," in I. Illich et al., *Disabling Professions* (Marion Bazars, 1977), pp. 41–67.

40. Michel Bourgon, "Echec ou victoire de la psychotherapie: les leçons de l'histoire," mimeographed Montreal, p. 5.

41. See, on this subject, the excellent article of Dimitri Roussopoulos "The Political Origins of the 1960's new Left and the Future," *Our Generation* 14, no.2 (1980): 5–11. In Québec, several factors distinguish the Québec "New Left" from its American counterpart: the national sovereignty question, the more politically aware working classes, the existence of a political partly (the Parti-Québecois) inspired by social-democratic ideals, and the particular structure of the new francophone middle class.

8

Britain: Possible Future
for the National Health Service

Rudolf Klein and Celia Davies

To speculate about the future, it is first essential to understand the past. The first section of this chapter therefore examines the origins and development of Britain's National Health Service, briefly delineating its organization, financing, and aims. The second section analyses the strains—political, organizational, and economic—that became evident in the NHS in the course of the seventies. The third, and last, section looks at some possible policy developments in the eighties, on a variety of assumptions about possible economic and political trends in Britain.

THE HISTORY AND STRUCTURE OF THE NHS

Britain's NHS is unique among the health care systems of the advanced industrial societies of the Western world. It was the first set up to provide a health *service*—as distinct from insurance coverage—for the whole population. That was in 1948, under a labor government. The creation of the NHS was part of a broad commitment in the postwar era to social welfare measures: a commitment which crossed class and party lines. In the field of health, politicians of all parties and the medical profession were agreed that some kind of a national service was both inevitable and desirable, although there was considerable conflict within this broad consensus about the precise nature of the service that should be set up.[1] The agreement reflected a number of factors: the new perspectives opened up by the wartime

206

experience of state intervention in the planning of medical services, the optimism about the possibility of using health services to lower the cost of medical care by improving the population's state of health, and the uneasy awareness of the near bankruptcy of the charity hospitals.

The special contribution of the then Labor minister of health, Aneurin Bevan, was to bring together under the same administrative umbrella the two quite distinct hospital systems that had developed in Britain over the previous century: the independent voluntary (or charitable) sector and the local government sector. At its inception, the NHS was therefore primarily a national hospital service. Primary care—that is, the care provided by general practitioners outside the institutional setting—remained in 1948, and remains today, an independent and largely autonomous enclave. While hospital doctors work in a bureaucratic setting and are paid salaries, general practitioners, in contrast, are independent contractors, paid primarily on a capitation basis. Their status has not been changed by the trend in recent years toward an increased salary element and the introduction of some minor fee-for-service payments. Furthermore, local authorities retained control of some health-related services—notably maternity and child health—thus creating problems of overlap and coordination but also creating some scope for consumer choice for those who understood and could manipulate the system.

The NHS was designed to be, and remains, a service financed overwhelmingly out of general taxation. Earmarked social security contributions and direct payments by patients are relatively insignificant: in 1978–79 the former contributed less than ten percent of total NHS revenue, and the latter contributed a mere two percent.[2] The guiding principle behind the creation of the NHS was that it should provide service free of charge at the point of delivery. Although that principle has been breached, charges to patients have remained marginal both individually and in total. Small payments have to be made by patients for such items as prescriptions, spectacles, and dental treatment, but large categories of the population—such as the elderly and young children—are automatically exempt. For example, by 1977 more than sixty percent of the prescriptions issued were to patients who did not have to pay.[3]

The insistence of the postwar Labor government on a free service was part of a larger commitment to the principle of guaranteeing equality of access to health care. The only criterion for the use of health services was to be need; the recognition of the problematic nature of this concept came only later. There was to be equality of access, irrespective of financial circumstance and geographical location. The distribution of health care resources—hospitals, general practitioners, and local authority services—inherited by the NHS in 1948, was markedly uneven. "It is one of the tragedies of the situation," Bevan told parliament when introducing his legislation, "that very often the best hospital facilities are available where they are least needed." The object of setting up a national service, he further argued, was to ensure that an "equally good service is available everywhere."[4] Thus, the achievement of equality in the distribution and use of resources was one of the main aims of the NHS from the start: an aim which has never been subsequently challenged, although there has been growing awareness of the conceptual difficulties of defining equality and, in particular, of moving toward equity.

Although the NHS was, from the first, designed as a national service to cover the entire population, it was not intended to be a monopoly provider of health care, nor has it become one. There is no limitation on either the right to practice or the right to seek medical treatment in the private sector. The private sector has remained small and marginal, however. In the mid-seventies spending on private health care accounted for only five percent, or so, of the NHS's budget. Although something like 2.5 million people—one in twenty of the population—are covered by private insurance (mainly corporate plans taken out by employers), the private sector tends to supply a specialized form of medical treatment, excluding both chronic and high technology medicine.[5]

Both the financial and the ideological foundations of the NHS lead to the same organizational consequence: centralization. Control tends to follow money, and one of the main themes of policymaking in the past thirty years has been that since central government effectively provides all the NHS's money, it must also exercise a detailed check on the way funds are spent. Similarly, the emphasis on the principle of equality encourages and justifies central control; for, how is it possible to bring about a more equal geographical distribution of resources unless central government acts as a rationing agent? Indeed, one of the main arguments used by Bevan in justifying his decision to set up a national service, instead of transferring control to local government, was precisely that local control would perpetuate inequalities between poor and rich parts of the country. Finally, under the British constitutional system, the secretary of state for social services (or the minister of health, as he was called until 1969) is answerable to Parliament for everything that happens in the NHS. For example, he can be questioned by Members of Parliament about what happens to individual patients. Once again this tends to reinforce central control over the periphery.

In practice, the principle of centralized control is circumscribed by three factors: the limits of administrative capacity, the availability of cognitive tools, and the autonomy of the medical professions.[6]

THE LIMITS OF ADMINISTRATIVE CAPACITY

The NHS is a vast and very heterogeneous organization currently employing some one million people. One of the dilemmas of central government is therefore how to retain the right of detailed intervention and control over strategic policymaking while divesting itself of responsibility for day-to-day management. From the start, responsibility for the detailed managment of services was delegated to a series of nominated boards, whose role has been to "act as the agents" (to use Bevan's phrase) of the center. Further complicating the task of central control has been the independent status of general practitioners and the existence of local authority controlled services. In addition, the 1948 model NHS gave teaching hospitals an autonomous status outside the administrative hierarchy of the rest of the health service.

The administrative history of the NHS can therefore be summed up in part as an attempt to make central control more effective while avoiding organizational overload at the center. In 1948, the Ministry of Health was a weak department that lacked outstanding civil servants and was conspicuously deficient in economic and statistical expertise. The departmental ethos was that of laissez faire: there was a reluctance to dictate to the periphery and a bias toward incremental planning. Ministerial circulars were often ignored by the field authorities or kept "continuously under review."[7]

It was not until the 1960s that this style of control began to change. This was the decade when planning became fashionable in Britain: when, for example, the 1964 National Plan was produced in imitation of the French planning system. And this enthusiasm for planning was reflected in the NHS. The Ministry of Health began to employ statisticians and economists. Indeed, in 1962 it had already produced the Hospital Plan:[8] a blueprint for a capital investment program for the provision of hospital beds, based on explicit norms and designed to bring about a rational and equitable distribution of new capital resources. Finally, a series of proposals for reorganizing the NHS were put forward, which were eventually implemented in an amended form with the 1974 reorganization of the NHS.[9] The intention of this scheme was to create a more rational bureaucratic structure and to facilitate planning by incorporating general practitioner services, some of the relevant local authority services, and the teaching hospitals within the same hierarchical administrative structure. It has since been criticized, however, for creating excessive bureaucratic complexity and failing to end the autonomous status of general practice.[10]

THE AVAILABILITY OF COGNITIVE TOOLS

In Britain, as elsewhere, the problems of administrative control and central planning have been aggravated by the nature of the cognitive tools available to policymakers. There are no simple macroindicators of performance (such as return on capital) in a health service. There are, in addition, severe conceptual problems involved in devising criteria for rationing resources. On the one hand, it is difficult to devise indicators of need.[11] On the other hand, although it is possible to change the distribution of resources (for example, since the fifties the NHS has tried to control and plan the distribution of medical manpower, i.e., general practitioners and hospital consultants), it is virtually impossible to control the output or outcomes resulting from resource allocation.

THE AUTONOMY OF THE MEDICAL PROFESSION

In 1948 Bevan recognized that it was both politically impossible and organizationally undesirable to attempt to make the medical profession hierarchically accountable. Central government controlled the budgets available to hospital doctors; but the hospital doctors enjoyed, and continue to enjoy, total autonomy within the limits of those budgets.[12] Ironically, they enjoy greater freedom than their counterparts in the United States and elsewhere,[13] since the fixed budget principle means that it is not necessary to try to check spending by means of detailed administrative controls over the actions of individual doctors. Similarly, general practitioners enjoy total autonomy: indeed, the absence of fee-for-service payments means that no one knows what they actually do, and the information required for administrative supervision is virtually nonexistent.

The 1948 model also explicitly recognized that the medical profession should be involved in the administration of the NHS: its representatives were given places at every level of the administrative hierarchy (a principle maintained at the time of the 1974 reorganization). In other words, the implicit premise—amply confirmed by the political activities of the medical profession—was that the NHS could only be administered with the consent of doctors. In practice, they claimed, and were conceded, a veto power over the policies of the NHS. This assertion must be sharply differentiated from simplistic theories of medical domination, however. Under the British NHS, the medical profession is certainly not able to impose its own policies on the government—for example, it has repeatedly been defeated in its attempts to impose its views regarding the level and structure of payments to doctors. It is, however, strategically placed to stop policies not to its liking, and its aims and ideology largely define the parameters of what is thought feasible by policymakers and what therefore appears on the political agenda.

So far, this review of the NHS has concentrated on delineating its main characteristics as they evolved in the fifties and sixties. Before turning to a more specific analysis of the new strains and stresses that appeared during the course of the seventies, it may be helpful to draw up a balance sheet of achievements and failures. The following summarizes the conclusions that might have been drawn about the NHS ten (or even five) years ago.

First, in terms of the original objective of achieving equality in the distribution of resources, the NHS is, at best, a qualified success story. Because of the controls over medical manpower, there is less maldistribution of doctors than in, say, France or the United States—both among different specialties and among different localities. Still, there remain gross inequalities in the distribution of health resources as measured in terms of per capita spending in different parts of the country.[14] The 1962 Hospital Plan has never been fully implemented. In the face of economic stringency, British governments are apt to cut capital spending, and the hospital building program has fallen victim to repeated changes of policy.

Second, in terms of cost containment, Britain's NHS has been a remarkable success story. In the mid-seventies, when the Organization for Economic Cooperation and Development (OECD) reviewed the international situation, Britain was spending 5.2 percent of its gross domestic product (GDP) on health care—slightly below the overall OECD average and well below the figures for France (6.9 percent), Sweden (7.3 percent) and the United States (7.4 percent). Further, taking the period 1962 to 1974, the same survey also shows that the elasticity of spending on health relative to the growth in GDP was considerably lower in Britain than in most other Western countries.[15]

Third, and helping perhaps to explain the incremental pattern of both spending and distribution policies, for most of its existence the NHS has lacked political salience and visibility. No great ideological issues separated the Labor and Conservative parties as far as the NHS was concerned, until the mid-seventies. In theory the two parties have always been sharply divided on the question of direct charges to patients. Nevertheless, though the Labor party has been committed in principle to abolishing all such charges, in practice it has been forced to keep them on grounds of financial expediency; and though the Conservative party has been positively committed to extending charges, in practice the administrative problems and costs of doing so have stopped successive Tory governments from carrying out their intentions.

Fourth, it has followed from the lack of salience of health policy issues that, until recently, policymaking has been largely left to what might be called the medico-bureaucratic alliance. This is not to suggest that the medical profession and the administrators were necessarily in harmony. Indeed, the fifties and sixties were punctuated by battles that often left a sense of bitter antagonism between the two sides. These battles were carried out according to certain accepted rules, however. The differences between the medical profession and the administrative bureaucracy were constrained by a shared agreement that they should not be pushed to the point of endangering the existence of the NHS. The situation was one of conflict within consensus.[16]

Until the 1970s the history of the NHS was characterized by the politics of the closed arena, or the politics of accommodation.[17] The number of actors within the arena was limited: no other group of health workers challenged the supremacy of the medical profession. Outside interest in the NHS was low: as far as the public was concerned, despite the waiting lists, the ancient hospital buildings and the resource poverty of many parts of the country, satisfaction remained high. Consequently in a situation where the existing configuration of resources and power had not yet been challenged, even the modest growth rate of the NHS was large enough to avoid conflict. The pattern of closed arena politics helps to explain both the success and the failure of the NHS: its success in containing costs and its failure to make any radical change in the inherited pattern of resource distribution.

CURRENT STRAINS:
AN EXPANDING POLITICAL ARENA
IN A CONTRACTING ECONOMY

In the 1970s the arena of health care politics in Britain has increasingly opened out. New actors have come onto the stage; new and more militant tactics have been adopted. At the same time, from the mid-seventies onward, the financial situation of the NHS has worsened, reflecting the overall performance of the British economy. The NHS is widely perceived to be in a state of crisis and, for the first time, ideological divisions are beginning to become apparent. On the Right, questions are being asked as to whether Britain can afford a universal, tax-financed health service. On the Left, those who had previously criticized the NHS for its shortcomings are beginning to adopt a militantly defensive stance.

Perhaps the most important factor in the opening up of the health care arena is the trend toward greater unionization—and the more militant strategies adopted by the trade unions. These developments are, to an extent, linked: greater militancy partly reflects the recruiting strategies of unions competing for members. Moreover, the NHS is in no sense unique; the developments in labor relations within it reflect wider societal trends. Strikes in the health service—inconceivable in the fifties and early sixties—have become more frequent. And they have not just been about pay. For example, in 1974 the trade unions put the issue of private practice onto the political agenda and helped to persuade the labor government to legislate about "pay" beds—those beds in NHS hospitals where hospital doctors could treat their private patients.

The medical profession, furthermore, has increasingly adopted trade union tactics. One reason for this is that the British system of centralized control over budgetary totals—while decentralizing responsibility for the way resources are used—means that it is the service providers who have to turn away patients. Thus, for the medical profession the price of freedom of decision making is accepting the blame for saying "No." On occasion, as in the case of patients requiring renal dialysis or transplants, this means turning people away to die because resources are inadequate. Renal dialysis is an example of an area in which Britain provides fewer resources, in proportion to the relevant population, than France and many other Western societies.[18] Compounding the resentment of the doctors is the fact that the profession tends to take its standards from the international medical community. It tends to look at the level of medical technology available in much richer countries and to assume that Britain should be providing the same level of facilities—as well as the same level of rewards for doctors.

The political arena has also been extended as a by-product of the 1974 reorganization of the NHS. This created a wider political arena in a number of ways. First, it conceded representation—on the medical model—to other skill groups among health care workers. In this sense it represented a move towards syndicalism—that is, the institutionalization of producer participation in the decision making cycle. Second, the 1974 reorganization also institutionalized public participation of a sort by setting up community health councils (CHCs).[19] There are some two hundred of these charged with representing consumer or community interests; and they have a statutory right to delay certain changes, such as the closure of hospitals. Thus, there is a new set of actors in the shifting coalitions that now influence policymaking. Moreover CHCs act as a platform for the various pressure groups that have sprung up over the past decade to represent the interests of particular client groups, ranging from the mentally ill and handicapped to psoriasis sufferers.

The 1974 reorganization had several further consequences. Before 1974, the geographical boundaries of the units of health care administration did not correspond to any existing political units. Following reorganization, the boundaries were aligned with those of the local authorities. Health authorities therefore gained in political visibility; there was now a natural constituency. In addition, reorganization in itself gave greater public salience to the NHS: the changes generated widespread discontent within the service, and the loud accusations of "excessive bureaucracy" helped to bring the NHS to the attention of the media and the public.

So much for the expanding political arena of the NHS. The point about the contracting economy hardly needs elaboration; the facts about Britain's economic performance in the second half of the seventies are well known. What needs noting, perhaps, is that the NHS remained largely sheltered from the effects of economic recession for at least the first three years of the 1974–1979 Labor government. Current spending (in volume terms) continued to increase, with the primary pressure for reductions placed on the capital budget for building. In fact, it was the planned rate of expansion in health care spending that was cut, not the actual budgets.

Two factors have contributed to a widespread perception that the service has actually been cut however. On the one hand, there are the demographic trends. Britain's population is aging, and consequently the demands on the NHS are increasing. Simply to maintain the existing level of services while accommodating these extra demands requires a one percent increase (in real terms) in the NHS budget every year. On the other hand, the extension of the political arena has created extra demands. Some of these are demands made by pressure groups on behalf of specific client groups. More importantly however, the opening up of the political arena has been accompanied by—and perhaps was a contributory factor in—the increasing emphasis on achieving the original 1948 aim of an equitable geographical distribution of resources. The principle of incremental resource allocation, characteristic of the era of the politics of accommodation, has been replaced by the principle of differential resource allocation according to need. Following the report of the Resource Allocation Working Party (RAWP) in 1976, a new formula for distributing resources was adopted, based on various dimensions of population characteristics.[20] The RAWP formula identified over and underprovided parts of the country, and the government accepted its recommendations that these inequalities be ironed out.

In a period of economic prosperity, and a rapidly expanding NHS budget, this policy would have been relatively painless. It could have been achieved reasonably rapidly by a policy of differential rates of expansion: everyone would have gained, but some would have gained more than others. Given economic stringency, however, redistribution has meant that some regions of the country have (allowing for demographic factors) been in a position of zero growth, at best. Moreover, a special problem has been encountered in inner-city areas—notably in London—where over the years the population has declined while hospital buildings and resources have remained. It has been felt necessary to cut the allocation of finance to such inner-city areas in order to free resources for the underprovided areas of the country.

The effects of economic stringency, exacerbated by the policies of RAWP, have led to the further politicization of health care issues. Old constituencies have become more militant and new ones have emerged. The threat of hospital closures acts to rally a variety of interest and pressure groups. It is not only trade unions which have adopted militant tactics—strikes and sit-ins—in the attempt to prevent hospital closures and protect the jobs of their members; so have local community groups and members of the medical profession. On occasion the result has been to create unprecedented alliances between consultants, CHCs and trade unions in defense of the status quo.[21] In turn, the radicalization of the unions over local issues reinforces demands for higher pay, increasing the cost to the NHS of any given input of labor. As costs go up, so do the stresses on the NHS budget, making further cuts necessary.

To sum up, then, the situation appears to be one of corporate stalemate[22]—making the NHS a micromodel of the problems that afflict Britain generally. That is, veto power among the producers has multiplied, with the result that decision making has become more costly and slower. The cost-containment strategies of earlier years are no longer as effective in the open political arena. The dynamics have changed markedly; and at a time when considerations of economic efficiency demand flexibility in the reallocation of resources, political forces have made such adjustments more difficult. Economic stringency has catapulted diverse groups into mobilization. Trade unions have supplemented their concern with defending jobs with interest in other issues. Above all, the medico-bureaucratic alliance is under threat; for, it is the logic of financial stringency to question ever more critically the use to which resources are put by the medical profession, particularly in the high cost areas of modern technology. The attempt to apply this logic, however, invades the hitherto sacrosanct arena of professional autonomy and threatens the basis of the implicit concordat between doctors and successive governments on which the NHS is founded.

POLICY OPTIONS IN THE 1980s

Before considering possible future developments in Britain, it may be helpful to outline a very simple model of a publicly regulated health care system. Let us assume that demands for health care of various kinds are generated by the socio-economic system: that this is where ill health is produced. The role of the health care system, in this basic model, is then simply to cope, as best it can, with the demands made on it. The only scope for policy discretion is the kind and level of health care offered (for even if the right to health care is conceded—however dubious such a concept may be in this particular context—this leaves open the question of precisely what it is a right to).

Next, however, let us introduce the possibility of feedback to allow for the fact that the behavior of the health care system is likely to affect demand—that is, the health care system may either encourage or discourage demand and introduce selective barriers to deflect specific kinds of demand. In addition, the health care system may, if it discourages demand sufficiently, externalize the problem; it may redefine a problem as social rather than medical. Such a redefinition may take different forms. So, finally, let us refine the model still further by assuming that the health care system may make demands on the socioeconomic system at the level of either the individual (and his or her family) or the economic sector. In the latter case, the problem is redefined as being the *production* of ill health and the emphasis will be on dealing with it at the point of production.

This model suggests various public policy strategies. In summary form they are as follows:

(i)   *Put the emphasis on a least-cost package of medical care*: that is, try to deal with the cost problem by acting on the mix of health care which is offered. For example, put increased stress on the primary care sector in the hope that this would minimize the need for more expensive and technology-intensive hospital treatment.

(ii) *Discourage demand (at least on the public sector of health care) by putting up barriers to access.* These barriers would be designed to increase the cost to consumers of obtaining health care, either by increasing the time cost (queuing, waiting lists) or by raising the financial cost (charges, cost sharing). If the result were to create a spillover of demand into the private sector, this would not matter, since the problem is perceived as one of how best to finance public expenditure rather than as one of excessive investment of national resources in health care.

(iii) *Redefine medical as social problems*: the demedicalization of health care. Such a strategy would seek to push the burden of care onto the family, the community, and other social services, using financial incentives and other supports (e.g., home help and nurses) to bolster the voluntary sector. The advantage, at least from the point of view of public expenditure management, is that this way many of the costs are invisible, particularly when they are carried by families.

(iv) *Try to reverse the trend whereby the costs of ill health are carried by the health care system rather than by the industrial producers.* Such a strategy would seek to impose the costs of ill health on the producers, to the limited extent that these can be identified. For example, there might be more emphasis on occupational health schemes financed by industry, which would then have to carry a higher proportion of the costs now imposed on the community at large. A more extreme version of this policy would call for the restructuring of, for example, the food industry and tighter controls on profit making in general, in the interests of the protection of health.

Such are the hypothetical strategies that can be derived from our model. Now let us examine the political and economic context in which these policy options will be debated in Britain in the eighties.

The New Political-Economic Context

At present, Britain has an essentially two-party system; but each of the two major parties—Labor and Conservative—is, in effect, a coalition. The Labor party is a coalition of, on the one hand, those who believe in a mixed economy (capitalism modified by significant state intervention and egalitarian social policies) and, on the other hand, those who believe in moving toward a planned economy (capitalism replaced by some form of socialist system). The Conservative party is a coalition of, on the one hand, those who also believe in a mixed economy (but with less state intervention and less egalitarian social policies) and, on the other hand, those who believe in moving toward a competitive market system. The possibility of a realignment of Britain's political parties during the course of the eighties cannot be ruled out. It is possible to conceive of a situation in which the Labor and Conservative parties would lurch toward their radical extremes, and the mixed economy advocates in both parties would join the Liberal party (at present not a significant political force) to create a new political party of the center. In what follows, however, we shall make the simplifying assumption that the structure of the British party system will remain basically unchanged during the coming decade.

As far as the health care system is concerned, few ideological or practical issues separate the mixed economy wings of the Labor and Conservative parties. This reflects the broad political consensus about the NHS that developed in the 1950s and 1960s. It is a consensus that embodies the century-old British tradition of paternalistic state intervention in social policies and which is sustained by the ethos of Britain's administrative elite in the civil service. It is well reflected in the 1979 report of the Royal Commission on the NHS,[23] which endorsed the present structure and recommended only incremental changes.

In examining the attitudes of the radical wings of the two parties, however, sharp ideological cleavages over health care issues become apparent. For Labor radicals, the present system is still an unsatisfactory compromise because of its tolerance of a private sector; indeed the Labor party conference has voted for the abolition of private practice. For the Conservative radicals, the present system is also an unsatisfactory compromise because it gives only a residual role to the private market. Hence, demands emerge for greater use of such market mechanisms as direct charges to patients and, further, the direct encouragement of the private health care system, leaving only a residual role for the NHS. It is important to note one point of apparent agreement between the two radical points of view. In contrast to the mixed economy center, the radical wings distrust bureaucracy. They are united in their suspicion of paternalist elitism in health (and other social) policies, although they part company when it comes to discussing possible alternatives. The radical Left emphasizes decentralization and participation in political decision making; the radical Right, emphasizes decentralization through the market system.

In speculating about possible developments in the British NHS during the eighties, we are clearly making assumptions about the interaction between two sets of variables: the political and the economic. Assuming three possible economic scenarios—a return to slow growth, zero growth, and negative growth or decay—each has implications both for the evolution of British politics and for the NHS.

We assume that a return to slow growth would be likely to mean a move back to consensus politics: that is, it would strengthen the mixed economy wings of both the Labor and the Conservative parties, so that political debate would be about marginal adjustments to the status quo. In contrast, zero growth—and, a fortiori, decay—would strengthen the radical wings of both parties and thus widen the ideological cleavages between them. In making these assumptions, we are of course simply extrapolating from past trends: in British postwar history, the fifties and sixties were marked by both economic growth (by national standards) and consensus politics, whereas the economic crises of the seventies have tended to produce ideological polarization.

Turning to the NHS, we assume that a return to economic growth would ease the strains described previously and limit change to incremental adjustments at the edges. In contrast, even a zero growth situation would sharpen ideological cleavages because the new demands produced by open arena politics would turn the battles over resource distribution (both geographical and sectional) into a zero sum game. More emphatically still, a situation of negative growth would almost certainly put radical and fundamental changes in the health care system onto the political agenda.

Alternative Strategies

In the light of these considerations, let us now examine alternative strategies that might be adopted in Britain, strategies derived from our initial model.

(i) *Putting the emphasis on providing a least-cost package of medical care.* Clearly, all governments will try some cost-containment strategies of this variety; however, their scope for doing so will depend both on their own ideological stance and the extent to which a sense of crisis allows new policy instruments to be adopted. The British health care system, as already stressed, is unique in that, while it does not give providers any incentives to maximize their work load, neither does it offer any policy instruments for shaping their behavior within the fixed budgets. This means, for example, that investing in the expansion of the primary care sector would not necessarily ease the load on the hospital sector: it might simply increase the leisure enjoyed by general practitioners.

Assuming expansion, it is difficult to foresee much change from the policies of the past twenty years—a mixture of exhortation and attempts at shaping provider practices through education and collective professional pressures.[24] As strains and ideological cleavages increase, however, one might expect more radical solutions to be adopted. Thus, a Labor government might be expected to try to introduce further restrictions on the behavior of general practitioners (i.e., a strategy of bureaucratic control)—and, indeed, might well return to its pre-1948 policy aim of making all general practitioners salaried employees, or functionaries, of the NHS. A Conservative government, in contrast, might attempt to introduce more fee-for-service payments designed to persuade general practitioners to take on responsibilities that would otherwise have to be carried by the hospital sector (i.e., a strategy of financial incentives) and might even abandon the present capitation system totally.

(ii) *Discouraging demand by putting up barriers to access.* Caught between ideology and political pressures, a Labor government would have little scope for adopting this strategy. Ideology makes it virtually impossible for a Labor government to increase financial barriers; and politically, the increasing salience of health care issues and the multiplication of various consumer pressure groups make the political costs of such an option prohibitive. Further, there is some evidence that suggests that the tolerance of queues and waiting lists—such a conspicuous feature of Britain's NHS—may be a wasting asset. The younger generation is increasingly more critical of delays (and other shortcomings) than the generation that grew up in the pre-NHS era.[25]

In contrast, a Conservative government would have an ideological bias toward imposing financial barriers, a bias that would become more pronounced if the party were to move from the center to the radical right. Indeed, the present Conservative government, whose policies are more ideological than those of any of its postwar predecessors, seems likely to put the emphasis on increasing the financial cost to NHS consumers, with the deliberate intention of using the private sector as a safety valve. Given a pessimistic economic scenario, a Conservative government might move even farther toward offering positive incentives to develop the private market in medical care—although the scope for such development is, at present, limited by the fact that the private sector offers a complement to, rather than a substitute for, the public sector, concentrating on routine surgery and on those procedures for which the time costs are particularly heavy (notably elective procedures), rather than on high technology medicine.

(iii) *Redefining medical as social problems.* The trend in this direction has been apparent in Britain for the past two decades and can be expected to continue irrespective of the economic situation or of the ideology of the party in power. Past experience suggests that this is far from being a costless strategy, however. Relabeling expenditures (and transferring costs from public services to the individual or the family) must not be confused with measures that save money. The burden on families of providing care is no less real for not appearing in the national accounts, and the feasibility of such a strategy depends crucially on its political visibility: that is, whether or not people see through it.

The British experience would suggest that a policy of restricting the scope of the health care system—by excluding "social" support—will lead to demands for other forms of expenditure: one of the growth areas of public expenditure in the seventies has been the increase in cash allowances to families to look after disabled members. Similarly, the trend toward women's participation in the labor force means—on the Swedish pattern—that the care previously provided in the home is being increasingly externalized and provided (by the same women?) in the public sector by social services, if not by the health care system. Indeed, a Labor government, under conditions of continuing high unemployment, might well adopt a deliberate policy of expanding the "caring" services[26] as a means of creating employment for semi- or unskilled men and women (i.e., substituting labor-intensive for capital-intensive services). In contrast, the ideology of a Conservative government in a similar situation might incline it to encourage women to stay at home.

(iv) *Making industry pay for the costs of ill health generated by its activities*. This would seem to be a particularly attractive option for a Labor government. However, given pessimistic assumptions about the economy, even a radical Labor government would come up against the problem which makes the adoption of such a strategy unlikely under a Conservative government: after all, imposing extra costs on industry (e.g., by developing occupational health schemes) might threaten the competitiveness of British exports.

In addition, two other limitations on such a strategy require noting. First, while some kinds of ill health have a direct impact on workers, others are more difficult to identify, reach beyond the industrial labor force, and sometimes require politically unacceptable restrictions on the behavior of individuals. For example, it is easy to demonstrate that a high consumption of sugar is associated with dental decay,[27] but what if consumers are happy to pay the price? Second, industry does not generate (although it may aggravate) the degenerative conditions associated with old age and chronic illness. Where health policies succeed in extending the span of life, they could, paradoxically of course, add to the demands on the health care system. Transforming society might well ease the problems of the health care system, but such problems are minor compared to the upheavals that might be involved in grandiose social engineering.

Probable Directions

Assuming a return to economic growth, and a consequent dominance of the ideology of the mixed economy, the most sensible assumption to make is that there will be no great change in the present system. There would, howeer, be differences of emphasis at the margin.

In the case of a nonradical Conservative government, it would seem reasonable to expect less emphasis on central control and on the achievement of equality in the distribution of access to health care. The two, of course, go hand in hand. Progress toward the achievement of greater equality would seem to depend on also achieving a greater degree of central control. Experience has shown that more equality of financing is unlikely to succeed and that detailed monitoring and intervention by central government is one way to promote equality of access to health resources. Given that a Conservative government is less committed to the goal of equality, it is therefore likely to tolerate a greater degree of inequality and diversity in exchange for less bureaucratic control.

In the case of a nonradical Labor government, the reverse would be true. It would almost certainly assert the achievement of equality as its prime policy goal. Consequently, there would be more emphasis, rather than less, on bureaucratic rationalization and control. The British tradition of paternalistic state intervention would continue and perhaps be reinforced. Indeed, since cost containment would remain an important policy objective even under favorable economic conditions, there would be growing pressures for more, rather than less, bureaucratic control over how the NHS's resources are spent by the professional providers.

In the more pessimistic economic scenarios, entailing increased ideological cleavages, we would assume more radical change. Given a situation where the gap between resources and demands widens, we would expect both a radical Labor and a radical Conservative government to adopt what might be called "blame diffusion" strategies: that is, strategies designed to divert criticism of the inadequacy of the NHS away from the central government by limiting the responsibility of the center for the provision of health care.

In the case of a radical Conservative government the strategy would be to expand the role of the private market and reduce the role, and responsibility, of the NHS. In the case of a radical Labor government, the strategy might well be to adopt a full-blown syndicalist model of health care—as proposed by G. D. H. Cole at the beginning of this century[28]—along the lines of the Yugoslav model.[29] Briefly, this would mean that health care would be provided by self-governing units of health service providers, perhaps negotiating terms of service with self-governing units of consumers. Such a strategy would fit in well with left-wing ideology on two counts. It would give recognition to the role of the workers, and it would be a response to the growing trade union demands for involvement in the control of the health services. Also, it would seem to meet the demands for less bureaucracy, smaller scale, and more consumer participation.

On balance, however, radical change seems unlikely. This is not because there is reason to be particularly optimistic about Britain's economic prospects. It is, rather, because there is reason to be pessimistic about the likelihood of radical alterations in Britain's health care system even in conditions that would seem to logically require such change. This pessimism is based on the organizational and political factors we have described: the categorization of the present situation as one of "corporate stalemate" not only helps to explain some of the strains on the NHS but also indicates why it is so difficult, organizationally and politically, to bring about change in Britain today. The more radical scenarios described are therefore catastrophe scenarios: that is, they seem likely only if economic conditions become so acute as to shake up the present social, political, and economic structure of the country.

POSTSCRIPT

When this chapter was completed in 1979, Britain was on the point of changing course politically. A Conservative government was elected into office with a strong ideological and rhetorical commitment to cutting public expenditure and encouraging self-help in a market economy; and in 1981 the fissures within the Labor party were to lead to the formation of a Social Democratic party. Looking back on our conclusions nearly three years later, we are therefore in a position to apply hindsight. What difference has a self-proclaimed radical Conservative government made in the field of health care policy? Have our predictions survived the test of time?

So far, our conclusions have proved remarkably robust. Certainly, events have sustained our central prediction that "radical change is unlikely." The architecture of Britain's system of health care remains much as it was three years ago, even if some of the paintwork looks shabbier. There have been no changes in the method of financing the National Health Service and only minor changes in its organization. Where there have been policy changes, they have been marginal in character and have been in the predicted direction.

Despite the public expenditure cutting rhetoric of the Conservative government, the budget of the NHS has been protected against the axe. Its budget has continued to rise, in real terms, if only at a barely perceptible rate (just about enough to keep pace with the extra demands made by an aging population); so in a period of declining national income, the NHS's share has risen. The Conservative government has also reorganized the NHS. The main aim of this reorganization, which was politically uncontentious, was to simplify the administrative structure by eliminating one of the tiers of management. In line with our analysis, however, the reorganization was also a "blame diffusion" exercise. Much stress was put by ministers on the delegation of responsibility to the periphery: on leaving responsibility for rationing scarce resources to the peripheral authorities.

More relevant to our argument is what the Conservative government has *not* done. It came into office committed to examining the options for transforming the financial basis of health care in Britain, that is, to moving toward an insurance based system. An elaborate paper exercise was indeed carried out at the Department of Health; but nothing more has been heard of it. The Conservatives remain committed to the NHS, as does the medical profession, at least until the next election.

Only at the margins have there been changes. The Labor policy of trying to restrict the private sector of health care has been reversed. Conservative policy has been to encourage its growth by relaxing the regulations governing the development of new facilities and by offering some minor tax incentives. However, the private sector remains small: its share of the national expenditure on health care is only about five percent of the total. Similarly, there has been a sharp increase in charges for prescriptions—though, again, nothing more has been heard of other Conservative plans for introducing a wider range of consumer charges. Lastly, Conservative rhetoric, if not policy, faithfully mirrors our expectations of an increasing emphasis on self-help in the community.

Overall, then, the record confirms that there has been no explicit or dramatic change of direction. But the record also suggests a point perhaps not fully appreciated in our original analysis. This is that overt government action may not be needed to shift the balance of health care. Simply by maintaining the status quo in a period of increasing demands on health care, governments may be able to divert more of the burden to the private and informal sectors—a diffuse, politically invisible, and gradual process.

NOTES

1. For the background to the foundation of the National Health Service, see: H. Eckstein, *The English Health Service* (Cambridge, Mass.: Harvard University Press, 1958); and A. G. Willcocks, *The Creation of the National Health Service* (London: Routledge and Kegan Paul, 1967). Readers may also want to consult more recent reassessments. These have been written from diverse perspectives and include some highly polemical interpretations. See, for example, B. Abel-Smith, *The National Health Service: The first 30 years* (London: HMSO, 1978); V. Navarro, *Class Struggle: The State and Medicine* (New York: Prodist, 1978); B. Watkin, *The NHS: The First Phase* (London: Allen and Unwin, 1978).

2. *Report of the Royal Commission on the National Health Service* (London: HMSO, 1979).

3. Department of Health and Social Security, *Annual Report, 1977* (London: HMSO, 1978).

4. Quoted in M. J. Buxton and R. E. Klein, *Allocating Health Resources*, Royal Commission on the NHS, Research Paper no. 3 (London: HMSO 1978).

5. Rudolf Klein, "Ideology, Class and Conflict in the NHS," *Journal of Health Politics, Policy and Law* 4, no. 3 (1979): 464–490.

6. These three factors should not, of course, be taken as the sole influence on policy development. The medical profession is only one element in the politics of decision-making; conceptual as well as cognitive tools require analysis. See, Celia Davies, "Hospital-Centred Health Care: Policy and Politics in the NHS," in P., Atkinson et al., eds., *Prospects for the National Health* (London: Croom Helm, 1979).

7. Rosemary Stewart and Janet Sleeman, *Continuously Under Review*, Occasional Papers on Social Administration no. 20 (London: G. Bell & Sons, 1967).

8. D. Allen, *Hospital Planning* (Kent: Pitman Medical, 1979).

9. R. G. S. Brown, *The Changing National Health Service*, 2d ed. (London: Routledge & Kegan Paul, 1978).

10. See, for example, P. Draper et al., *"The Organization of Health Care: A Critical View of the 1974 reorganization of the NHS,"* in D. Tuckett, ed., *An Introduction to Medical Sociology* (Tavistock, 1976).

11. R. F. L. Logan, J. S. A. Ashley, R. E. Klein, and D. M. Robson, *Dynamics of Medical Care*, London School of Hygiene and Tropical Medicine, Memoir no. 14 (1972).

12. For a discussion of the freedom of hospital consultants in the early NHS, see Celia Davies, "Professionalism in Organizations: Some Preliminary Observations on Hospital Consultants," *Sociological Review* 20 (1972). Recent accounts of the dynamics of local decision-making also stress the role of doctors. See, for example, R. Taylor, "The Local Health System: An Ethnography of Interest Groups and Decision-making," *Social Science and Medicine* 11 (1977); D. J. Hunter, "Coping with Uncertainty: Decisions and Resources within Health Authorities," *Sociology of Health and Illness* 1 (1979).

13. David Mechanic, *Future Issues in Health Care* (New York: Free Press, 1979).

14. M J. Buxton and R. E. Klein, "Distribution of Hospital Provision," *British Medical Journal*, 8 February 1975.

15. Studies in Resource Allocation, *Public Expenditure on Health* (Paris: OECD, 1978).

16. Rudolf Klein, "Conflict within Consensus," mimeographed (paper given at conference on Instruments der Gesundheitspolitik, organized by Hans-Seidel Stiftung, Munich, June 1977).

17. For an analysis of the relationship between the success in controlling budgets and closed arena politics, see Rudolf Klein, "Costs and Benefits of Complexity" (paper given at the Loch conference on the Challenge to Governance Project, June 1978; Beverly Hills, Calif.: Sage, forthcoming).

18. Office of Health Economics, *Renal Failure* (London: 1978).

19. Rudolf Klein and Janet Lewis, *The Politics of Consumer Representation* (Centre for Studies in Social Policy, 1976).

20. Department of Health and Social Security, *Sharing Resources for Health in England* (London: HMSO, 1976).

21. See, for example, Jane Leighton, "Fighting for Better Health Services: The role of the CHC," in G. Craig et al., eds., *Jobs and Community Action* (London: Routledge and Kegan Paul, 1979).

22. The corporatist character of the NHS was first identified by H. Eckstein, *Pressure Group Politics* (London: Allen and Unwin, 1960). For subsequent developments of this theme, see Rudolf Klein, "The Stalemate Society," *Commentary*, 56 (November 1973), and "The Corporate State, the Health Service and the Professions," *New Universities Quarterly* (Spring 1977).

23. See note 2.

24. For a classic description of this style of management, see Sir George

Godber, *Change in Medicine* (London: Nuffield Provincial Hospitals Trust, 1975).

25. Rudolf Klein, "Public Opinion and the National Health Service," *British Medical Journal*, 12 May 1979.

26. Roy Parker, "The Future of the Personal Social Services," mimeographed (paper given at seminar to mark the 10th anniversary of the Seebohn Report, University of Bath, September 1978).

27. Gordon Best, "Notes on the Marcro-Economics of Illness and Health," mimeographed (December 1978).

28. Rudolf Klein, "Control, Participation and the British National Health Service," *Milbank Memorial Fund Quarterly* 57, no. 1, (1979).

29. For a description of the Yugoslav model, see Stephen J. Kunitz, "Health Care and Workers' Self-Management in Yugoslavia," *Int. J. Health Services* 9, no. 3 (1979).

9

The United States: A Social Forecast

Paul Starr and Theodore Marmor

The point of forecasting is not to predict the future, but rather to change it.* We know too much about the failure of even the most sophisticated demographic and economic projections to hope that we could accurately predict the changing structure of institutions. Writing in 1980, we cannot possibly predict the shape of things ten or even five years hence. What forecasting can usefully do, though, is to suggest the path of change if only a given set of variables were to work themselves out. Undoubtedly, other factors and events outside our present field of vision will come into play, but a forecast allows us to plan against the visible trends in progress. The future will be different from what we now imagine, but one reason may be our having imagined at least part of it beforehand and acted to shape it.

For medical care in America, simple extrapolation into the future on the basis of recent history is likely to be mistaken. The economy will almost certainly not allow the future to be like the past. Between 1950 and 1980 medicine increased its share of the gross national product from 4.5 to 9.1 percent.[1] Moreover, these figures probably understate the growth in expenditures on health because they do not include the vast increases in preventive expenditures imposed by federal regulation in the areas of environmental protection, consumer product safety, and occupational health.[2] Since the expenditures required by the new wave of health and safety regulations enacted in the 1960s and 1970s were made by private corporations, they do not show up in the federal budget, nor do they appear in an accounting of total medical costs. This deficiency of social accounting helps to perpetuate the erroneous view that America increased its spending on medical services but not on prevention.

While the decades since World War II have seen a steady growth in health expenditures, the orientation of public policy has shifted more than once, and these shifts have deeply affected medical institutions. Beginning in the late 1940s, national policy emphasized the expansion of medical resources. Federal programs generously aided medical research and hospital construction and helped build up the infrastructure of a highly technological system of health services centered in medical schools and their affiliated institutions. Under the impact of federal aid and the growth of private health insurance, American hospitals became progressively more elaborate, sophisticated—and expensive.

In the 1960s, the emphasis of policy shifted to the redistribution of services. With the enactment of Medicare and Medicaid in 1965 and the inception of the War on Poverty, public policy became more explicitly concerned with correcting class and racial inequities. And, with the adoption of programs to increase the number of physicians, set up community mental health centers and other neighborhood clinics, and bring about other changes in the pattern of services, federal policy shifted from its earlier preoccupation with hospitals to a broader interest that included primary care. The new programs of the 1960s did not initially replace those adopted in the 1940s because policymakers did not yet see any need for a choice of priorities or for regulation of growth. In the late 1960s, public concern about environmental and safety issues also increased, and by the early seventies a host of new laws had been enacted in those areas as well.[3]

These programs were not entirely unsuccessful. Between 1960 and 1975 the infant mortality rate was cut by thirty-eight percent.[4] The age-adjusted mortality rate dropped sixteen percent for coronary artery disease and twenty-two percent for stroke between 1970 and 1976.[5] Accidental deaths in the work place fell by half in the decade after new occupational health and safety legislation was passed.[6] However, the exact causes of these gains have not been well understood; it is unclear what share of the credit goes to better prevention, what share to more effective and more accessible medical care, and what share to other changes.

Paradoxically, in the same period that these successes were taking place, a new skepticism was setting in about both medical and preventive expenditures.[7] Critics charged that growing medical costs made little difference in health. They pointed to evidence from the period before the early 1970s—when a plateau in health status seemed to have been reached—and they cited studies that showed no effect on the health of populations in different regions when the level of medical resources varied. Some, following Ivan Illich, drew the conclusion that medical care did not matter at all. What such studies demonstrated, however, was only that the effect on health is small in the range that medical resources vary in advanced societies. One cannot extrapolate and conclude that if medical resources were reduced to zero, health would be unaffected. Nor can one conclude that future innovations in medical science will have no effect once they are generally diffused. The evidence against medical care suggested that one ought not to expect significant gains in health from incremental changes in medical resources,[8] but the improvements in health status in the 1970s were already suggesting that in some areas such gains may be possible.

The other assault on growing expenditures has focused on the costs imposed by health and safety regulations. Conservatives have argued that such regulations are inflationary; that they not only fail to achieve their objectives but also often have perverse effects; and that they constitute a form of governmental paternalism out of place in a free society.[9] Whether or not these charges are justified, by the late seventies they were increasingly believed. The effort to increase energy production and to revive basic industries such as steel produced strong pressure to override recent environmental protection and occupational health and safety measures. The new economic conditions created by stiff international competition and higher energy costs seemed to rule out any growth in social investment in environmental protection over what has already been committed.

For reasons grounded partly in empirical research and partly in the individualistic character of American thought, recent health policy in the United States has emphasized preventive measures available to individuals, such as reduced smoking, more exercise, and better diet.[10] But such measures run up against powerful interests, such as the cigarette and packaged food industries, and against the deeper cultural patterns that reinforce unhealthy forms of individual behavior. While behavior-oriented preventive policies have some appeal, they seem unlikely to substitute either for environmental measures, which are more likely to improve health, or for medical care, which commands popular faith and political influence.

The widespread skepticism about the benefits of further growth in medical expenditures and the conservative criticism of health and safety regulation represent two powerful forces opposing greater social investment in health. But there are currently other forces at work as well; and some of these may help to generate even higher levels of medical expenditure than are now being experienced. These trends in progress are the subject of the first part of this analysis. But as indicated earlier, forecasting such trends falls short of predicting the future. Besides the trends, which may change, there are major, unpredictable contingencies. The second part of the chapter examines several possible alternative scenarios under varying political and economic conditions. To leave the future open in this way is not merely a confession of limited knowledge. It is also a statement about our capacity to create the future, subject to the constraints not only of our objective circumstances but of our collective will and imagination.

TRENDS IN PROGRESS: A MICROANALYSIS
OF THE FUTURE

*[margin handwritten note: Δ's affecting costs *]*

Two current developments affecting the future of medical care will put significant pressure on costs. The first is the shift in the age distribution of the population toward the elderly. The second is a dramatically rising supply of physicians.

Most of the increase in the elderly population will actually come after the turn of the century. People over sixty-five, eleven percent of the population, will increase to about 12.5 percent by the year 2000 and to an estimated 20.9 percent by 2030, if current demographic patterns persist.[11] However, in the 1980s and 1990s the most rapidly increasing group among the aged will be those over eighty-five, who have the highest rates of morbidity and institutional care. Partly reflecting this prospect, one recent estimate suggests that between 1978 and 2003 the number of persons with activity limitations will rise by 35 to 48 percent.[12]

The use of medical care is not only a function of the burden of disease and disability. In a third-party insurance system, like that of the United States, the use of medical care also depends on the level of insurance and the availability of services. The effect of insurance is clear: the more insurance coverage people hold, the more they and their doctors are willing to undertake expensive procedures. The effect of supply, particularly the supply of physicians, has frequently been demonstrated in research.[13] The more surgeons in a region, for example, the higher the rate of surgery. The demand for medical services emanates not only from patients, who make the initial contact with doctors, but also from physicians, who decide whether complex tests and procedures, hospitalization, drugs, and further visits are required. Under fee-for-service arrangements, doctors have a clear incentive to increase the number of services they provide. Hence, an increase in the supply of doctors will probably show up as an increase in services as well.

[margin handwritten note: moral hazard]

The levels of insurance coverage and physician supply are both likely to increase in the next fifteen years. Insurance levels depend in part on the uncertain resolution of national health insurance proposals. Even if no universal plan is enacted, however—and it now seems unlikely that one will be—private insurance coverage may increase because of the inflationary pattern in medical expenditures. The process is self-reinforcing. The more medical costs go up, the more people seek insurance to protect themselves against those costs; and the more insurance, the higher the costs are likely to go. Since about ninety percent of the population now has coverage for at least some hospital costs, the future increases are likely to come mainly in coverage for physicians' services, nursing care, X-rays, dental services, and drugs.[14] This has already been the pattern for the last two decades, and it may continue. (In February 1983 the Reagan administration proposed limiting tax incentives for health insurance. But the political obstacles to such measures are formidable.[15] And even if tax incentives are changed, the established pattern of insurance purchasing may well continue in the absence of any other means of personal protection against medical expenses.)

The increasing supply of doctors is a result of policies adopted in the 1960s and 1970s, when a widespread consensus held that the United States faced a doctor shortage. As a result of federal aid, thirty-eight new medical schools have opened since 1965; in addition, enrollments at existing schools have increased. The number of graduates—7,500 a year in the mid-sixties—has now doubled to more than 16,000. Because population growth has been slow, the increase relative to population is considerable. In 1960, there were 148 doctors for every 100,000 Americans; by 1975, there were 175. By 1995 there will be nearly 250.[16]

The original aim of government aid to expand medical schools was to relieve the shortages of physicians in small towns and poor neighborhoods of big cities. But it soon became apparent that the new physicians were prepared neither to work in such locations nor to go into primary health care. Instead, they gravitated toward the wealthier suburbs and prestigious specialties. In the 1970s, policy-makers adopted measures to counteract these tendencies. One was a national health service corps, a program to assign volunteer physicians and other medical personnel to "underserved areas." At first, the program was small, as there were few volunteers. But then Congress shifted its aid to medical schools from direct grants to the institutions to scholarships for students. In return, medical students had to agree to serve in the national health service corps for as many years as they received financial assistance. This measure promised to bring significant numbers of doctors to areas in need, until the Reagan administration cut the program, on the grounds that doctors were voluntarily locating in underserved areas.[17]

In the 1970s Congress also began to require medical schools to channel students into primary care. Though this effort may bear some fruit, it is difficult to prevent a young doctor who has gone into pediatrics or internal medicine (defined as primary care fields) from later developing a subspecialty. The United States lacks the centralized planning of advanced training programs that would make such restrictions feasible.

Yet even if the attempts to redistribute doctors to underserved areas and primary care succeed, there is every likelihood that more doctors will generate higher medical costs, if the fee-for-service system continues to predominate. These additional doctors will demand more tests, more operations, more drugs, and more visits. They may also expand the conception of what types of health services are "needed," because of the great culture authority their advice will continue to exert.

There are several possibilities, however, for minimizing, if not erasing, the inflationary effect on costs. One would be to attempt to reverse the increase in the number of doctors, but this would be politically difficult because of the demand for places in medical schools; in any event, a flood of new doctors is already in the pipeline. A second, and more

interesting, possibility would be to change the financial
arrangements governing medical practice. A third would be
to change the relationships that now obtain between doctors and hospitals.

The inflationary consequences of the present fee-for-
service, third-party payment system are widely recognized.
Alternative systems have received some legislative support. The most important of these is an American invention:
the health maintenance organization (HMO). HMOs are
organizations that offer a wide array of medical and hospital
services for a flat sum each year. They vary greatly in
structure. Some are group practices with their own clinics
and hospitals; others are financial entities that reimburse
their doctors on a fee basis, within the limits of their budgets. They are not insurance plans; they provide health
services directly. Like a national health service, they must
work within a fixed budget—determined, in their case, by
the total number of subscribers. But unlike a national health
service, they must compete for subscribers with insurance
organizations and with each other in areas where more than
one HMO exists.

Some HMOs were established in America as long ago as
the 1920s. During the Great Depression, they were seen as a
radical innovation and were called "medical cooperatives"
when established under consumer control. But the most
significant development came after World War II under the
sponsorship of the industrialist Henry Kaiser, who expanded a medical program for shipyard workers into the
Kaiser Foundation Health Plan, which now serves over
three million subscribers. Kaiser's record in controlling
medical costs brought the prepaid alternative to the attention of conservative forces in America. With support from
President Nixon, the Congress in 1973 enacted a law to
encourage the spread of HMOs throughout the country.

This legislation did not have the expected effect for a
variety of reasons, most notably regulatory requirements
that made HMOs less competitive with health insurance;
hence, the growth in HMO enrollment has been much

slower than anticipated. It now stands at only about five percent of the population.[18]

Should HMOs grow substantially in the future, they could alter the effects of the rising supply of physicians. More doctors mean higher costs under fee-for-service; they generate extra expenditures without engaging in price competition that would cut costs. However, an increased supply should enable HMOs to recruit young physicians at lower salaries. Thus, while raising costs in the fee-for-service sector, a growing doctor supply may lower costs among the HMOs. If the gradient were steep enough, it might accelerate the movement of patients toward HMOs from fee-for-service.[19]

The other possibility for relieving the inflationary effects of additional doctors involves changes in their relationship to hospitals. Unlike Europe, where hospital doctors generally form a separate group from general practitioners. America has a system in which nearly all community practitioners follow their patients into the hospital and continue to decide what tests and procedures are needed. American doctors have been free to be oblivious to administrative concerns about the costs of their decisions. The insurance system, in any event, has freed the hospitals from the need to exercise such controls, since more tests and procedures have brought them more money in the form of higher insurance reimbursements. In recent years, however, when the federal government has considered setting limits on hospital revenues, the restricted capacity of administrators to modify doctors' clinical decisions has assumed greater importance. If the government tells hospital administrators they must keep expenditures within certain bounds, the administrators do not necessarily have the means to alter medical decisions accordingly. They can cut back only on those departments subject to their direct control, such as food and housekeeping; they cannot necessarily require more cost-effective forms of treatment.[20]

But this is where the increasing supply of doctors becomes relevant. While the number of doctors has been rising, the number of hospital beds has been relatively stable. Hence the ratio of hospital beds to doctors has been falling (from about 3.15 general beds per active medical doctor in 1968 to about 2.83 in 1976).[21] This changing ratio limits the ability of doctors to generate demand for hospital care; it also provides the opportunity for hospitals to gain more control over physicians. In the past, hospitals have competed with one another for the favor of doctors who could keep their beds filled, but as more doctors become available, that relationship may change. The hospitals may be in a position to demand compliance with more economical rules of practice, although they would have to be motivated to make such demands either by changed methods of insurance reimbursement or by federal limits on their budgets.

Such constraints on physicians are as yet a matter of speculation.* The Carter administration proposed a limit on hospital revenues, but Congress rejected the measure. However, other restrictions on the sovereignty of American doctors were enacted earlier in the 1970s as part of a general movement toward increased government regulation in the health services sector.[22] This regulation was, in large measure, a response to the increase in government health spending and to the growing sense of diminishing returns on public investment in medical care.

Several major points stand out about this expanded state intervention. First, although the government's share of health spending has increased, public ownership of medical facilities has actually diminished. Medicare and Medicaid made it possible for patients formerly dependent on public institutions to receive care in private hospitals and from private physicians. As a result, public facilities have had an increasingly vestigial and vulnerable role. Second, in the absence of direct control through ownership, the

---

*In 1983 Congress adopted a new system of prospective payment for Medicare beneficiaries' hospital care. This new system has given hospital management an incentive to scrutinize some physician practices more closely.

government enacted regulatory controls—but in such a fragmentary form that they were often ineffective and even worked at cross-purposes. And third, the outcome of this partial, compromised regulation was increased conflict without change—an intensified level of political antagonism without much institutional reform.[23]

Before the Reagan cutbacks, what the United States had mainly to show for this intervention was a new infrastructure of health regulation and planning. Among the new regulatory systems was a network of professional standards review organizations (PSROs), which, in cases of patients who receive federal funds, subjected doctors' judgments on hospitalization and other aspects of treatment to an audit by a board of colleagues. The medical profession retained its collective autonomy, although individual physicians did not entirely retain theirs. The law established agencies to allow some doctors to set and enforce standards governing the practice of their colleagues. From the viewpoint of cost control, the results were not intoxicating. What effect, if any, the PSROs had on the quality of care is disputed.

Disagreement has also surrounded the new generation of planning bodies called health systems agencies, (HSAs) that emerged in the 1970s. Born of concern over previous fragmented and ineffective efforts at planning, but then compromised in the process of enactment, the health planning legislation of 1974 still did not centralize effective authority. Financing and planning remained separate. The new law gave consumer representatives a major role, but it did not establish any means by which consumers could effectively hold their ostensible representatives accountable.[24]

The HSAs were given a mix of planning and regulatory responsibilities but little authority. In annual implementation plans, they were to rank local health priorities and identify promising proposals to satisfy community goals for medical care. However, they had no money to carry out any of these proposals. Their power was severely restricted,

almost entirely negative in character, and certainly insufficient to reshape the local medical system. Although HSAs
were required to review institutional proposals for capital
expenditures over $150,000, they only advised the state
agencies that had legal authority to issue "certificates of
need." HSAs were to review the "appropriateness" of all
medical facilities in their area, but they had neither the
positive authority to make improvements nor clear sanctions for controlling present operations. It was not a
model of planning likely to generate confidence, and the
HSAs, like the PSROs, were subject to federal cutbacks
under President Reagan. The states retain some health
planning functions, primarily veto power over large capital
expenditures.[25]

In one way planning has changed. Between 1945 and
1973 health planners were concerned mainly with the planning of expansion. Since the mid-1970s they have been
concerned with the planning of retrenchment. Their task is
perhaps more difficult now because the loss of existing jobs
and resources usually occasions even greater agitation than
the distribution of new ones. The planners who once aspired to bring health services to the poor now are assigned
the unhappy role of deciding which public facilities to close,
whom to fire, what population to neglect. The continued
likelihood of fiscal restraint makes it all the more likely that
the next fifteen years will be a period of medical austerity,
with tough and even "tragic choices" for the planners of
containment.

So passed a golden age. The last decades of expansion
were not only a boon to physicians and hospitals; they were
also a splendid era for reformers. The growing expenditures
on medical care offered simultaneously the reason for reform and the means of reform. Expanding resources create
the opportunity to avoid zero-sum conflict, but as the game
grows tight, each party is likely to dig in its heels that much
harder. Health care reform may not be entirely dead for the
next fifteen years, but if it succeeds, its success will be more
bitter.

ALTERNATIVE SCENARIOS: A MACROANALYSIS OF THE FUTURE

How do the broader currents of change in American society and politics impinge on medicine? And what types of changes may we expect to see in the next fifteen years?

Some changes that affect the structure of society are quiet; others are noisy. The quiet changes are those that take place in the structure of institutions and the patterns of culture so steadily that they rarely make the news or become issues in political debate. The noisy changes are the social movements and political reforms that dominate the surface of events and occasionally alter the entire geometry of power and decision making.

We have already alluded to one "quiet" change in American society that holds profound implications for medical care in the future: the changing age distribution. More difficult to specify, but no less important, are changes in class structure. Probably the most significant change in class relations since the Second World War involves the growth of a professional class, flowing out of an expanded higher education system, and the growing mutual dependency of sections of that class and the poor as a result of an expanded system of social services. The professional class in America is by no means radical in its politics, although it has given disproportionate support to the antiwar and civil rights movements. Public opinion analysts suggest that while liberal in their attitudes toward civil rights and "cultural" issues such as abortion, professionals are conservative in their economic views. However, because many professionals such as teachers, social workers, and nurses depend upon government for their incomes, they look more favorably upon the growth of government than the old bourgeoisie. In particular, they often form alliances with their clients on behalf of social welfare programs.

The expanded role of government in medical care has begun to create, within medicine, this same "progressive" professional class. Its members work in the expanded academic medical centers, in neighborhood clinics, and in public health and planning agencies. In a sense, the rift between these health professionals and private practitioners repeats the larger split between the new professional class and the older bourgeoisie. Like teachers and social workers, progressive health professionals are more sympathetic to the concerns of the poor (though, at the same time, they are often involved in antagonistic relations with them, as at teaching hospitals where the poor become "clinical material"). The significance of this group is that it introduces a division of interests and ideals in the medical professions— and the word *professions* is plural here because one can no longer think of doctors as the only powerful professionals in medicine. The result may be a diminished capacity to resist government intervention in the future.

Another development undermining traditional patterns in American medicine is the growth of the feminist movement and increasing support for sexual equality. Here the effects on medicine come not only from the demand of women for greater control and knowledge of their bodies but also from an increase in the number of women physicians. As of the mid-1960s, women still represented only six percent of incoming medical students. They are now close to thirty percent. As dramatic as the growth in numbers, however, is the shift in outlook. The women who formerly constituted a small minority in the profession did not demand any changes in its organization; they accommodated themselves to the prevailing system and were drawn into the less prestigious specialties, such as pediatrics and child psychiatry. Today, however, women doctors may be less inclined to restrict their ambitions and demands. "They appear unwilling," one observer has written, "to give up the female presence in a male dominated atmosphere, and are not flattered to be considered 'one of the guys.' They are not ready to sacrifice home, husband, and outside interests to a hard-driving career, but differ from their older colleagues in that they will not accept a second-class career as a compromise. In making more demands of the system to bend to what they perceive to be their legitimate needs, they have caused male colleagues to question their own attitudes, lifestyles, and career models with the result that greater flexibility is now being sought for men as well as women."[26]

Whether feminist demands—from women as patients or as doctors—will be quietly co-opted or will require some major adjustment of institutions remains to be seen; but the emergence of feminism, like the rise of the new class of health professionals, may tend to strengthen the liberal forces in medicine.

Besides shifts in class structure and sexual composition, American medicine is also experiencing important changes in organizational structure. The service sector is now the frontier of corporate business. Medical care, long the province of independent practitioners and independent, nonprofit hospitals, is now witnessing the growth of for-profit hospital chains as well as nonprofit multihospital systems and diversified health care companies of all kinds. HMOs, which were nearly all nonprofit and locally controlled in 1970, are increasingly operated by large national corporations, some of them insurance firms. The movement of doctors into group practice has accelerated; now more than a quarter of the profession practices in groups, as compared with just 2.6 percent in 1946 and 12.8 percent in 1969. Throughout the health sector, institutional consolidation is taking place, as practitioners, hospitals, and health plans struggle to maintain their position in the market. These changes, particularly the growing corporate role in American medicine, seem likely to continue over the next two decades.[27]

Conservatives have welcomed the amalgamation of hospitals and medical services into national corporations as likely to introduce better management; but there is actually little evidence of reductions in cost by the hospital chains or other national companies. Indeed, one of the skills claimed by corporate managers—"reimbursement maximization"— seems likely only to drain more money from governmental and private payers.

Against the interest of professional and corporate providers in maximizing payment run the pressures for cost containment mentioned earlier. Given the currently projected growth of military expenditures, resistance to higher taxes, and continued government deficits, there is no reason to believe that these demands for cost containment in medical care will diminish. Indeed, the demands may well escalate from cost containment to medical austerity.

What would austerity in medical care look like? It would depend, of course, on the political auspices under which it took place. In the unlikely event that the Left presides, the tendency would be to move toward a more centrally budgeted system along the lines of the British model, although it would probably stop short of a national health service. The great advantage of the British system, from the perspective of cost containment, is that it simultaneously introduces a single national budget for medical care and eliminates the inflationary incentives of fee-for-service by paying practitioners on a capitation basis.[28] The unified budget has allowed the British to keep their medical expenditures below six percent of GNP—a smaller proportion than in any other of the advanced societies. Introducing a centralized budget and eliminating fee-for-service could not cut American expenditures to this level. But the British option offers the greatest hope of controlling costs while pursuing the traditional objectives of the Left in social equality and public health.

Should conservatives preside in a time of medical austerity, as they do today, the pattern would be different. The Right faces a different "contradiction" from the one faced by the Left. Whereas the Left seeks to control costs while augmenting equality, the Right seeks to control costs while limiting state control and preserving the traditional prerogatives of physicians, hospitals, and insurers. These objectives are no easier to combine than the dual objectives of the Left. Just as the Left in power might be forced to compromise its desire to expand access for the poor, so might the Right be forced to compromise its opposition to government regulation and control. Such compromises were the hallmark of conservative health reforms in the 1970s. The Reagan administration repudiated these regulatory programs, but its own competitive strategy has found little support. Conservatives have succeeded in cutting the growth of public expenditures on health programs, and under medical austerity, the cuts would go deeper; but because so much financing originates in the private sector, public retrenchment is unlikely to resolve the broader problems of health care costs. For many conservatives, the most attractive measures involve the suppression of demand, as through increased patient cost sharing in health insurance and greater business supervision over—and participation in—management and decision making in the medical care industry.

While the currently bleak economic conditions suggest that medical austerity is a genuine possibility, there remains the possibility of a return to relative affluence and economic growth. How would medical care be affected by that turn of events?

Again, one must consider the political auspices. Were the Left to preside over an expanding economy, its inclination in health policy would most likely be to move in the direction of the Canadian system. In a sense, this would mean resuming the course of development that began in the 1960s with Medicare, a liberal national health insurance system. Canadian health insurance began with nationwide hospital coverage in the late 1950s and a decade later added full-scale physician benefits. Expanding by services, the Canadian way differs from the incremental additions of population groups to government programs in the United States. Monopsonistic bargaining by the ten Canadian provinces has restrained the rate of growth in medical expenditures even with universal coverage. Though the United States and Canada started the 1970s with similar outlays— roughly 7.3 percent of GNP—at the end of the decade Canada devoted only 7.5 percent of GNP to medical care; by contrast, the United States now spends 10 percent.[29] Cost controls under the Canadian option are less centralized than under the British model. Practitioners would retain greater autonomy, and fee-for-service would continue for those physicians who prefer it; but there would be universal coverage and an increased interest in social investment for prevention. These policies would draw support from the new professional class, and they would expand that class at the same time.

Were conservatives to preside over a period of renewed prosperity, their inclination would be either not to change the medical system in any significant way or, at most, to introduce reforms along the lines of the German model. The German system provides for almost universal health insurance, but under private rather than governmental control. Most conservative health insurance proposals in America have adopted this orientation, though in varying forms. Such an approach would, in a sense, round out the private health insurance system, just as the Canadian option would round out a public system. The German model, however, is more corporatist in character than Americans would be likely to accept: it calls for collective annual negotiations between "sick funds" and physicians—an arrangement not possible under United States antitrust laws. The American Right is more individualistic, and it would most likely leave in place the individualistic system of physician reimbursement that now exists.

At this point, even the modest changes required for the German option of universal private health insurance do not seem likely, much less the more drastic reforms required for the British or Canadian models; but the present inertia and stalemate should not be accepted as a guide to the future.

Medical care, like other social institutions in the United States, has seen cycles of reform activity and political quiescence. Over the course of this century, three waves of reform have brought changes to health and medical care along with a host of other measures. The Progressive Era saw the passage, for example, of workmen's compensation and federal drug regulation. The New Deal witnessed the introduction of Social Security. The Great Society and its aftershocks in the seventies brought Medicare, Medicaid, and health and safety legislation. The rhetoric of reformers notwithstanding, these measures were part of a conservative development which relieved tensions that otherwise might have erupted in more radical threats to the political order. The reforms provided new protections to workers and consumers without fundamentally jeopardizing the position of the privileged or altering the capitalist order.

The United States is now in the midst of one of its periods of stalemate, but all the elements of some future crisis are already present. International economic and political instability seem the most likely sources of that eventual crisis. But whatever the causes, such a crisis is likely to shatter the present stalemate in social policy and once again set in motion the dialectic between radical social movements and conservative political reform that characteristically produces institutional change in America. At that moment, the icy glacier will move an inch, and the thunder will be heard for decades.

NOTES

*This article was first written in 1980, and edited and revised in 1983. If it had been written de novo in 1983, there would have been more emphasis on the rise of corporate health care, discussed at greater length by Paul Starr, in *The Social Transformation of American Medicine* (New York: Basic Books, 1982).

1. *Health—United States: 1981*, p. 263. For a discussion of the reasons for this increase, see Alain Enthoven, *Health Plan: The Only Practical Solution to the Soaring Cost of Medical Care* (Reading, Mass.: Addison-Wesley, 1980); Paul Starr and Gosta Esping-Anderson, "Passive Intervention: How Government Accommodation of Private Interests Increases Medical and Housing Costs," *Working Papers for a New Society* (July–August 1979): 15–25; and Theodore Marmor et al., "The Politics of Medical Inflation," *Journal of Health Politics, Policy and Law* 1 (Spring 1976): 69–84. For a discussion of the factors distinguishing the U.S. experience from the Canadian, see "The Development of the Welfare State in North America," by R. T Kudrle and T. R. Marmor, in Peter Flora and Arnold

Heidenheimer, eds., *The Historical Development and Contemporary Problems of Welfare States* (New Brunswick, N.J.: Spectrum, 1980).

2. For example, Bruce Ackerman and William Hassler estimate that pollution control "scrubbing" requirements for coal-fired power plants alone will have a national cost of $3 billion annually. See their book, *Clean Coal, Dirty Air* (New Haven, Conn.: Yale University Press, 1981).

3. This capsule summary of postwar developments is only meant to highlight a few points relevant to this analysis. For a more serious effort at understanding the recent history, see Paul Starr, *The Social Transformation of American Medicine* (New York: Basic Books, 1982), bk. 2, chaps. 3–5.

4. Maternal mortality fell 71% in the same period. For these and other figures showing marked improvements in health, see David E. Rogers and Robert J. Blendon, "The Changing American Health Scene: Sometimes Things Get Better," *Journal of the American Medical Association* 237 (April 18, 1977): 1710–1714.

5. "Health of the American People," in Executive Office of the President of the United States, *Outlook Report* (Washington, D.C., February 15, 1979), pp. 683–684. Adrian Ostfeld attributes a large part of the decline in stroke mortality to mass screening programs, widespread dietary change, and use of hypertension medication.

6. Steven Kelman, "Regulation That Works," *The New Republic*, November 25, 1978, pp. 17–18.

7. Paul Starr, "The Politics of Therapeutic Nihilism," *Working Papers for a New Society* (Summer 1976).

8. See, for example, Marc Lalonde, *A New Perspective on the Health of Canadians: A Working Document* (Ottawa: Government of Canada, 1974).

9. For an attempt to document the conservative critique, see Murray Weidenbaum, *Costs of Regulation and Benefits of Reform* (St. Louis, Mo.: Center for the Study of American Business, 1980).

10. *Healthy People: The Surgeon General's Report on Health and Disease Prevention* (Washington, D.C.: U.S. Government Printing Office, 1980).

11. Stephen Crystal, "Health Resources for All the Aged by the Year 2000: A Prospectus for New Strategies," (Paper prepared for the Institute of Medicine, Committee on U.S. Health Goals for the Year 2000).

12. "Health of the American People," p. 733.

13. See Jack Hadley, "Physician Supply and Distribution," in J. Feder, J. Holahan, and T. Marmor, eds., *National Health Insurance: Conflicting Goals and Policy Choices* (Washington, D.C.: The Urban Institute, 1980).

14. See Douglas Conrad and Theodore R. Marmor, "Patient Cost Shar-

ing," in Feder, *National Health Insurance*, for a discussion of trends in insurance coverage.

15. See Enthoven, *Health Plan*, pp. 19–21.

16. Paul Starr, "A Coming Doctor Surplus?" *Working Papers for a New Society* 4 (Winter 1977): 18; and Hadley, "Physician Supply and Distribution."

17. Hadley, "Physician Supply and Distribution," pp. 235–240.

18. For a general discussion of HMOs and the failure of the HMO act, see the analysis in Paul Starr, "The Undelivered Health System," *The Public Interest*, no. 42 (Winter 1976), pp. 66–85; and Harold Luft et al., "Health Maintenance Organizations," in Feder, *National Health Insurance*.

19. On other possible consequences of the growing doctor supply, see Starr, *Social Transformation of American Medicine*, bk. 2, chap. 5.

20. Jeffrey E. Harris, "Regulation and Internal Control in Hospitals," *Bulletin of the New York Academy of Medicine* 55 (January 1979): 88–103.

21. National Center for Health Statistics, *Health Resources Statistics, 1976–77* (Washington, D.C., 1977), pp. 141, 305.

22. For a more general analysis, see Starr, *Social Transformation of American Medicine*.

23. For a more complete treatment of these developments, especially hospital regulation, see Andrew Dunham, "Hospital Regulation" in Feder, *National Health Insurance*.

24. Theodore Marmor and James Morone, "Representing Consumer Interests: Imbalanced Political Markets, Health Planning and the HSA's," *Health and Society* 58 (Winter 1980): 125–165.

25. For case studies at HSAs, see Drew Altman, Richard Greene, and Harvey M. Sapolsky, *Health Planning and Regulation: The Decision-Making Process* (Washington, D.C.: AUPHA Press, 1981).

26. Naomi Bluestone, "The Future Impact of Women Physicians on American Medicine," *American Journal of Public Health* 68 (August 1978): 760–767.

27. The corporate transformation is discussed more thoroughly in Starr, *Social Transformation of American Medicine*, bk. 2, chap. 5.

28. For a clear explication of the model, see the essay in this volume by Rudolf Klein and Celia Davis.

29. For a discussion of the Canadian experience for U.S. policy purposes, see Theodore Marmor and Edward Tenner, "National Health Insurance: Canada's Path, America's Choice," *Challenge* 20, no. 2 (May/June 1977): 13–21.

Part IV
CONCLUSION

10

The Future of Health Policy:
Constraints, Controls,
and Choices

John R. Kimberly and Victor G. Rodwin

In Western industrialized nations, the notion that the welfare state can provide an abundance of health services for all citizens is now recognized as an illusion, especially in the context of slow economic growth. The new political discourse about health policy calls for understanding of constraints, design of administrative controls, and explicit decisions about difficult choices. Along with the cherished official rhetoric about providing equality of access to quality medical care, there is now a new emphasis on improving management, limiting professional autonomy, and promoting self-help in health care.

Some common themes—as well as some variations in health policies—emerge from the case studies presented in this book. In this concluding chapter, we shall highlight the more important themes as well as the emerging trends that are likely to shape the character of the health sector, and speculate about the future of health policy.

COMMON THEMES AND VARIATIONS

Idealism and Realism

Two common phases may be distinguished in the evolution of health policy in the nations we have considered: (1) an expansionary phase characterized by efforts to improve access to health services and coordinate health sector

growth; and (2) a containment phase characterized by efforts to control rising health care costs and redistribute
resources within the health sector. The first phase reflected
an idealistic quest, especially pronounced in the postwar
period, for a more humane world, and a faith in the capacity
of the state to create that world by strategic interventions
that would correct market inadequacies through economic
and welfare planning. The second phase was a response to
slow economic growth in the seventies and to the failure of
expansionary policies to handle the persistent problems of
structural unemployment, inflation, and resource allocation in the face of financial and other constraints.

THE EXPANSIONARY PHASE

During the expansionary phase, the growth of the health
sector was fueled on the demand side by massive infusions
of public funds, which significantly reduced the financial
barriers to medical care.

In France, the national health insurance program, originally instituted in 1930, was progressively extended, until
by 1960 seventy-five percent of the population was covered.
Subsequently, coverage was extended to agricultural workers (1961), then the self-employed (1965), and most recently
to virtually the entire population, including the clergy.

In Québec, hospital insurance was passed in 1960 and
extended to ambulatory care in 1970. In Britain, universal
coverage was achieved almost immediately with the creation of the National Health Service in 1948.

In the United States, Medicare and Medicaid were enacted in 1965, providing national health insurance for the
elderly and the poor. Although universal coverage has still
not been achieved, the large majority of the population is
now insured against the risk of hospitalization through
private health insurance.

On the supply side, state intervention in the health sector
emphasized modernization and new construction of hospital infrastructure, as well as subsidies for biomedical
research.

In France, state policies aimed at reorganizing the supply of health services focused on hospital construction and reform. In 1958, the Hospital Reform Act was passed, merging the best equipped regional hospital facilities with teaching hospitals and initiating a gradual shift in reimbursement of hospital based physicians from fee-for-service toward salary payment. Like the impact of the Flexner Report (1910) and the regional medical programs (1965) in the United States, the effect of this legislation in France was to consolidate the position of high technology medicine. By the late 1960s, France's public hospital infrastructure had been successfully modernized and acute beds in private cliniques had grown to include one-third of the total by the early 1970s.

In Québec, the Hospitals Act was passed in 1962, requiring legislative authorization for all hospitals and administrative compliance with provincial regulatory authorities. Following this legislation, public hospitals grew as former religious institutions were gradually financed by the provincial government.

In Britain, immediately following the creation of the NHS, supply-side policy also focused on hospital modernization. Although during the first years of the NHS only one new hospital was built, in 1962, while Enoch Powell was minister of health, a ten-year plan for balanced hospital development was produced. Its effect was not merely to promote hospital expansion, but also to replace small rural hospitals with modern district hospitals.

And, in the United States, the Hill-Burton Hospital Survey and Construction Act of 1946 provided federal aid to states for subsidizing the construction and modernization of hospital facilities in the private sector. In addition, in 1965, the Heart Disease, Cancer, and Stroke Amendments (Public Law 89–239) created Regional Medical Programs in fifty-six regions in order to speed up the application of biomedical knowledge by establishing cooperative arrangements among health care institutions, medical schools, and research institutions.

THE CONTAINMENT PHASE

During the present containment phase, in all four countries health care costs have threatened to get out of hand, and policymakers have been increasingly preoccupied with the task of regulating the demand, supply, and distribution of health resources. They are designing incentives to promote the substitution of ambulatory for hospital care; attempting to impose controls on hospital expansion and on capital expenditures in order to reduce excess capacity and improve access to medical services; calling for reimbursement and quality controls on hospitals and physicians; and urging changes in methods of provider reimbursement from fee-for-service to capitation or prepaid systems—in which physicians are encouraged to work on a salaried basis, to share in the risk of overspending, and to emphasize health maintenance. Finally, legislation has been passed and regulations devised to set national health priorities and establish national and regional health planning machinery.

In France, since 1960, health care costs have risen at a faster rate even than in the United States.[1] The legislative response to this situation was the Hospital Law of 1970, which sought to improve management in the public sector, control the unrestrained growth of the private sector, and promote a "harmonious" distribution of health services. In 1973 a national commission was charged with producing a national health plan. In addition, two regional commissions were established in each of France's twenty-one administrative regions to plan for health service needs and authorize construction of new cliniques or extensions of existing ones in the private sector.

In Québec, with the passage of Bill 42 in 1970, the Ministry of Health and the Ministry of the Family and Social Welfare were merged into the new Ministry of Social Affairs. This ministry was charged with setting priorities, planning, programming, and evaluation. In 1971, with the passage of Bill 65, twelve regional councils (CRSSSs) were created to determine the health and social service needs of the population, prepare regional health plans, and coordinate investments in health sector infrastructure, particularly with regard to the newly created local community service centers (CLSCs). Also as minister of health, Castonguay suspended a large number of ongoing hospital construction projects to channel the funds into domiciliary care programs, CLSCs, and other programs in social medicine.

In England, with the administrative reorganization of the NHS in 1974, NHS planners sought to eliminate the fragmentation of the former tripartite structure and to improve coordination by linking health services provided by the NHS with the social services provided by local authorities. In addition, by streamlining management functions and instituting a formal planning system, they sought to increase central control over resource allocation decisions.

Finally, in the United States, with the passage of the National Health Planning and Resources Development Act of 1974, a network of health planning agencies was established at area-wide and state levels to produce annual and long-term health plans and to regulate hospital expansion and capital expenditures.

Political Stalemate in Health Care Reform

If there is a single guiding theme which underlies all four cases studied, it is surely that of political stalemate in efforts to reform the health sector.[2] In the case study of Britain, Klein and Davies write of "corporate stalemate," which refers to the multiplication of veto power among producers which causes decision making to be slower and more costly. In the case study of Québec, Renaud criticizes the "shifts and displacements" in the initial goals of health care reform. In the case study of France, we note that none of the major measures undertaken since 1967 has succeeded in controlling health care costs. And, in the United States, as Marmor has remarked, the campaign to pass national health insurance has been faced with "progressive stalemate."

In Western industrialized nations, the growth of the health sector, the emergence of new health professions, and broader participation by diverse interest groups have converted the health sector into a political arena for the resolution of competing claims. As health care costs have risen, proposals for health care reform have increased; but so have the obstacles to effective implementation. Powerful forces will continue to cause health care costs to mount. There are also signs that policymakers will extend their control over the direction and quality of health sector growth.

In the case study of France we noted that consumption of medical services, in current prices, increased at an average annual rate of fifteen percent between 1960 and 1980. Neither the negotiations and collective contracts with the medical profession, nor the Hospital Reform Act, nor the reform of social security, nor even the Hospital Law of 1970 and its regulatory controls have succeeded in containing the growth of health care costs. A review of alternative revenue increasing mechanisms and cost-containment strategies disclosed that each of these methods provokes vigorous reactions from major interest groups—hospital associations, physicians, industry, and consumers. As yet there is little evidence that the French government intends—or is able—to change significantly the financing of health expenditures or the organization of health care. This has been true under the former government of Giscard d'Estaing as well as under the present regime of François Mitterand.

In the case study of Québec, Renaud associates health care reforms with the influence of broader economic and social forces—modernization and the emergence of a francophone middle class employed by a growing public sector. Although these reforms were probably the most ambitious undertaken by Western industrialized nations in their pursuit of equitable access to comprehensive health services, the goal of economic efficiency predominated—often to the detriment of the ideals that underlay the reforms. Instead of pursuing, above all, the goal of redistributive justice, as originally outlined in the Castonguay Commission report, cost control and budget cutting have become the central preoccupation of policymakers in Québec. Instead of promoting broader participation in decision making, the "bureaucratic rationalizers" have increased their power. Instead of equalizing privilege among health care providers, there has been increasing professionalization. Finally, instead of promoting broad primary prevention programs, there has been the introduction of a "new morality in health," including the emergence of "victim blaming," so that the moral responsibility for health is placed upon the individual.

Klein and Davies report that "in terms of cost containment, Britain's NHS has been a remarkable success story." Offsetting this success, however, they note the extent to which centralized control of the NHS has been circumscribed by the limits of administrative capacity, the inadequacy of cognitive tools (e.g., management information systems), and the autonomy of the medical profession. In analyzing current strains on the British NHS, Klein and Davies highlight the problem of an "expanding political arena in a contracting economy." They point up the trends toward greater unionization of health service employees and institutionalized public participation by health care workers as well as the public (through community health councils); and they note that issues of resource allocation in the health sector have become increasingly politicized. In the context of economic stringency, this has made adjustments in health policy all the more delicate. For these reasons they conclude that radical changes in Britain's NHS are unlikely.

In the United States, Marmor and Starr highlight opposing trends that are expected to limit the possibility of major transformation in the health sector. The shifting age distribution of the population and the increasing supply of doctors will increase the demand for health care services; and the growth of third-party reimbursement mechanisms on a fee-for-service basis will reinforce this trend. There is increasing skepticism, however, about the potential benefits of continued growth in health expenditures. Along with such skepticism, the high rate of general inflation and the fiscal strains affecting all levels of government are powerful factors that resist the growth of health expenditures and suggest that the "economy will almost certainly not allow the future to be like the past." In contrast to the major health initiatives throughout the golden age of the sixties, the next fifteen years are likely to be a period of medical austerity, with few prospects for major reform.

During the health sector's expansionary phase there was a conviction among most policymakers in Western industrialized nations that the state could insure against most economic and social claims. Through public investment policies, it was thought that the state could assure not just full employment and steady economic growth but also reasonable security against social hazards, including the ravages of illness. During the containment phase, the welfare state has come under attack. Policymakers in France, Québec, Britain, and the United States—as well as in other Western industrialized nations—have reassessed the assumptions underlying their policies in the health sector. It is interesting in this regard to compare the case studies with respect to some of the issues discussed earlier in this book: the role of the state; prevention policy; and the emergence of health care rationing.

The Role of the State

France, Québec, Britain, and the United States are all liberal democratic polities in which the state has gradually expanded its activities in the health sector. None has developed a health system that corresponds to any of the pure models discussed in chapter two: the professional model, the free enterprise model, the Illich model, or socialized medicine. Likewise, the role of the state in these countries does not correspond to the ideal of the radical or conservative perspective as outlined in chapter two. Of the three perspectives on the state, the liberal one appears to characterize best the role of the state in France, Québec, Britain, and the United States. All of the case studies indicate that prevailing opinion in each country accepts the justification for state intervention and the notion that health policy ought to be guided by criteria such as rationality, equity, and accountability.

Within the liberal perspective, there is, of course, much variation. For example, France is noted for its unitary political system and extreme administrative centralization. Québec, although part of a federal political system, is characterized by a highly centralized provincial administration and an active, "narcissistic" state preoccupied with extending its legitimacy over civil society. Britain, although historically more decentralized than France and more evolutionary in its style of political change, is associated with nationalization—the creation of the National Health Service accomplished in one swoop by the National Health Service Act of 1946. Finally, the United States, although characterized by its separation of powers, pluralistic mode of decision making, and vigorous private sector, is noted for its general movement toward increased government regulation.

Despite these variations, and despite the fact that within each country proponents of the conservative perspective urge increased reliance on the market mechanism and proponents of the radical perspective urge greater use of bureaucratic and moral incentives, France, Québec, Britain, and the United States have, for the most part, relied on a similar mix of policy instruments.

The case studies document the use of bureaucratic incentives, in particular substantial legislative and regulatory activities that aim to achieve administrative control over the health sector. For example, in France the Hospital Reform Act, the Social Security Ordinances of 1967 and the Hospital Law of 1970 are all examples of important legislative activity. Elaboration of standards to control capital expenditures and of statistical profiles to monitor physician behavior are evidence of increased regulatory activity. Similar examples abound in Québec, Britain, and the United States. In Britain, however, with respect to physician profiles, since fee-for-service reimbursement to physicians is relatively infrequent there is no billing information on the activities of general practitioners; nor are there policy instruments to influence their behavior.

The case studies also provide examples of market incentives. In the United States, removing tax incentives for health insurance, raising levels of patient cost sharing, and promoting health maintenance organizations are all fashionable policy instruments to control rising health care costs through the use of market incentives. In Québec, although Renaud argues that the state has largely replaced the market, he concludes by predicting an increasing role for conservative ideas in the formulation of health policy. In France, copayments for medical care are an important policy instrument and are likely to survive the current socialist regime. And in Britain, where market incentives are least developed, private insurance has grown under the Thatcher government. As noted by Klein and Davies, policy instruments to discourage demand, such as the introduction of new patient charges and increased cost sharing, are key policy options for the eighties.

Along with bureaucratic and market incentives, the case studies reveal ample use of moral incentives as policy instruments. Most often, these have been directed to issues of disease prevention and health education.

Prevention Policy

In chapter three, Ratcliffe, Fagnani, Wallack, and Rodwin note that since the eighteenth century there have been two distinct traditions in the evolution of medical knowledge—the individual clinical heritage and the collective public health movement, which focused on issues of disease prevention. As health policy has evolved from the expansionary to the containment phase, the case studies suggest that issues of disease prevention, particularly health promotion campaigns, have received renewed attention.

In the case study on France, prevention programs were considered in relation to cost-control strategies. Although reinforcing moral crusades against health hazards such as tobacco and alcohol is not likely to prove cost-effective in the short run, the new socialist government in France has embraced the collective public health notion of prevention and paid lip service to the strategy of health protection. Selected regions will be granted special budgets to establish prevention programs. However symbolic, this new effort will encourage the growth of epidemiology and perhaps even promote a series of health care reforms.

In the case study on Québec, Renaud reviews how the Castonguay reforms encouraged a more preventive approach to medicine, exemplified by community based comprehensive services in the local health and social service centers (CLSCs) and new public health and community health specialists in the departments of community health (DSCs). To some extent, these new institutions pursued a strategy of health protection: they promoted various forms of social and political action to attack the social causes of illness. For the first time, new professions such as community nurses, social workers, and specialists in family medicine were mobilized around primary care.

Renaud observes, however, that this emphasis on disease prevention played into the hands of government rationalizers who, faced with rising health care costs, squeezed budgets and invested in community-based health and social services. Instead of actively promoting health protection programs, the new emphasis on prevention, in Québec, reinforced health promotion campaigns. Rather than assume collective responsibility for prevention it was easier, politically, to place the burden of responsibility onto the individual and to wage moral crusades against tobacco, alcohol, obesity and all individual behaviors which are potentially dangerous to health.

In Britain, prevention policy has been associated with

cost-control strategies since the creation of the NHS. Klein and Davies note the optimism about the possibility of using health services to lower the cost of medical care by improving the population's state of health. Such optimism resulted from an implicit assumption that the need for health care is finite. The experience of Britain, however, suggests that this assumption is unfounded. There are queues for needed services, and there are increasing pressures to rationalize resource allocation within the health sector in order to meet growing demands.

Among the four principal policy options noted by Klein and Davies, three are inspired by the idea of prevention. The strategy of emphasizing least-cost packages of medical care requires the development of the primary care sector to reduce the need for more costly technology-intensive treatment. The strategy of redefining medical as social problems encourages placing the burden of care onto the family, the community, and other social services in order to avert costly medicalization and institutionalization of health care. Finally, the strategy of shifting the costs of health care to industrial producers would seek to prevent disease and injury by restructuring industry, vigilantly enforcing safety standards, and promoting occupational health programs.

In the United States, as in France, Québec, and England, primary prevention issues have also received renewed attention. The health maintenance organization, for example, is an ingenious institution for altering financial incentives to favor substitution of primary care for hospital based care. As in Québec, behavior oriented prevention policies have received disproportionate attention in the United States; for example, the promotion of measures available to individuals to reduce smoking, increase physical exercise, and improve diet. In contrast, in response to slow economic growth, broad macrosocial interventions—such as pollution control, safety standards, and housing and income maintenance programs—have suffered; and there has been pressure to override environmental protection measures as well as occupational health and safety rules.

The Emergence of Health Care Rationing

Given the growth of new medical technology, price inflation in the health sector, and systems of social insurance to reimburse these costs, it would seem that regulation of hospital beds and capital expenditures is merely an indication of the kinds of rationing mechanisms that are likely to emerge. Explicit health care rationing occurs at the clinical and at the institutional, as well as the regional or national, level. On the supply side, policymakers may ration health care by modifying the organization, quantity, and distribution of manpower, beds, and equipment. On the demand side, policymakers may ration health care by affecting utilization through pricing policies—applied to both money and time costs—and through prevention policies to reduce the need for acute services.

The case studies suggest that France, Québec, Britain, and the United States have all pursued a variety of rationing strategies with varying degrees of commitment and success. In France, on the supply side, policymakers have limited the growth of new hospitals, established standards and a review process for capital expenditures on medical equipment, and imposed new restrictions on the number of medical school graduates; they are currently considering alternative schemes to finance public hospitals on the basis of closed budgets. On the demand side, the national health insurance fund (CNAMTS) has maintained a small copayment for all ambulatory care; however, this is not significant, for most consumers have private insurance (mutual aid funds) to cover most of their copayment.

In Québec, supply-side rationing is more decentralized. It occurs at the level of individual institutions through prospectively set global budgets for hospitals and at the regional level through a bargaining process organized by the regional councils (CRSSSs). Renaud notes that the directors of different health institutions within a region were forced to sit at the same table and negotiate the allocation of resources for different institutions in a given region. On the demand side, although all medical services are free at the point of consumption, Québec has aggressively developed primary health care and social services.

In contrast to France and Québec, in Britain, on the supply side, the central government has acted as a rationing agent for the NHS since its inception. Since the Report of the Resource Allocation Working Party (RAWP) in 1976 the consequences of rationing decisions have been examined and explicit criteria developed to guide this process. As Klein and Davies note, however, the system of centralized control over budgets and decentralized responsibility for the way resources are used means that service providers are left with the task of rationing at the clinical level. In the case of renal dialysis, for example, Britain provides fewer resources than France, Québec, or the United States. On the demand side, British rationing operates in the form of queues, notably for elective surgery and ambulatory specialty care; however, queuing appears to have been less of an explicit rationing strategy than a miscalculation on the part of NHS planners about the relativity of need for medical care.[3]

In the United States, rationing has traditionally been imposed by the market on the demand side. As third-party payments have increased to cover roughly seventy percent of all health expenditures, supply-side controls have become firmly established. As noted by Marmor and Starr, health systems agencies (HSAs), certificate of need (CON) legislation, and appropriateness review have become critical to the planning of retrenchment, "although the fate of some of these programs under the Reagan administration is unclear." Also, health maintenance organizations (HMOs) have provided an institutional vehicle for rationing health care through the substitution of ambulatory services for inpatient hospital care.[4] Finally, the growing supply of physicians has made competition among hospitals for physicians less difficult. Soon, hospitals will be in a better position to demand compliance with more economical rules of medical practice, such as those promoted by the physician standards review organizations (PSROs).

EMERGING TRENDS

In light of the common themes and variations suggested by the case studies, it is tempting to speculate about emerging trends likely to shape health policy in Western industrialized nations. There are trends that impinge directly on the domain of medicine and trends that occur outside the domain of medicine whose effects are likely to be important to health policy.

Trends in the Domain of Medicine

The trends in the domain of medicine challenge the traditional autonomy and independence of the medical profession. They raise the issue of control in ways that would have been unthinkable even fifteen years ago. As a consequence of the increasing economic significance of the health care industry, these trends are no longer surprising, however; in fact, some are already being reflected in new policy initiatives. Though the breadth of their likely impact is unclear, their presence is incontrovertible.

EFFORTS TO DEFINE PRODUCTION FUNCTIONS FOR MEDICAL CARE.

It has long been argued that it is neither feasible nor desirable to evaluate physician performance. Proponents of this position advise against estimating production functions for medical services—which would relate patterns of resource consumption to outputs. They especially question the possibility of systematic and effective managerial monitoring and control of physician productivity. This line of argument has been strongly reinforced by medical ideology, which emphasizes the uniqueness of each "product" and which, in effect, mystifies the work of the physician by denying the possibility that a nonphysician can evaluate its outcomes. The absence of production functions, or their analogs for medical practice, has frustrated efforts at rationalization and control and produced a pattern of public response that might appropriately be called "management without objectives."[5]

It is a widely recognized fact, however, that physician judgments about the services appropriate for each patient account for a significant proportion of the costs of health care. So it is hardly surprising that efforts are underway in many quarters to define much more carefully the resource consumption consequences of physician practice decisions.[6] The assumption is that detailed descriptions of what physicians do will help us assess how they are utilizing resources and question the appropriateness of patterns identified; such information can ultimately be used for purposes of institutional management, area-wide planning, and reimbursement.

In the case study of Québec, Renaud refers to such application of basic management tools to the health sector as "the introduction of a productivist logic." In no country is the development of this logic more advanced than in the United States. For example, in an experiment currently being conducted in the state of New Jersey, the state Department of Health, in collaboration with all third-party payers and the state hospital association, has agreed to tie reimbursement directly to standardized costs identified by microanalysis of case mix and resource consumption.[7] The most innovative aspect of this experiment is the application of an administrative technology—diagnosis related groups (DRGs)—capable of establishing a common language between doctors and administrators. The technology enables physicians to examine patterns of resource consumption for similar patients in their own practices, over time, and also permits one physician to be compared with another and one institution with another. Thus, a new and potentially powerful mechanism exists for increasing the visibility of physician practice—a mechanism that permits nonphysicians to observe deviations readily, and to pursue their implications. Furthermore, the logic and technology of case-based prospective reimbursement is now being applied to Medicare patients on a nation-wide basis.

ALTERNATIVE ORGANIZATIONAL FORMS FOR MEDICAL PRACTICE

Alternative organizational forms incorporate a variety of devices designed to give the physician more control over his time; rationalize practice patterns by spreading the work load over several physicians (often with active use of paraprofessional personnel); provide incentives to minimize the use of inpatient facilities; and permit regular and systematic assessments of inpatient admissions, lengths of stay, and medical care.

In France, fee-for-service solo practice remains the predominant form of ambulatory care; but group practice is growing, and within hospitals all physicians are salaried. In Québec, the local health and social service centers (CLSCs) represent a significant organizational innovation, and the competing polyclinics (multispecialty group practice) suggest that solo practice may one day become an institutional anachronism. In Britain, solo practice general practitioner surgeries are slowly being transformed into health centers and group practice surgeries. It is in the United States, however, that one sees the greatest proliferation of organizational alternatives.

There is, for example, the growth of both single specialty and multispecialty forms of fee-for-service group practice and of prepaid group plans—health maintenance organizations (HMOs). The simultaneous development of fee-for-service group practice models and prepaid group practice models has some contradictory implications for the future. The fee-for-service model enables physicians to regularize their work schedules and to realize certain economies of scale while maintaining levels of income. This model reinforces the status quo in medical practice and, in one sense, consolidates the power of physicians by incorporating their interests at an organizational, as opposed to an individual, level.

The prepaid group models, in contrast, portend the possibility of change. In the HMO, for example, members pay a flat yearly fee for all the medical services they require (with the exception of prescriptions, glasses, and in some cases, dental care). Physicians work on a salaried basis across the range of medical specialties. The incentive structure in HMOs discourages inappropriate or excessive use of ancillary services and of inpatient facilities, while maintaining incentives for quality. An HMO whose reputation for quality is questioned will suffer from disenrollment and will not find it easy to attract new members.

Such data as are available suggest that HMOs do achieve savings in comparison with conventional forms of fee-for-service reimbursement.[8] Although widely hailed as the delivery model of the future, only five percent of the population at most is currently enrolled in HMOs. The recent failure of a number of HMOs and the fact that others are currently facing severe problems is raising concern about the future.[9] Some argue that the regulation of HMOs inhibits economies and rationalization and therefore leads to failure. But the root problem may be managerial incompetence. If so, the solution lies in the formal training of a corps of managerially sophisticated individuals to work in HMOs.[10]

CONTROLS OVER THE SUPPLY AND CERTIFICATION OF PHYSICIANS

The case studies of France and of the United States noted parallel concerns about the growing supply of physicians. In contrast to the late 1950s and early 1960s, when manpower planners were concerned about how to increase the number of physicians, attention is currently focused on how to limit their numbers.

The question of how many doctors a country needs is fraught with controversy; but in the United States, there is some agreement that, given demographic projections, the country faces a short-term oversupply.[11] This situation is likely to intensify intraprofessional competition in the large metropolitan areas that have historically been the choicest practice locations, particularly for specialists. There is some evidence that "demetropolitanization" of specialty practice is already occurring as a consequence of competition; specialists are beginning to locate or relocate in the suburbs. Whether this is desirable from a policy perspective is debatable, depending upon whether one believes in a "demand-push" or "availability-pull" theory of medical services consumption.

In any case, policy attention in France and the United States—and no doubt in the other developed nations—will focus on the question of geographical maldistribution of physicians and how to increase the availability of medical manpower in "underserved" areas. Production of physicians will be curtailed, either through decreases in state subsidies to medical schools or through the imposition of direct quotas and stricter admission screening. No doubt, the medical profession will be divided over what policy initiatives to support.

Although less visible in the case studies than the issue of supply and distribution, the issue of certification and recertification of physicians is likely to receive increased attention. Ways of assessing current returns on social investment are likely to be demanded, and greater returns are likely to be sought. Requirements for relicensure and recertification are entirely compatible with the notion that there exists a short-term oversupply of physicians. Needless to say, such requirements are unlikely to be warmly embraced by the medical profession. Whether or not they ever become a reality, they represent another intrusion on professional hegemony occasioned by the end of the illusion of abundance.

ALTERNATIVES TO THE MEDICAL MODEL

The case studies suggest that community based services, holistic health, and primary prevention may receive more attention in the future. Each of these represents an alternative to the traditional medical model for health care, and none is really new. Each, however, has historically been marginal; none has been able to command levels of social investment even approaching those of medicine. There are signs, however, that these alternatives are becoming increasingly visible to ever larger segments of the population. With increasing visibility may come increasing legitimacy.

In the United States and Québec in particular, the media have been instrumental in informing consumers about alternatives to the traditional medical model for health care. Although the long-term effects on costs are not easily estimated, people are being urged to take more personal responsibility for their own well-being. What is most interesting about these alternatives are the different assumptions about well-being on which they are based, and the different implications for social investment that they contain. To the extent that their legitimacy grows and they capture more resources, they will compete with medicine. Certainly they can no longer be ignored; neither the media nor the competing professionals will permit it.

INTENSIFICATION OF ETHICAL DILEMMAS

Advances in technology coupled with the likelihood of health care rationing will create increasingly numerous and publicly visible ethical dilemmas. Western industrial nations will need to develop mechanisms for making difficult choices in a socially acceptable fashion. For example, who shall have access to what treatment modalities under what circumstances? Who shall decide? When is it legitimate to withdraw life-support systems from people? And who will get renal dialysis?

The medical profession will play a central role in whatever structures are created, but in our judgment, multidisciplinary committees will most likely be charged with developing ethical guidelines and making decisions. The composition of these committees, as well as the nature of the appeal and review procedures, will provoke controversy and will undoubtedly create a whole new field of social administration and research.

Similar problems loom with regard to the appropriateness of various kinds of basic biomedical research. Controversies over the ethical implications of genetic engineering are but the tip of the iceberg. In response to these issues some form of international negotiation mechanism will in all likelihood emerge—perhaps at the initiative of the scientific community—to help make difficult choices about general principles and to develop appropriate criteria for case-by-case decisions.

Trends Outside the Domain of Medicine

Three other trends are likely to influence the development of the medical field: the infusion of private capital into the health care sector; the rise of the ideology of managerial efficiency; and the growth of corporate strategizing.

3 trends

THE INFUSION OF PRIVATE CAPITAL INTO THE HEALTH CARE SECTOR

Private capital has always played a strong role in the development of such industries on the periphery of health care as medical instruments, drugs, prosthetics, and supplies; but the role of private capital in the core of the system has been more variable and less significant in the past. In the United States, for example, private (and, to a large extent, physician) ownership of health facilities was quite common toward the end of the nineteenth century and in the beginning of this century. As efforts to achieve greater social control over medical care intensified, however, and as the capital requirements for its provision increased (the advent of the modern hospital), the role of the private sector diminished.

Since the passage of Medicare and Medicaid, hospitals have been borrowing in the private capital markets. In the last fifteen years, however, hospital ownership and management has grown more attractive to private investors.

The proportion of beds under proprietary ownership in the United States has increased sixty-one percent in the past ten years and is continuing to increase, although there are signs that the rate of increase may be slowing.[12] The new growth has come primarily from the aggressive investment policies of the investor owned chains that have realized profits through the construction of new facilities as well as the acquisition of existing facilities. The latter strategy has involved both hospitals in the voluntary sector *and* hospitals in the proprietary sector. Many hospitals that were formerly physician owned (and hence proprietary) have been acquired by the large chains. Thus, figures showing the increasing penetration of the private sector underestimate the activity of the chains.

Another important facet of private sector involvement in the hospital industry is management contracting—private firms in the business of managing hospitals for a fee. Despite debate among the corporate giants in the field about the profitability of this activity, management contracting is big business.[13] Moreover, it is a growing export product. International competition for management contracts in the developing nations is intense.

The Rise of the Ideology of Managerial Efficiency

All of the case studies reflect government efforts to reform the health sector through the promotion of managerial efficiency. Especially in the United States, the level of managerial sophistication in hospitals is increasing rapidly, particularly in the area of financial management. In fact, the proprietaries have built their competitive edge on their ability to systematize, routinize, and program the management of nonmedical support services. And the "nonprofits" are rapidly catching up. Where hospitals have not had the necessary sophistication in-house, they have gone outside to purchase it. The remarkable growth in the past seven years of the management contracting industry is attributable to the increasingly widespread belief (accurate or not) at the level of corporate governance—boards of directors and boards of trustees—that considerable cost savings can be realized through more efficient management of nonmedical support services. It is striking that so many hospitals that have hitherto prided themselves on their autonomy and independence should in such a short period of time come to rely so heavily on outside expertise to manage their internal affairs.

The ideology of managerial efficiency raises two questions for the future. First, health care institutions will become increasingly populated by individuals whose cultural orientation is less and less incompatible with administrative rationalization. They will share a common language and frame of reference. Will this serve to narrow the gulf between the hospital industry and the state, or will it exacerbate fundamental incompatibilities?

Second, will the ideology of managerial efficiency penetrate the medical arena directly? As we noted earlier, efforts are currently underway in the United States to apply managerial techniques commonly used in industry to analyze in-patient care in hospitals. These efforts represent a significant departure from traditionally accepted practice. They are encountering resistance in predictable quarters. Perhaps what is truly significant is not the relative success or failure of particular efforts but rather how the social role of medicine and its traditional imperviousness to any form of social control will be affected by their cumulative impact.

THE GROWTH OF CORPORATE STRATEGIZING

Health care is big business, but many of the tools, techniques, and perspectives of big business are being applied to this sector for the first time. They encompass far more than the arena of operations management; for example, they include state-of-the-art work in the areas of strategic planning, marketing, and finance. They represent a dramatic departure from past practices in most health care institutions.

In the United States, managerial sophistication has increased not only in the investor owned chains but also in certain nonprofit multi-institutional systems and even many community hospitals. There is active technology transfer from the industrial sector to the health care sector in the managerial sphere, and this trend is likely to continue well into the 1980s.

Corporate strategizing is likely to have an important impact on the future structure of health care delivery.[14] First, there is likely to be continued growth in multiunit systems, both in the proprietary and the nonprofit sectors. This represents a strategy of growth through horizontal expansion, particularly through mergers and acquisition, in both domestic and in foreign markets. Second, strategies of growth through vertical integration are also likely to be vigorously pursued as opportunities for horizontal expansion become more limited and less attractive. In the next fifteen years, there will be active investment by health corporations in extended care facilities—in nursing homes, in out-patient surgical centers, and in other "businesses" related to the core business of patient care. The corporation is also likely to move into domains unrelated to health care. The classic strategy of corporate diversification is already observable in some cases in which corporations that began in health care have formed holding companies that have invested in everything from apartment buildings and shopping centers to amusement parks.

In the wake of such corporate growth strategies, health corporations may themselves become attractive acquisition targets for larger corporations seeking to diversify their holdings. The recent acquisition of Hospital Affiliates in the U.S. by the insurance giant INA (Insurance Company of North America) and the subsequent sale of its hospital business to the Hospital Corporation of America, is perhaps an omen of things to come. As the business of patient care becomes subject to the same sort of corporate scrutiny as the sale of dog food and becomes embedded in large and powerful corporate structures, will the business of health policy itself be co-opted by the interests of the private sector?

The lines between profit and nonprofit enterprises in the health care system of the United States are also likely to become increasingly blurred and perhaps even disappear.

A recent review of the nonprofit status of hospitals in the United States by a noted legal scholar[15] concluded that the nonprofits enjoy an unusually privileged status in the American system and questioned whether, from the perspective of social policy, this should be permitted to continue. That the question should even be raised is interesting in itself, and when coupled with the fact that many of the nonprofits are virtually indistinguishable from their investor-owned counterparts in terms of strategy, structure, and performance, one wonders about the future of the nonprofit, independent, community voluntary hospital.

As American health care corporations begin to expand their investments to international markets, there will be increasing domestic competition. French companies, for example, will be formed to compete with United States firms on French soil and in international markets as well. The British are already in the French market. The era of the multinational health corporation is just beginning to dawn. If, and as it develops, national health policy will perforce acquire an international flavor. The areas of similarity in policies between one nation and another will likely become larger, as has begun to happen, for example, in the regulation of standards for automobile production. The role of the state in health policy, as dependent as it is on the particular configuration of economic conditions and political ideology at any given time, will be strongly influenced by the conservative orientation of the developing corporate systems.

Not least, the Third World is a potentially vast market for the health care corporation of the 1980s and 1990s. It provides markets for both the technology and the managerial expertise developed in the West. What is more, other countries, Japan in particular, are already making strong efforts to penetrate these markets.

THE FUTURE OF HEALTH POLICY

The emerging trends outlined in the previous section are not all occurring in all the countries covered in the case studies; nor are they all new. Each trend is rather like a separate piece of a puzzle whose future shape is unknown. For those who believe that the structure of health systems is unlikely to change in the short run, the emerging trends are like pieces that will be molded to fit the puzzle as it is now shaped. For those who believe in the possibility of structural change, the trends represent new pieces of the puzzle which are less likely to be shaped by than to shape its future geometry.

At the seminar in Megève where the general idea for this book was first discussed, we agreed that social forecasting is a perilous endeavor, given the fact that we are unable even to predict the state of the economy over a five-year period. We also agreed that there were no magic solutions to problems in the health sector. The remedies for improving access to services and containing health care costs are well known and already tested (e.g., in Québec). The problem, however, is to make such solutions politically acceptable. The case studies suggest that this will not be easy.

The slow rates of economic growth in Western industrialized nations no longer allow generous health care reforms; but draconian measures to limit the growth of health care expenditures are unlikely in the short run. In this context, the most likely course for the near future is a series of incremental changes and administrative reorganizations that do not seriously threaten the status quo. The case studies provide ample examples of such reform. In the longer run, however, it will not be possible to forestall significant change indefinitely; it will be necessary to rethink the architecture of health systems.

How, then, will health policy evolve in Western industrialized nations? The emerging trends we have noted provide an indication of the changes that loom ahead. Although the case studies make no predictions, they do highlight important issues and identify alternative scenarios. Perhaps as important as the issues they highlight is the question that none of the case studies addresses: What will be the characteristics of the health sector in the future? The collective silence on this point may well be attributable to the lack of any agreed-upon blueprints about what constitutes an ideal health care system for the "good society." The vision and idealism of the sixties has waned in the eighties. The illusion of abundance for all has come to an end.

As for alternative scenarios for the future, all of the case studies emphasize the importance of both economic and political conditions in determining what H. G. Wells has called the "shape of things to come." The shape will depend on whether economic conditions are relatively austere or prosperous and whether left- or right-leaning parties are in power.

Under conditions of recession, the case studies suggest that if the Right comes to power there will be an increase in the role of the market in allocating health resources. For example, in France, there would likely be an erosion of acquired privileges under national health insurance, an increasing role for the private sector in underwriting "minor risk" and greater use of consumer copayments and deductibles. In Québec, although Renaud does not specify scenarios, one may infer that the Right would lead the way in curing Québec of the "narcissism" of the state. In Britain, also, the Right would place less emphasis on central control, and on the achievement of equality, and encourage the growth of private insurance. This strategy has already been initiated by Prime Minister Thatcher. As for the United States, once again, should the Right preside in times of medical austerity, it would seek to cut government programs while limiting government control and protecting— to some extent—the prerogatives of physicians, hospitals, and insurers. Indeed, this is now occurring under the Reagan administration.

If the Left comes to power under conditions of recession, there is likely to be a trend toward increased regulatory control over the health sector. For example, in France and the United States pressure is likely to mount to establish a national health service along the lines of the British NHS. In Britain there will be pressure to increase local syndicalism and to decentralize administrative control.

In contrast, should there be a return to conditions of economic growth and prosperity, health policy will be likely to take a quite different turn. Under a left-leaning government, all the case studies suggest that there would be greater efforts to promote equity in access to health services. In Britain, Klein and Davies note that there would be more emphasis—rather than less—on bureaucratic rationalization and control. In the United States, there would be a move in the direction of universal public health insurance, as in Canada.

Under a right-leaning government, there would be less pressure for government intervention in the health sector. In France this would probably result in little change, along the lines of the trend extrapolations of scenario one. In Britain, there would be less concern with equality; and in the United States there would most likely be a move in the direction of private and quasi-public health insurance systems like those of Germany and France.

Renaud observes that the Right currently defines the frame of reference for policy debate in Québec. As for the Left, he notes the emergence of a quiescent New Left that refuses to place itself in traditional political struggles, is "disillusioned by the failure of socialism and communism in the world," and has a "tendency toward introspection." The situation is similar in Britain and the United States. In France, however, since the election of President Mitterand, the Left is clearly defining the framework for debate.

Based on the experience of health care reform in Québec, Renaud argues that "no one cares whether the traditional Left or Right gains power. In any case, nothing will change." Klein and Davies concur with this view. They predict that radical change is unlikely; indeed, the Conservative government has not questioned the principle of a national health service. As for France and the United States, it is perhaps too early to assess the possible scenarios. Neither Mitterand's early promise of considerable administrative decentralization of health care, nor the Reagan administration's flirtation with procompetitive legislation limiting the role of the state in health care, has yet led to significant change.

It is often tempting to conclude that nothing will change. What such a conclusion fails to take into account, however, are the effects of the very significant trends occurring both within and outside the domain of medicine. The convergence of these trends, particularly the pressures for rationalization, the rise of new organizational forms of medical practice, and the growth of multinational health care corporations are now spurring the growth of proprietary ownership in the United States. Neither the Left nor the Right nor the principal actors in the health sector have come to grips with the issues which these changes portend. Sooner or later, however, there are likely to be some strong reactions. For the shape of the health care puzzle is likely to be quite different in the future: not as radically different as its many detractors would wish, but sharply different from what its staunchest defenders cherish.

NOTES

1. V. Rodwin, "The Marriage of National Health Insurance and *La Médecine Libérale*," *Milbank Memorial Fund Quarterly* 59, no. 1 (1981).

2. In this connection, see R. Alford, *Health Care Politics: Ideological and Interest Group Barriers to Reform* (Chicago: University of Chicago Press, 1975); and V. Rodwin, *The Health Planning Predicament: France, Québec, England, and the United States* (Berkeley, Los Angeles, London: University of California Press, 1984), chap. 9.

3. M. Cooper, *Rationing Health Care* (New York, Toronto: John Wiley, Halstead, 1975). For further reading on health care rationing, see A. Culyer, *Need and the National Health Service* (Oxford: Martin Robertson, 1976); and D. Mechanic, *Future Issues in Health Care: Social Policy and the Rationing of Medical Services* (New York: Free Press, 1979).

4. H. Luft, "Health Maintenance Organizations and the Rationing of Medical Care," *Milbank Memorial Fund Quarterly* 60, no. 2 (1982).

5. For three contrasting analyses of these issues by the editors of this book, see J. de Kervasdoué, "Les politiques de santé, sont-elles adaptées à la pratique médicale?" *Sociologie du Travail* 3 (1979); J. R. Kimberly, "Managerial Innovation and Health Policy," *Journal of Health Politics,*

Policy and Law 6, no. 4 (Winter 1982); and V. Rodwin, "Management Without Objectives: The French Health Policy Gamble," in G. McLachlan and A. Maynard, eds., *The Public/Private Mix for Health: The Relevance and Effects of Change* (London: Nuffield Provincial Hospitals Trust, 1982).

6. See, for example, R. B. Fetter et al., "Case Mix Definition by Diagnosis-Related Groups," *Medical Care* 18, no. 2 (February 1980).

7. See the four-volume evaluation of this experiment: *DRG Evaluation* (Rocky Hill, N.J.: Health Research and Educational Trust, 1982).

8. H. Luft, "Assessing the Evidence on HMO Performance," *Milbank Memorial Fund Quarterly/Health and Society* 58, 4 (1980).

9. See, for example, D. Harrison and J. R. Kimberly, "HMOs Need Not Fail," *Harvard Business Review* (July–August 1982).

10. D. Harrison and J. R. Kimberly, "Private and Public Initiatives in HMOs," *Journal of Health Politics, Policy and Law* 7, no. 1 (Spring 1982).

11. See, for example, Health Resources Administration, DHHS, *Summary Report of the Graduate Medical Education National Advisory Committee*, vol. 1, DHHS Publication no. (HRA) 81–651, (Washington, D.C.: U.S. Government Printing Office, April 1981).

12. *AHA Guide to Hospitals 1981* (Chicago: American Hospital Association, 1981).

13. See, for example, Linda Punch, "Leading Firms Boost Contract Business 18.2%," *Modern Health Care* 12, no. 7 (July 1982).

14. A critical perspective on this issue can be found in C. Pollitt, "Corporate Rationalization of American Health Care: A Visitor's Appraisal," *Journal of Health Politics, Policy and Law* 7, no. 1 (Spring 1982).

15. R. C. Clark, "Does the Non-Profit Form Fit the Hospital Industry?" *Harvard Law Review* 93, no. 7 (May 1980).

INDEX

Advertising, 73
Alcohol drinking, 10, 70, 72–73, 153
Alford, Robert, 175
AMA (American Medical Association), 42, 117
American Public Health Association, 67

Barre, Raymond, 22, 158
Behavior modification, 71–75
Bevan, Aneurin, 207, 208–209, 210, 211
Beveridge report of 1942, 6
BMA Handbook. See *Handbook of Medical Ethics*
Bosquet, Michel, 190–191
Braverman, Harry, 189
Brenner, Harvey, 70
British Medical Association (BMA), 117
British National Health Service. See NHS (Great Britain)
Burke, Edmund, 35

Caisse Nationale D'Assurance Maladie des Travailleurs Salariés. See CNAMTS (Caisse Nationale d'Assurance Maladie des Travailleurs Salariés)
Cancer, 67, 74, 78, 100, 106; treatment of, 88, 91, 93–94
Cardiovascular disease, 70, 235–236, 253 n. 5
Castonguay-Nepveu Commission, 172–174, 183, 187, 263
CAT scanners, 92–93, 95–98, 102
CHCs. See Community Health Councils (CHCs)
Cigarette smoking, 72–73
Cirrhosis of the liver, 70
Clark, Joe, 22
CLSCs. See Local health and social service centers (CLSCs)

CNAMTS (Caisse Nationale d'Assurance Maladie des Travailleurs Salariés), 137, 140, 269
Community Health Councils (CHCs), 216
Confédération des syndicats médicaux français (CSMF), 42
Conservative government (Great Britain): health policy of, 224–230; NHS and, 213, 221–222, 228
Conservative perspective, 35, 36–37, 41–45, 52, 54 n. 18. *See also* Free enterprise model; Professional model
Cost containment, 24–29, 258
Cost containment (Canada), 23, 187
Cost containment (France), 23, 145–153, 260; alcohol drinking and, 153; carte sanitaire and, 151–152; CNAMTS and, 145, 148, 149, 150; consumers' role in, 153–154; demand side policies and, 147–148; expenditure reductions and, 147–153; hospitals and, 148–152, 161; insurance and, 147–148; market regulation of, 157–160; medical school enrollment and, 152; Ministry of Health and, 150–152; NHI reductions and, 157–158; nomenclature and, 141, 148; physical autonomy and, 161; public health programs and, 160–161; regulation increases and, 160–161; revenue increases and, 146–147; stalemate in, 262; supply side policies and, 148–149
Cost containment (Germany), 23
Cost containment (Great Britain), 23, 29, 227–228; NHS and, 213, 214, 261; strategies for, 220–221, 223–227, 230–231
Cost containment (Québec), 187, 260–261

Designer: UC Press Staff
Compositor: Trend Western
Printer: Braun-Brumfield
Binder: Braun-Brumfield
Text: 11/13 Palatino Roman
Display: Palatino Roman